# Beyond Tech Fixes

Christo El Morr • Yahya El-Lahib
Rachel da Silveira Gorman
Editors

# Beyond Tech Fixes

## Towards an AI Future Where Disability Justice Thrives

Springer

*Editors*
Christo El Morr
School of Health Policy and Management
York University
Toronto, ON, Canada

Yahya El-Lahib
Faculty of Social Work
University of Calgary
Calgary, AB, Canada

Rachel da Silveira Gorman
School of Health Policy and Management
York University
Toronto, ON, Canada

ISBN 978-3-031-93021-8 ISBN 978-3-031-93022-5 (eBook)
https://doi.org/10.1007/978-3-031-93022-5



This Springer imprint is published by the registered company Springer Nature Switzerland AG
The registered company address is: Gewerbestrasse 11, 6330 Cham, Switzerland

*For Valentina and Alexi—who embody compassion and resistance.*
*To all people who are struggling with the disabling and debilitating effects of AI systems in Gaza, Palestine, Congo, Sudan, and across the globe, we dedicate this book as a form of resistance and hope.*

# Foreword

I came to this book not only as a technologist and requirements engineer, but as someone who has long reflected on the uneven consequences of innovation. In both research and practice, I have witnessed how the pursuit of technical progress and economic growth often leaves certain communities behind—especially those already marginalized. This book insists on a different path. It listens carefully. It does not treat disability as a technical edge case or a problem to be solved. Instead, it reimagines technology through the lenses of justice, dignity, and care.

I often think of Haben Girma, the deafblind lawyer and disability rights advocate, whose life and work offer a powerful reminder: success does not have a single definition. For some, success means refusing to be limited by the assumptions and imaginations of others. That idea stays with me, especially when I think about how we design, teach, and implement AI systems. Too often, we create technologies grounded in narrow assumptions shaped by our own lived experiences and the convenience of dominant norms.

Today's AI systems, particularly large foundation models, are trained on vast Internet-based datasets that overrepresent Western, white, male, and able-bodied perspectives. As a result, the experiences of disabled people and other marginalized communities are often excluded, distorted, or ignored. These systems are typically developed by teams that also lack demographic and experiential diversity. Even when technically advanced, such models tend to optimize for efficiency, scale, and commercial return rather than accessibility or justice. Without intentional efforts to rethink data practices, diversify design teams, and center disability justice, AI will continue to replicate and intensify existing forms of exclusion.

This book offers a much-needed intervention. It opens with foundational reflections on accessible and inclusive AI, emphasizing that both data and design must account for the full range of human experience. In chapter "A Framework for Social Justice-Oriented Practices for Accessible and Inclusive AI", Fernandes et al. examine how biased datasets and homogeneous teams lead to systems that disadvantage disabled users. Chapter "AI and the Disability Divide: Towards a Transdisciplinary Approach", by Taleghani, introduces user-centered and transdisciplinary approaches that integrate marginalized voices throughout the design process.

Chapter "Understanding the Digital Disability Creation Process and Bridging the Gap Between Responsible AI Design and Disability Frameworks", by Metoui, brings ethical, legal, and conceptual disability frameworks into conversation with AI development, showing how systems can either reinforce or challenge disabling environments. Chapter "Evaluating AI Assistive Technologies for Older Adults Living with Dementia Using a Disability Justice Framework", by Zeid, offers a concrete application of Fraser's theory of social justice to assistive technologies for older adults, identifying structural gaps and outlining future research needs. Chapter "An Opportunity to Use AI to Support Content Creators in Creating Born-Accessible Documents", by Lazar et al., advocates for a "born-accessible" approach to content creation. By embedding accessibility features during authoring, they propose a shift away from remediation and toward a more equitable default. In chapter "Assessing AI's Role in Digital Accessibility", Makati expands the conversation with a mixed-method study on how AI technologies can simultaneously challenge and reproduce ableism. Chapter "Empowering Voices: The Role of Emerging Technologies in Workplace Inclusion for Individuals with Speech Impairments", by Davies and Desai, uses a co-creation methodology to explore inclusive design for employment tools, especially for individuals with speech impairments.

The educational context comes to the forefront in chapter "AI Opportunities and Challenges for Students with Learning Disabilities", where Dehghantezerjani et al. discuss how AI might support students with learning differences. Chapter "Toward an Emancipatory AI Pedagogy: The Dos and Don'ts of an Anti-Racist/Anti-Ableist Approach to Writing Instruction Using GenAI", by Han and Johnson, considers the role of generative AI in postsecondary education, emphasizing emancipatory uses that confront linguistic and structural barriers. In chapter "Challenges with Recruitment, Collection, and Analysis: A Research Study on Physiological Signals and Emotional Experiences in Youth with Severe Motor and Communication Impairments", Vowles et al. focus on youth with severe motor and communication impairments, showing how AI can support emotional expression and social connection.

The final chapters broaden the lens to systems and representation. Chapter "The View from Elsewhere: Investigating Infrastructural Inequities at the Intersection of Disability and AI-Enabled Interactive Technologies", by Hamidi et al., explores the lived experiences of forced migrants with disabilities in Germany, revealing policy and infrastructural inequities. Chapter "Mechanisms of Disability Evasiveness in AI-generated Flash Fiction", by Barron et al., analyzes AI-generated stories about disabled children, introducing the concept of "disability evasiveness"—the tendency to erase disability under the guise of inclusion. Chapter "Decoloniality and AI: Possibilities and Pitfalls", by Lallani, investigates whose values and cultural assumptions are reinforced through global AI systems. In chapter "An Affirmation of Weakness: Reimagining Disability Through Derrida and AI as a Prosthetic", Sherbert challenges ableist ideals of independence and strength, instead positioning interdependence and vulnerability as powerful design principles. Chapter "Disability Data Futures: Achievable Imaginaries for AI and Disability Data Justice", by Newman-Griffis et al., calls for disability data justice, highlighting the importance of co-design, intersectionality, and transdisciplinary work. Finally, chapter "Toward a Disability Justice Framework for Artificial Intelligence", by Khan and El-Lahib, proposes a disability justice framework for understanding and addressing AI bias, offering a vision of systems rooted in equity, care, and collective empowerment.

This book does not treat disability as a problem to be fixed. It asks us to start from the margins, where insights into care, justice, and interdependence are most clearly articulated and to build from there. In doing so, it invites us to reimagine technology as a space of collective possibility. AI must not become a tool of inequality masked as innovation. This book demands more and offers a path forward. One where technology does not merely include the margins but begins there.

Maleknaz Nayebi
York University
Toronto, Canada
CIFAL-UNITAR, York University
North York, ON, Canada
May 2025

# Preface

This book was born out of a double silence: the silence of AI research about the lived realities of people with disabilities, and the silence within social sciences and humanities about the profound and often violent impact of artificial intelligence. At the intersection of these silences lies a critical void—the absence of sustained critique of AI—that this volume seeks to fill, or at least, begins a dialog about within transdisciplinary spaces. The book emerges from a deep concern over the persistence of the medical model in AI research and the lack of awareness among technologists about the social, political, economic, and ethical stakes of their creations.

We are living through a moment of convergence: AI is no longer a distant innovation—it is now embedded in the infrastructures of daily life. At the same time, we are witnessing a global erosion of rights, the resurgence of fascist ideologies, and the weaponization of AI in the service of war, displacement, and systemic violence, including the disabling and killing of marginalized peoples. The urgency to respond—to refuse silence—is now.

This book speaks from and to the margins. It draws on the lenses of disability justice, decolonial critique, feminist thought, and Global South epistemologies. It does not pretend to offer solutions wrapped in techno-optimism. Instead, it offers pathways—toward solidarity, toward resistance, toward collective imagining.

This book creates space for AI researchers, disability scholars, activists, families, and allies to understand what is at stake. It invites us to engage in the deeper issues, struggles, and stakes.

We offer this work as an invitation: to carry forward a vision of equal dignity for all. To struggle not for inclusion into unjust systems, but for their transformation. To reimagine a world where justice is not an afterthought, but the starting point.

Let this be a beginning.

Toronto, ON, Canada — Christo El Morr
Calgary, AB, Canada — Yahya El-Lahib
Toronto, ON, Canada — Rachel da Silveira Gorman

# Acknowledgments

We extend our heartfelt gratitude to the students who walked alongside us in this intellectual and political journey.

To Sabine Fernandes, Sarah Taleghani, Maimuna Khan, Bushra Kundi, and Habiba Rahman—thank you for your curiosity, your critical questions, your research support, and your unwavering commitment to justice. Your engagement helped shape the contours of this work, and your presence reminds us that the future of scholarship is in good hands.

This book carries traces of your thought, labor, and passion. We are deeply grateful.

This book was made possible in part through the generous support of the Social Sciences and Humanities Research Council (SSHRC) Knowledge Synthesis Grant (Grant No. 872-2022-1025), awarded for the project "Towards an Accessible Inclusive Artificial Intelligence (AI2)." We gratefully acknowledge this funding, received by Christo El Morr, Rachel da Silveira Gorman, and Yahya El-Lahib, which provided a critical foundation for the research and collaboration that shaped this volume.

This book also emerges from the rich conversations, critical insights, and collective engagements of *The First AI & Disability Justice Symposium*, held at York University in Toronto, Ontario, Canada, on November 14–15, 2024. The symposium brought together scholars, activists, technologists, and community members committed to reimagining AI through the lens of disability justice, and its spirit of solidarity and critique animates the pages of this volume.

# Contents

# Contributors

**Samah Al-Shaghdari** NOW! Nicht Ohne das Wir, c/o Handicap International e.V., Berlin, Germany

**Nge Nge Aye Maung** NOW! Nicht Ohne das Wir, c/o Handicap International e.V., Berlin, Germany

**Melanie Baljko** Lassonde School of Engineering, York University, North York, ON, Canada

**Alireza Baneshi** Educational Research, Faculty of Psychology and Education, Tehran, Iran

**Katherine Barron** Faculty of Education, York University, North York, ON, Canada

**Mackenzie L. Collins** Department of Mechanical and Materials Engineering, Queen's University, Kingston, ON, Canada

School of Medicine, Queen's University, Kingston, ON, Canada

**Ryan Collis** Faculty of Education, York University, North York, ON, Canada

**T. Claire Davies** Department of Mechanical and Materials Engineering, Queen's University, Kingston, ON, Canada

Mechanical and Materials Engineering, Queen's University, Kingston, ON, Canada

**Mahnaz Dehghantezerjani** Faculty of Education, York University, Toronto, ON, Canada

**Shital Desai** Social and Technological Systems (SaTS) Lab, School of Arts Media Performance and Design, York University, Toronto, ON, Canada

**Yahya El-Lahib** Faculty of Social Work, University of Calgary, Calgary, AB, Canada

**Christo El Morr** School of Health Policy and Management, York University, Toronto, ON, Canada

**Sabine Fernandes** School of Health Policy and Management, Critical Disability Studies, York University, Toronto, ON, Canada

**Rachel da Silveira Gorman** School of Health Policy and Management, York University, Toronto, ON, Canada

**Foad Hamidi** Information Systems Department, University of Maryland, Baltimore County (UMBC), Baltimore, MD, USA

**Yoonmee Han** Department of Science and Technology Studies, York University, North York, ON, Canada

**Michaela Hynie** Department of Psychology/Centre for Refugee Studies, York University, North York, ON, Canada

**Rajiv Jain** Adobe, Inc., San Jose, CA, USA

**Mary Ann Jawili MJ** Adobe, Inc., San Jose, CA, USA

**Sammy Jo Johnson** School of Health Policy and Management, Critical Disability Studies, York University, North York, ON, Canada

**Abhinav Kannan** College of Information, University of Maryland, College Park, MD, USA

**Maimuna S. Khan** School of Social Work, McMaster University, Hamilton, ON, Canada

**Annette Korntheuer** Munich University of Applied Sciences, Munich, Germany

**Mishall Lallani** Department of Political Science, York University, North York, ON, Canada

**Jonathan Lazar** College of Information, University of Maryland, College Park, MD, USA

**Tlamelo Makati** School of Computer Science, Technological University Dublin, Dublin, Ireland

**Gillian Mason** Independent Consultant and Disability Advocate, Newcastle, NSW, Australia

**Nadia Metoui** Faculty of Technology, Policy, and Management, Delft University of Technology, Delft, The Netherlands

**Zainab Mohamedhasn Abdlamer Abol-Hawa** NOW! Nicht Ohne das Wir, c/o Handicap International e.V., Berlin, Germany

**Denis Newman-Griffis** School of Computer Science & Centre for Machine Intelligence, University of Sheffield, Sheffield, UK

**Yalpi Shiva Prasad** Adobe, Inc., San Jose, CA, USA

**Habiba Rahman** School of Health Policy and Management, Critical Disability Studies, York University, Toronto, ON, Canada

**Aaron Richmond** Independent Researcher, North York, ON, Canada

**Mahdieh Roshanbin** Faculty of Psychology and Education, University of Tehran, Kish Island, Iran

**Robert Savage** Faculty of Education, York University, Toronto, ON, Canada

**Michael G. Sherbert** Postdoctoral Fellow, Connected Minds Program, Queen's University, Kingston, ON, Canada

**Alexa Siu** Adobe, Inc., San Jose, CA, USA

**Bonnielin Swenor** Disability Health Research Center, Johns Hopkins University, Baltimore, MD, USA

**Sarah Taleghani** School of Health Policy and Management, York University, Toronto, ON, Canada

**Garreth W. Tigwell** School of Information, Rochester Institute of Technology, Rochester, NY, USA

**Rick Treitman** Adobe, Inc., San Jose, CA, USA

**Rupa Valdez** School of Engineering and Applied Sciences, and School of Medicine, University of Virginia, Charlottesville, VA, USA

**Ellouise Van Berkel** Faculty of Education, York University, North York, ON, Canada

**Caryn J. Vowles** Department of Mechanical and Materials Engineering, Queen's University, Kingston, ON, Canada

**Janna Zeid** Cognitive Systems, The University of British Columbia, Vancouver, BC, Canada

# Part I
# Foundations

## 1.1 Introduction

This opening section lays the conceptual groundwork for engaging critically with the intersection of artificial intelligence (AI) and disability. Rather than positioning AI as a neutral tool, the chapters in this part emphasize the importance of embedding social justice, disability theory, and intersectional thinking at the core of AI development and deployment. Contributors challenge us to move beyond mere technical fixes, inviting a deeper engagement with the power structures, historical exclusions, and possibilities for inclusive and transformative design.

# AI and Disability Justice: Why Beyond Tech Fixes?

**Yahya El-Lahib, Rachel da Silveira Gorman, and Christo El Morr**

## Introduction

Contemporary global realities, with the rise of AI systems and open, interactive, and generative artificial intelligence, have dominated public spaces and recently generated global media attention. Such new development has shifted the discourse on AI and its impacts in ways that dismiss concerns about AI and serve the interests of multi-national corporations invested in the new wave of AI and machine learnings. What is clearly promoted in these discourses is reflected in the race for the most effective AI system and the financial costs associated with its production to make it available for the masses. As with any innovation, corporate interests will always secure their own head start to maximize their profit and ensure their product is competitive and is able to dominate the market. In this context, it is worth noting the tensions between accepting the fact that AI and all its sub-products are here to stay and recognizing that the social, political, environmental, and economic impacts of AI systems have yet to be addressed or even acknowledged by those who are steering the world into an absolute reliance on AI. Accordingly, we titled our book *Beyond Tech Fixes: Towards an AI Future Where Disability Justice Thrives* as a call to question the ways AI systems have been promoted, utilized and accepted as the way forward for efficient and effective use of technology and its development.

By "beyond tech fixes," we mean rejecting the notion that AI can be "fixed" by adding ethical guidelines, improving datasets, or tweaking bias-detection

Y. El-Lahib
Faculty of Social Work, University of Calgary, Calgary, AB, Canada
e-mail: yellahib@ucalgary.ca

R. da Silveira Gorman · C. El Morr (✉)
School of Health Policy and Management, York University, Toronto, ON, Canada
e-mail: gorman@yorku.ca; elmorr@yorku.ca


C. El Morr et al. (eds.), *Beyond Tech Fixes*,
https://doi.org/10.1007/978-3-031-93022-5_1

algorithms. Similarly, we reject the false promise that improving access, inclusion and participation of disabled people can be fixed with technical solutions. Instead, we call for a fundamental reckoning with AI's role in perpetuating ableism, colonialism, and neoliberal oppression in the same ways we call for challenging these systems that foster oppression and marginalization of the disabled other. Our argument does not dismiss AI's potential to benefit disabled people, but it insists that AI in its current form prioritizes corporate and state interests over disability justice.

Beyond tech fixes is our way of asserting a position that not only calls to question the over-reliance on AI in recent years but also challenges the premise of AI development that neglects every aspect of human interconnections in the name of innovation, efficiency, effectiveness and productivity to name a few. As we set the ground for such critical dialogue on AI and disability, we argue that AI, as a tool, can be beneficial to disabled people navigating their everyday realities as they survive this ableist world. However, we also assert that in the current climate, the threats that AI pose to disabled people have yet to be investigated and examined. We posit that these threats are multi-faceted and can be understood on a global scale and on an individual level.

## AI as a Product of Imperial and Colonial Dominance

Our call to question and interrogate AI is situated within our understanding of it as a tool that has the potential to support and improve the lives of disabled people; nonetheless, AI also can serve as a mechanism that further erases, marginalize and sideline disabled people from any public space and discourse. What has been promoted as innovative AI systems that would improve the everyday lives and independence of disabled people also has the potential to facilitate their further marginalization and erasure in many complex ways that require more attention. This is especially true in the current global climate of colonial modernity and corporate threats to the means of social existence. The rapid development of AI systems in the last two decades has been integral to the calls we advance in this book as they are indicators of the world to come, where issues of justice, decolonization, and sovereignty (individuals and statehood) are faced with unprecedented challenges that are worth posing and asking the question: Why beyond tech fixes? We assert the need for AI development and promotion to move beyond tech fixes for many reasons, as we outline below.

First, to challenge the various forms of contemporary corporate coloniality that have been obscured through centering techno-specific functioning of AI operations on serving the interests of the technological, industrial complex. Whether it is the neocolonial operation of AI that very few nations (say Western states and corporations) have a say in across the globe or the many threats of erasure or challenges to the sovereignty and independence that countries in the Global South face (Arora et al., 2023; Garcia, 2019; Madianou, 2019b, 2022). The contemporary race toward AI development is a storm that is taking everything in its way to serve the interests of a few Western states and corporations that dictate the new anticipated world order promised by AI dominance and control. Mingolo and Walsh (2018, p. 116) remind us that colonialism is “a practice of domination involving the subjugation of one people by another through military, economic and political means.” Further, Quijano (2000) developed coloniality of power to maintain that the subjugation of the colonized continues in new means after the direct colonial rule and exploitation. As such, of significant relevance here are the power dynamics and relations between the Global North and South and the ways neocolonialism, technocolonialism, and digital colonialism manifest in the current global order. The dominance of Western states and corporate hegemony and their ability to control the monopoly of AI systems gives the Global North many advantages to maintain its subjugation, exploitation and control over the Global South in new and unprecedented ways (Mignolo & Walsh, 2018; Madianou, 2019a, b; Vaidhyanathan, 2018).

While the Global South continues to struggle with the impacts of the Global North’s exploitation and subjugation of its land, resources and people, it remains home for the majority of disabled people globally (Grech, 2009, 2012; Grech & Goodley, 2011). There are many examples that speak about the use of AI systems to maintain Western hegemony in the Global South. However, we highlight here the Western weaponizing of AI in the current ongoing genocides against Palestine in Gaza and the West Bank. The use of AI for surveillance and autonomous arms systems has been responsible for the destruction of land and the continued violence, killing and erasure of Palestinian people. Of significant importance here is the role that AI autonomous arms systems play in the production of impairments allowing Israel and its Western allies to eliminate any resistance to their settler colonial objectives and pave the way for these colonial entities to construct themselves as the saviours once the genocide is over and rebuilding efforts start taking place. Such subjugation of Palestinians through AI speaks volumes of the necessity to move beyond tech fixes and call for AI accountability and responsibility. This also demonstrates the marriage between the military-industrial complex and the technology-industrial complex and highlights the many threats such marriage imposes on humanity and the global order. Taking a stand against such marriage is to resist the use of AI as it serves neocolonial interests and imperial goals. Indeed, such marriage has proven to be not only a threat to the world as we know it but also a threat to the relationship between people and their governments, as well as the interconnectedness between different global players, to say the least. A new world order where multinational corporations threaten state sovereignty is only the beginning of such a marriage if not questioned or challenged. Indeed, the challenges posed by AI and its state and corporate beneficiaries will only further marginalize and erase disabled people if we only keep focusing on tech fixes. Below, we turn to discuss AI as a tool for technoableism and state control experienced at the individual and personal level.

## Technoableism: AI as a Tool for State Surveillance and Control

As we continue to grapple with the global implications of the marriage between the military-industrial complex and the technology-industrial complex, there is a need to call into question how this marriage is affecting people beyond state borders; similarly, the race to achieve AI superiority needs to be understood not only on a global scale, but also on individual levels and the interconnectedness between people, their statehood, and their overall access to rights and protection. One of the key examples that highlight these issues is the current global debates about the loss of rights due to a surveillance technology that has been gaining momentum since the introduction of AI. Citizens, civil and human rights activists and organizations across the globe have raised alarms about the concerns over intensified and intrusive surveillance and the use of AI systems to facilitate the criminalization of any descent of mainstream narrative and discourse. Social media surveillance is an example, and the constant attempts to silence, erase, and shadow-ban any discourse that does not fit the colonial and imperial agenda. These surveillance mechanisms are intensified when issues of Western interest are questioned and challenged. The ability to control such a powerful AI tool hold the world hostage to the manipulation of Western imperial narratives and dictates many aspects of the world priorities and interests.

An important example to consider here is the implications of technocoloniality that manifest in various forms and affect people beyond time and space continuum. Technocolonialism, which describes the conjunction of "digital developments with humanitarian structures and market forces reinvigorates and reshape colonial relationships of dependency" (Madianou, 2019a, b, p. 2). This highlights role that AI and recent technological advancements play in reshaping power dynamics and relations between the Global North and the Global South. Of importance here is also the role that humanitarian interventions of Western players in the Global South play in not only shaping the everyday realities of Global South countries, but also their complicity in shaping dependency of various social groups including disabled people on Western knowledge, funding and discourses of disability rights, priorities and focus.

Technocolonialism as a phenomenon needs to be understood as a dynamic that facilitates the relationship between international humanitarian efforts, market forces and digital development that perpetuates and reinforces colonial thoughts, patterns and structures. Within the current neoliberal globalized world, this becomes an important factor that needs to be investigated and accounted for as we approach a world filled with AI systems that replace human in many sectors under the guise of efficiency, effectiveness and productivity (Madianou, 2019a, b). Disability related humanitarian interventions in the Global South play a significant role in perpetuating Western agenda that erases disabled people and their priorities, while constructing Western players and NGOs as saviours (Wehbi et al., 2009). This manifests in various forms of surveillance and control over local priorities to serve the interests of these international players.

As we set the context for the discussion on why beyond tech fixes is a necessity to understand the global and local implications of the marriage between the military-industrial complex and the technological-industrial complex, we also assert our position as disability scholars and activists who are invested in holding AI systems and those involved in its development accountable for the misuse of a potentially good tool. AI as a tool has the potential to improve the quality of life in many areas, including health care, communication, and the overall well-being of people regardless of their status and affiliation. However, like many great tools and inventions, AI serving the interests of military interventions and technology markets can be destructive and pose many risks to the world as we know it. This is to assert our position that none of our discussion rejects AI advancements for the betterment of the world and its people; instead, our concerns are centered around promoting and investing in AI development and advancement without any consideration of its use as a weapon to maintain Western hegemony on a global scale and facilitate the normalization of fascist oppressive manifestation on a local level, to say the least.

AI systems have been promoted and presented as a life-changing opportunity for disabled people. Whether through its potential use in assistive devices or health care diagnosis and operation, AI systems have been presented as a life-altering tool for disabled people with a promise of "normal" life and independence. Although this might be true in certain cases, we argue that such a promise is inherently ableist as it facilitates a false notion of independence without any consideration of human-to-human interaction. On the surface, AI advancement in the case of disability may present an opportunity, but the question remains: For whom is the opportunity? Living with disability in an ableist world designed only for non-disabled people will not be resolved by adding some tech fixes to an inherently ableist and exclusionary design. The need to move beyond tech fixes speaks to the necessity required to understand AI as a tool that also has the potential to further maintain the hegemonic control of disabled people in unprecedented ways. Similar to disability critiques of medical rhetoric and fixation on curing and rehabilitating disabled people, tech fixes or technoableism critiques technological promises of "empowerment while reinforcing ableist tropes about body-minds" (Shew, 2020, 2022). In other words, despite its promise of independence, AI fixes drive individuals to fit in their environment rather than the other way around.

AI and interactive/generative AI have reached the abilities to make decisions within the parameters specified by their use. In the age of over-reliance on AI systems to provide health care, diagnosis, and even termination of life, such as MAiD, AI has been given control over our bodies and minds in challenging and uncontrolled ways. AI's abilities to make informed decisions on various healthcare issues have been justified by small margins of errors, but the implication of such ability goes beyond the technicalities to have direct impacts on the lives of those subjected to such control. Within the current neoliberal system, disabled people have been subjected to denial of services because of reviews of eligibility criteria conducted through some forms of AI systems. A setback of the welfare state where citizens with disabilities are removed from accessing their rights to welfare and income support. Such loss of rights serves neoliberal policies made possible by the introduction of AI to facilitate access to rights and citizenship.

## Conclusion

Our call into question in this book is an attempt to shift the focus of AI from being promoted as effective and productive and assisting disabled people in their everyday realities to considering AI accountability to the power imbalance created by AI and those benefiting from it. The promise that AI can offer disabled people opportunities for better lives obscures the moral claim about the purpose of technology, and AI systems hides the underlying power dynamics and relations (Madianou, 2021, 2022). Similarly, Lawrence (2023) reminds us of the racist algorithms that not only maintain racism but also play a significant role in deepening and empowering systemic racism. With the rise of AI and the power invested in its success to facilitate neoliberal imperial and colonial control of the land, its resources and its people, our effort in this book is to resist conforming but also holds some hope.

So far, we have outlined a grim picture of AI not only for disabled people but for the world, which begs the question, is a better AI possible? We hope for a more politicized, accountable and responsible technology decenters profit and investors and seek AI advancement for the betterment of people. The trends we see nowadays in AI use are not so promising, but perhaps a decolonial approach to AI is possible. A decolonial AI that centers on the well-being of marginalized groups starts with interrogating power and highlights the fact that "AI is part of larger genealogies of enumeration, measurement and classification that were originally developed by imperial powers to control colonial subjects (Madianou, 2021, 2022, p. 854). A decolonial AI would move beyond tech fixes and would reject technocolonialism and data colonialism, a system that values other ways of knowing, being and doing. A decolonial AI would embrace the diversity of beings in the same way it would celebrate all forms of being. If we can imagine a decolonial world, we hope that industries, states and key players still have the ability to see and imagine a better world beyond their tech fixes.

## References

Arora, A., Barrett, M., Lee, E., Oborn, E., & Prince, K. (2023). Risk and the future of AI: Algorithmic bias, data colonialism and marginalization. *Information and Organization, 33*(3), 1–7. https://doi.org/10.1016/j.infoandorg.2023.100478

Garcia, E. (2019). The militarization of artificial intelligence: A wake-up call for the Global South. SSRN. https://doi.org/10.2139/ssrn.3452323

Grech, S. (2012). "Disability and the majority world: A neocolonial approach." In D. Goodley, B. Hughes & L. Davisv (Eds.), Disability and Social Theory: New Developments and Directions (pp. 52–69). *Palgrave Macmillan*. https://doi.org/10.1057/9781137023001_4.

Grech, S. (2009). Disability, poverty and development: Critical reflections on the majority world debate. *Disability & Society, 24*(6), 771–784. https://doi.org/10.1080/09687590903160266

Grech, S., & Goodley, D. (2011). Doing research in the majority world: An alternative framework and the quest for decolonizing methods. *Journal of Human Development, Disability and Social Change, 19*(2), 43–55. https://doi.org/10.7202/1086899ar

Lawrence, C. D. (2023). *Hidden in white sight: How AI empowers and deepens systemic racism.* CRC Press.

Madianou, M. (2019a). Technocolonialism: Digital innovation and data practices in the humanitarian response to refugee crises. *Social Media and Society, 5*(3), 1–13. https://doi.org/10.1177/2056305119863146

Madianou, M. (2019b). The biometric assemblage: Surveillance, experimentation, profit and the measuring of refugee bodies. *Television and New Media, 20*(6), 581–599. https://doi.org/10.1177/1527476419857682

Madianou, M. (2021). Nonhuman humanitarianism: When 'AI for good' can be harmful? *Information, Communication & Society, 24*(6), 850–868. https://doi.org/10.1080/1369118X.2021.1909100

Madianou, M. (2022). Technological futures as colonial debris: "Tech for Good" as technocolonialism. In J. Zylinska & Goldsmith Media (Eds.), *The future of media* (pp. 281–294). Goldsmiths Press.

Mignolo, W., & Walsh, K. (2018). *On decoloniality: Concepts, analytics, praxis.* Duke University Press.

Quijano, A. (2000). Coloniality of power and Eurocentrism in Latin America. *International Sociology, 15*(2), 215–232.

Shew, A. (2020). Ableism, technoableism, and future AI. *IEEE Technology and Society Magazine, 39*(1), 40–85. https://doi.org/10.1109/MTS.2020.2967492

Shew, A. (2022). How to get a story wrong: Technoableism, simulation and cyborg resistance. *Including Disability, 1*(1), 13–36.

Vaidhyanathan, S. (2018). *Anti-social media.* Oxford University Press.

Wehbi, S., Elin, L., & El-Lahib, Y. (2009). Neo-colonial discourses and disability: The case of Canadian International Development NGOs. *Community Development Journal, 45*(4), 404–422.

# A Framework for Social Justice-Oriented Practices for Accessible and Inclusive AI

**Sabine Fernandes, Habiba Rahman, and Rachel da Silveira Gorman**

## Introduction

The purpose of this literature review is to explore and synthesize emerging social justice-oriented practices within data and design fields to advance the Accessible and Inclusive Artificial Intelligence (AI2) project. The project assesses AI use for people with disabilities, its current advantages and challenges. The outcomes will support future research agendas, practices and policies.

As artificial intelligence (AI) is increasingly being used in social systems—from healthcare to social media—it reveals opportunities and challenges for accessibility and inclusion. A major challenge is the presence of biases in AI systems, arising from datasets used for training and the perspectives of those who develop AI systems. AI biases result in discriminatory outcomes across various sectors, including healthcare, employment, industry, and criminal justice. In addition to concerns about bias, users also experience concerns about privacy and the lack of user-friendliness with AI, which stresses the importance of integrating user perspectives into the creation of AI systems. The lack of diversity among AI development teams, particularly with respect to marginalized and underrepresented populations, amplifies AI bias and concerns, highlighting the critical need for more accessible and inclusive design practices. Diversifying datasets and design teams can support AI systems that are more accessible and inclusive.

To mitigate AI bias and support more accessible and inclusive AI, traditional ethical frameworks often focus on individual accountability. However, these frameworks are

S. Fernandes (✉) · H. Rahman
School of Health Policy and Management, Critical Disability Studies, York University, Toronto, ON, Canada
e-mail: h5rahman@yorku.ca

R. da Silveira Gorman
School of Health Policy and Management, York University, Toronto, ON, Canada
e-mail: gorman@yorku.ca


C. El Morr et al. (eds.), *Beyond Tech Fixes*,
https://doi.org/10.1007/978-3-031-93022-5_2

critiqued for their individualist approaches to systemic issues. As such, Kinnula et al. (2021) recommend adopting "distributed responsibility" among all stakeholders—designers, developers, and users, as a more effective approach to address AI bias. This approach encourages the integration of ethical considerations throughout the AI lifecycle. Initiatives like the Accessible and Inclusive Artificial Intelligence (AI2) workshop aim to tackle these complex issues and foster AI that genuinely serves all individuals.

Proponents of a social justice-oriented AI development advance a paradigmatic shift in which accessibility and inclusion are prioritized over technological progress, with participatory governance as an essential strategy (Moon, 2023). By incorporating diverse viewpoints into governance structures there is potential to more effectively identify and address biases, privacy concerns, and usability issues within AI systems, aligning them with the access and inclusion needs of the people they are designed to serve. However, while the push for inclusive AI is commendable for emphasizing the integration of ethical considerations into design, it often lacks detailed strategies for implementing participatory governance and design and fails to adequately address power imbalances.

As a result, this literature review explores emerging social justice frameworks which address injustices in data and design to promote diversity and foster a culture of shared responsibility, toward creating truly accessible and inclusive AI. The proposed framework emphasizes Data Sovereignty, Community-Based Co-Design, and Design Justice, ensuring marginalized communities control their data, shape design processes, and experience genuine, long-term engagement.

## Methods

Given the time-sensitive nature of the deliverable, a rapid review methodology was employed. While systematic reviews are considered the gold standard, they often require extensive time. Rapid reviews, as described by Khangura et al. (2012), are increasingly used to synthesize evidence efficiently for policymakers and stakeholders. Guidelines from the National Centre for Methods and Tools (NCCMT) informed the review process (Dobbins, 2017).

To identify relevant literature, several Google Scholar searches were conducted using exact-phrase queries with specified inclusion and exclusion criteria, limiting results to studies published post-2015.

- Inclusive Co-Design: The query "inclusive co-design" in the title yielded 11 results (June 28, 2023).
- Data Justice: The query "data justice" produced 205 results (June 22, 2023). Studies focusing on humanitarian, anti-poverty, health, environmental, surveillance, and education were included, while topics like biodiversity, entrepreneurship, and cryptocurrency were excluded.
- Community Co-Design: A search for "community co-design" yielded 45 results (June 22, 2023). Reviews or studies informing future co-design efforts were excluded.

- Community-Led Co-Design: The query "community-led co-design" resulted in 22 relevant studies (June 22, 2023).
- Design Justice: Searching for "design justice" produced 118 relevant results (June 22, 2023).

This method ensured a targeted inclusion of 401 studies of data and design frameworks with attention to marginalized communities and social equity in research. Two authors (SF and HR) scanned the articles (n = 401) for attentiveness to racism, colonialism, and ableism. As a result, the authors (SF and HR) selected 29 studies for review. SF and HR used the qualitative data analysis software Dedoose to code the studies (n = 29).

## Results

The results of the search are summarised in Table 1.

## Data Approaches

### *Data Justice*

Emerging from the tensions between development studies and surveillance studies in the mid-2000s, Data Justice is a framework developed by Linnet Taylor (2017). It addresses the dual nature of data: its potential to reveal injustices and its capacity to exacerbate surveillance of marginalized and underserved communities (Akbari, 2019; Albornoz et al., 2019; Heeks & Shekhar, 2019; Krishna, 2019; Masiero & Das, 2019; Sivajothy, 2019; Vera et al., 2019; Dagne, 2021; Goldkind et al., 2021; Hoefsloot et al., 2023; Leslie et al., 2022; Shaw & Sekalala, 2023). The advent of mobile phone technology in low-income countries generated vast amounts of data, which development researchers and major technology corporations were eager to exploit (Taylor, 2019). Development practitioners hailed the ability to collect data on poverty and inequities, hoping these datasets would help address these issues. However, surveillance studies warned against the unchecked collection of data from low-income countries, noting concerns about power imbalances, data extraction, and exploitation (Dencik et al., 2016; Taylor, 2019). To address the tension between the right to be seen and counted and the right to privacy, Taylor (2017) proposed three pillars of data justice:

1. Visibility
2. Access to representation
3. Informational privacy

**Table 1** Results

| | Reference | Population | Approach | Intervention |
|---|---|---|---|---|
| 1. | Taylor (2017) | General populations impacted by data practices | Data Justice | Explores frameworks for data governance addressing visibility, privacy, and non-discrimination |
| 2. | Akbari (2019) | Marginalized populations affected by surveillance | Data Justice | Highlights data practices that aim to balance visibility and privacy concerns |
| 3. | Heeks and Shekhar (2019) | Populations in developing regions | Data Justice | Examines data governance models to mitigate data-related injustices |
| 4. | Leslie et al. (2022) | Various populations affected by AI and data | Data Justice | Proposes data ethics frameworks to prevent discrimination and uphold privacy |
| 5. | Barreneche and Lombana-Bermudez (2023) | Populations affected by surveillance practices | Data Justice | Investigates the impact of surveillance on data rights and social justice |
| 6. | Masiero and Das (2019) | Low-income communities | Data Justice | Analyzes data-driven discrimination in anti-poverty programs |
| 7. | Sivajothy (2019) | Marginalized communities | Data Justice | Examining the role of "transparency" in data governance |
| 8. | Shaw and Sekalala (2023) | Marginalized communities | Data Justice | Assesses data visibility's role in humanitarian and health-related contexts |
| 9. | D'Ignazio & Klein (2020) | Marginalized groups in data science | Data Feminism | Advocates for intersectional approaches in data science prioritizing marginalized voices |
| 10. | Hoefsloot et al. (2023) | Women and marginalized data groups | Data Feminism | Analyzes intersectional approaches to enhance inclusivity in data science |
| 11. | Chinn (2022) | Diverse populations in data ecosystems | Data Feminism | Introduces feminist theories to restructure traditional data systems |
| 12. | Coombes et al. (2022) | Gender-diverse and marginalized populations | Data Feminism | Uses feminist epistemologies to challenge dominant data practices |
| 13. | Goldkind et al. (2021) | Indigenous and marginalized communities | Data Sovereignty | Explores ethical governance practices promoting data ownership for indigenous communities |
| 14. | Reyna (2022) | Indigenous and marginalized communities | Data Sovereignty | Promotes data control frameworks to counter data colonialism |

(continued)

**Table 1** (continued)

| | Reference | Population | Approach | Intervention |
|---|---|---|---|---|
| 15. | Albornoz et al. (2019) | Marginalized global communities | Data Sovereignty | Focuses on ethical governance to address data colonialism |
| 16. | Dagne (2021) | Marginalized communities in Africa | Data Sovereignty | Examines data control by local communities as a counter to colonial data practices |
| 17. | Costanza-Chock (2018a, 2018b) | Marginalized and oppressed communities | Design Justice | Proposes equitable design processes to oppose systemic oppression |
| 18. | Costanza-Chock (2020) | Communities affected by white supremacy | Design Justice | Advocates for anti-oppressive design frameworks centered on marginalized communities |
| 19. | Poudyal (2023) | Various marginalized groups | Design Justice | Investigates design practices that resist structural oppression |
| 20. | Huffstetler et al. (2022) | Marginalized communities | Design Justice | Develops design principles that resist systemic bias |
| 21. | Das et al. (2023) | Vulnerable populations | Design Justice | Analyzes equitable design models focused on resisting oppression |
| 22. | Bray et al. (2022) | Community-based groups | Community-Based Co-Design | Establishes collaborative design methods with community insights for equitable outcomes |
| 23. | Bhatia (2020) | Community members with lived experience | Community-Based Co-Design | Uses community expertise to guide design for equitable results |
| 24. | Stanley (2020) | Local communities | Community-Based Co-Design | Emphasizes co-design with community members as design experts |
| 25. | Till et al. (2022) | Across geographic locations and cultures | Community-Based Co-Design | Highlights challenges of co-design in low-constraint settings across geographical locations with different languages and cultural dynamics |
| 26. | Krishna (2019) | Underrepresented community groups | Community-Based Co-Design | Highlights participatory approaches to incorporate community perspectives |
| 27. | Vera et al. (2019) | Community groups with specific needs | Community-Based Co-Design | Engages community expertise in co-design for targeted interventions |
| 28. | Roy et al. (2019) | Local communities | Design Probes | Utilizes creative prompts to facilitate community engagement |
| 29. | Murphy (2022) | Marginalized populations | Design Probes | Uses creative tools to capture local insights and concerns for co-design |

Additionally, Taylor (2017) emphasized:

- (Dis)Engagement with technology
- Sharing in data's benefits
- Autonomy in technology choices
- Non-discrimination
- Ability to challenge bias
- Preventing discrimination

Recent critiques have shifted focus from Western-centric knowledge production to the struggles of community activists advocating for equity in digital and data systems (Leslie et al., 2022). Heeks and Renken (2016) call for integrating data justice frameworks with human rights, while Dencik et al. (2016) advocate for collaboration between data justice frameworks and civil society activists.

Heeks and Shekhar (2019) identify several dimensions of data justice: procedural (use of data), instrumental (outcomes of data use), rights-based (adherence to data rights), structural (societal support for just data outcomes), and distributive (inequality in data outcomes). The literature highlights the importance of the structural dimensions of data justice (Akbari, 2019; Goldkind et al., 2021), and Akbari (2019) suggests incorporating political and intersectional perspectives into data justice.

Data justice has been applied across various fields, including journalism, human rights, and international development (Goldkind et al., 2021). Specific examples include health data justice, which focuses on addressing the needs of marginalized communities in healthcare (Shaw & Sekalala, 2023), and environmental data justice, which integrates environmental and data justice frameworks to address related conflicts (Vera et al., 2019; Barreneche & Lombana-Bermudez, 2023).

Overall, the field of data justice is evolving to expand beyond a Western-centric perspective, addressing issues such as datafication, informational capitalism, privacy, and social justice, while incorporating non-Western viewpoints (Leslie et al., 2022).

## *Data Feminism*

Data feminism, as conceptualized by D'Ignazio and Klein (2020), is an approach that seeks to challenge hegemonic power structures by examining how data is used to sustain them (Costanza-Chock, 2020; Goldkind et al., 2021; Hoefsloot et al., 2023; Poudyal, 2023). D'Ignazio and Klein adopt a broad definition of feminism, encompassing perspectives beyond the dominant white male viewpoint, including those that oppose sexist and oppressive systems (Goldkind et al., 2021). Proponents of data feminism draw on feminist epistemologies, such as intersectionality theory, which emphasize lived experiences, positionality, and grounded knowledge. The principles of data feminism include:

- Examine power
- Challenge power
- Elevate emotion and embodiment
- Rethink binaries and hierarchies
- Embrace pluralism
- Consider context
- Make labor visible (D'Ignazio & Klein, 2020)

Data feminism offers a critique of Taylor's (2017) focus on visibility as the right to not be "seen" in data. Instead, data feminism emphasizes the need to address the undermining and invisibility of multiply marginalized and underrepresented communities in datasets and data governance (Hoefsloot et al., 2023). According to Hoefsloot et al. (2023), the underrepresentation of individuals who are sick, disabled, queer, trans, Black, Indigenous, and people of color in data contributes to these communities being underserved or harmed due to unchecked racism, sexism, and other intersecting systems of oppression in data.

One method for identifying and disrupting oppression through data is feminist counter-mapping or counter-data (Goldkind et al., 2021; Poudyal, 2023). Feminist counter-mapping involves activist techniques and technologies that challenge dominant power structures by documenting and mapping narratives that reveal the politics of geography and model alternative realities (Hodgson & Schroeder, 2002). Poudyal (2023) highlights María Salguero's Los feminicidios en México project as a prime example of counter-mapping. In response to the government's lack of public data on femicide in Mexico, Salguero created an open-access map to track femicides. This project not only tracks these events but also seeks to memorialize the victims and analyze the material conditions contributing to their murders.

Los feminicidios en México exemplifies data feminism's shift away from racist, patriarchal, and elitist approaches to data science, which often treat the field as esoteric and driven by numbers. Instead, feminist data practices promote intersectional pedagogies that aim to dismantle, rather than perpetuate, systems of oppression. Data feminism employs these practices to engage multiply marginalized and underserved communities in data science and governance, fostering equity and co-liberation.

### *Data Sovereignty*

The importance of protecting Indigenous and traditional data is well-documented in the literature (Stanley, 2020; Dagne, 2021; Goldkind et al., 2021; Reyna, 2022). In the African context, Dagne (2021) underscores the importance of recognizing the collective contributions of Indigenous farmers as original sources of traditional knowledge and farm data, despite their data not meeting the legal definitions for individual data subjects. Challenges in safeguarding traditional knowledge often arise from methodological concerns, such as whether to use Western methods or acquire intellectual property rights (Stanley, 2020).

One emerging response to these challenges is the concept of data sovereignty. This framework aims to grant Indigenous communities, other marginalized groups, and governments affected by data colonialism control over their data, including its collection and application (Goldkind et al., 2021). Goldkind et al. (2021) explains that data sovereignty involves shifting from a "data for development" model, which often extracts data from marginalized communities without equitable returns, to one where data is managed and controlled by the communities from which it originates.

In practice, data sovereignty allows communities to apply Indigenous data practices, such as using traditional knowledge frameworks to govern data collection, interpretation, and sharing (Goldkind et al., 2021). This approach is not just theoretical but involves real-world implementations, including the development of Indigenous data governance protocols and ethical guidelines for data collection and use (Goldkind et al., 2021; Stanley, 2020).

Reyna (2022) highlights the importance of respecting and incorporating Indigenous perspectives and knowledge into data governance frameworks. For example, the First Nations Principles of OCAP (Ownership, Control, Access, and Possession) are essential for ensuring that First Nations communities have control over their data and that data use is conducted with their explicit consent and benefits (Reyna, 2022). This approach emphasizes that sovereignty over data is crucial for empowering Indigenous communities and preserving their knowledge systems in the face of ongoing data colonialism.

In summary, data sovereignty represents a significant shift in how data is conceptualized and managed, aiming to empower communities that have historically been marginalized and exploited. This approach promotes equitable data governance practices and supports the protection and respect of traditional knowledge.

## Design Approaches

### *Design Justice*

Design Justice, rooted in participatory design, is both a theoretical framework and a practical approach that focuses on addressing inequities in design processes and outcomes influenced by systemic issues such as white supremacy, heteropatriarchy, capitalism, and settler colonialism (Costanza-Chock, 2018a, 2018b, 2020; Arista et al., 2021; Vera et al., 2019; Chinn, 2022; Reyna, 2022; Huffstetler et al., 2022; Das et al., 2023; Poudyal, 2023). Established by a community-based network of organizers and designers in 2015, the ten principles of Design Justice are:

1. Use design to sustain, heal, and empower communities while seeking liberation from exploitative and oppressive systems.
2. Center the voices of those directly impacted by design outcomes.

3. Prioritize the impact of design on the community over the designer's intentions.
4. View change as emerging from an accountable, accessible, and collaborative process rather than as an end point.
5. See the designer's role as that of a facilitator rather than an expert.
6. Recognize everyone as an expert based on their lived experience, contributing unique insights to the design process.
7. Share design knowledge and tools with communities.
8. Aim for sustainable, community-led, and controlled outcomes.
9. Pursue non-exploitative solutions that reconnect us with the earth and each other.
10. Identify and build upon existing community-level solutions, honoring traditional, Indigenous, and local knowledge and practices.

Sasha Costanza-Chock describes Design Justice as "a dual pragmatic/utopic approach that simultaneously offers concrete suggestions for immediate implementation to improve people's quality of life while also calling out power inequalities and larger structural forces that impact people's life chances in the long run" (Costanza-Chock, 2020, p. 134). Drawing on Black feminist theories of intersectionality and the matrix of domination (Collins, 2002), as well as disability justice, Costanza-Chock has further developed Design Justice practices. This framework promotes a multifaceted approach to addressing both procedural and distributive justice aspects by advocating for the participation of marginalized and underserved communities in technology design processes and ensuring an equitable distribution of design costs and benefits.

To support these goals, Costanza-Chock (2020) reiterates recommendations from the Tech4SJ (Tech for Social Justice) initiative:

- Adopt co-design methods.
- Develop specific, concrete mechanisms for community accountability.
- Center community needs over tools.
- Invest in education (both formal and informal) that teaches co-design methods to more practitioners.
- Create tech clinics, modeled on legal clinics.
- Avoid "parachuting" technologists into communities.
- Stop reinventing the wheel.

Design Justice emphasizes design practices that consider the material conditions of transnational systemic oppressions and inequities. It foregrounds the potential of design to either perpetuate structural violence or subvert it (Das et al., 2023). The literature stresses the need for design practitioners to ensure an equitable distribution of both burdens and benefits, ensuring that the most impacted communities do not withstand the most design harm while others reap the rewards (Reyna, 2022). Practitioners should critically assess the limitations of "good" intentions and prioritize the material consequences for affected communities (Poudyal, 2023). The potential of co-design is highlighted as a practice that supports equitable power and resource distribution between impacted communities and design practitioners. Design Justice encourages community leadership in design activities and decision-making, incorporating community-based design traditions. Overall, Design Justice aims to empower communities, advance social transformation, and shift decision-making power and resources from institutions to community members, aligning with participatory design principles to foster inclusive practices for collective liberation and ecological sustainability (Huffstetler et al., 2022).

## *Community-Based Co-Design*

Community-led co-design practices are recognized in the literature as essential for supporting equity-informed design research, activities, and outcomes for historically marginalized and underserved communities (Bhatia, 2020; Stanley, 2020; Costanza-Chock, 2020; Dagne, 2021; Bray et al., 2022; Leslie et al., 2022; Till et al., 2022; Hoefsloot et al., 2023; Poudyal, 2023). Co-design is a form of participatory design (PD) that extends beyond traditional PD methods to involve users more deeply in the design process. According to Bray et al. (2022), "Co-design aims to bring people outside formal design and research spaces into the design process. This method promotes deeper collaboration with designers and non-designers across disciplines and cultures, emphasizing the acknowledgment of lived expertise" (para. 1). Costanza-Chock (2020) differentiates PD and co-design from Human-Centered Design (HCD), noting that the former includes end-users throughout the design process, while the latter includes them only as needed, making HCD more efficiency-driven and co-design more oriented toward social justice.

Despite its potential advantages over HCD and PD, Bray et al. (2022) argue that co-design alone may not adequately support equitable participation due to inherent power imbalances in academic research methods, which often influence collaborative design practices. To address these imbalances, community-led co-design can enhance the equity of design research, activities, and outcomes (Bhatia, 2020; Stanley, 2020; Till et al., 2022).

The literature highlights community-based co-design (CBCD) as a proven method for empowering communities most affected by design processes to lead cooperative efforts with institutional researchers and practitioners. Till et al. (2022) define CBCD as "the application of co-design techniques with the active involvement of the community being designed with, while embracing their values and norms" (p. 2). By incorporating community traditions and principles, CBCD fosters a democratic transformation of design processes. For instance, Stanley, (2020) utilizes CBCD to protect Indigenous Knowledge within African communities, emphasizing the importance of aligning research with community values and concerns. If communities do not perceive value or benefit from the research, adjusting objectives and adopting flexible practices can better align outcomes with community preferences. Stanley, (2020) illustrates this with the ovaHerero community, where elders initially questioned the relevance of working on computers during a drought. However, after explaining the research's purpose and potential benefits, the community agreed to participate. This case highlights CBCD as a collaborative, culturally sensitive approach that prioritizes the needs and traditions of the involved communities.

### *Design Probes*

Design probes are a co-design tool that researchers can use to gain an empathetic understanding of the community at the beginning of the design process (Roy et al., 2019; Bray et al., 2022). According to the authors, probes act as a gateway to co-design, enabling co-researchers to engage with various prompts and generate insights into the knowledge held by impacted communities and the questions they seek to answer. While design probes are investigative, they also foster creativity. Most notably, design probes respect and incorporate the lived experiences and expertise of co-researchers. For example, Stanley (2020) describes a technology probe conducted with a community co-designer. This probe involved learning to use a tablet, critiquing technologies that were unsuitable for the community, and refining the technology to better meet community needs.

## Limitations of "Justice" Approaches

### *Data "Justice"*

The literature discusses the pervasive influence of extractive logics in research, particularly in environmental data practices. Even well-intentioned researchers may unintentionally replicate colonial and racial research methods, given that institutions have historically been shaped by these forces. Extractive logics are ingrained in how environmental data is understood, often influenced by industries such as mining and fossil fuels. Data is described as capable of healing and destruction—on the one hand it can help address the crises like climate change, and on the other hand it can harm marginalized groups through systems racist predictive policing, digital discrimination, and surveillance.

The literature critiques the notion of data as raw or neutral, referencing Gitelman et al. (2013), who argue that data is always embedded in political contexts (Vera et al., 2019). The extractive logics of data production reinforce interlocking structures of oppression—what Black feminist scholar Patricia Hill Collins calls the "matrix of domination" (Collins, 1990; Costanza-Chock, 2018a, 2018b). The literature also highlights that marginalized populations, such as the homeless, those without government identification documents, or those living on the peripheries of mainstream societies, are often rendered invisible by data initiatives, while elites benefit from these practices without being held accountable (Heeks & Shekhar, 2019). Moreover, even when members of communities do become visible through data, they often lose control over how they are represented, illustrating the "ambivalence of legibility" (Heeks & Shekhar, 2019, p. 18).

Further, the literature reviews data justice as a field which has historically been dominated by Western perspectives, leading to biased identification of issues and solutions (Leslie et al., 2022). This has limited representation of non-Western values, as reflected in critiques of data governance, where datasets often privilege whiteness and serve private interests (Sivajothy, 2019; Noble, 2018). For instance, Stanley, (2020) emphasizes that technological interventions, particularly for Indigenous Knowledge, are often inappropriate for African contexts, perpetuating colonial dynamics.

Thus, the literature emphasizes that extractive logics underpin all data practices, including those aimed at achieving justice. Datasets and their uses are embedded in the extractive and intersecting systemic violences of white supremacy, heteropatriarchy, ableism, and settler colonialism, despite the social justice-oriented intentions and efforts of researchers.

## *Design "Justice"*

The literature critiques the pursuit of decolonial-feminist computing, hospitable data, and design justice, particularly from privileged spaces with access to innovation labs, big data tools, and sizeable funding (Poudyal, 2023). One major concern is the risk of perpetuating epistemic violence, where the voices of a few marginalized individuals may be assumed to represent the entire marginalized group in question, leading to essentializing and incomplete portrayals of underrepresented communities in social justice-oriented designs.

Poudyal (2023) argues the "social justice checklist," which aims to promote accessible and inclusive practices, can inadvertently become a tool for exploitation if it prioritizes social justice language over meaningful practices to combat injustice. The exploitation of communities couched in social justice tick boxes is exacerbated by neoliberal identity politics, white saviorism, and the commodification of diversity, accessibility, and inclusion within academic and professional contexts. Thus, the co-optation of social justice by wealthy corporations championing design "for" marginalized and underrepresented communities can lead to the further exploitation of these communities, particularly from the Global South, while academics and design practitioners can advance their careers under the brand of social justice.

Moreover, despite a theoretical commitment to Design Justice, practical limitations are apparent. According to Chinn (2022) many Design Justice Network (DJN) members, while promoting justice, often work on projects funded by extractive corporations, revealing a conflict between their stated values and their actual practices. While some design justice practitioners apply design justice principles in less contradictory ways, they continue to collaborate with international NGOs and corporations that perpetuate extractive practices. The use of social justice language as a marketing tool by designers working with exploitative entities further escalates this issue. Consequently, Design Justice can translate into a superficial branding exercise rather than a meaningfully transformative approach to accessibility and inclusion.

## Discussion

### *Opportunities Across Data and Design Approaches to Support Accessible and Inclusive AI*

The literature reveals that the various data and design approaches identified can address power imbalances and enhance accessibility and inclusion by promoting community involvement, challenging systemic biases, and ensuring that the benefits and burdens of data and design are distributed more fairly. They advocate for practices that respect and empower marginalized communities, contributing to more accessible and inclusive outcomes across various fields.

### *Supporting Equity*

Data Sovereignty, Community-Based Co-Design, and Design Probes focus on equity and accessibility for marginalized communities by affording them access to and control over data and design processes. Data Sovereignty ensures that Indigenous and marginalized communities manage their data and apply traditional knowledge, promoting autonomy and equitable outcomes (Goldkind et al., 2021; Reyna, 2022; Albornoz et al., 2019; Dagne, 2021). Community-Based Co-Design involves communities directly in the design process, respecting their values and expertise to create meaningful and beneficial solutions (Bray et al., 2022; Bhatia, 2020; Stanley, 2020; Till et al., 2022; Krishna, 2019; Vera et al., 2019). Design Probes engage communities early to gather insights on access needs and ensure that their lived experiences and accessibility needs shape the design outcomes (Roy et al., 2019; Murphy, 2022).

### *Incorporating Community Insights*

Data Justice, Data Feminism, and Design Justice emphasize the need to address systemic inequities and power imbalances. Data Justice promotes visibility, representation, and privacy for marginalized communities, ensuring their data benefits are balanced with rights protection. Data Feminism challenges hegemonic structures and highlights the importance of including underrepresented groups, advocating for systemic change to rectify biases (D'Ignazio & Klein, 2020; Hoefsloot et al., 2023; Chinn, 2022; Coombes et al., 2022). Design Justice centers the voices of impacted communities, ensuring that design processes are inclusive and address structural inequalities (Costanza-Chock, 2018a, 2018b, 2020; Poudyal, 2023; Huffstetler et al., 2022; Das et al., 2023).

### *Participatory Processes*

Across these approaches, there is a strong emphasis on empowerment. Data Justice and Design Justice advocate for community involvement in data governance and design processes, respectively, ensuring that decisions reflect the needs and voices of most impacted. Community-Based Co-Design and Design Probes further these ideals by integrating community input from the outset and throughout the design lifecycle, fostering a collaborative approach to the empowerment of marginalized and underserved communities in design (Bray et al., 2022; Bhatia, 2020; Stanley, 2020; Till et al., 2022; Krishna, 2019; Vera et al., 2019; Roy et al., 2019; Murphy, 2022).

## Challenges Across Data and Design Approaches to Support Accessible and Inclusive AI

Both data justice and design justice face limitations related to epistemic violence, commodification, tokenism, and challenges in practical implementation. Addressing these limitations requires a critical examination of these frameworks' theoretical and practical aspects, ensuring that efforts towards justice are genuine and impactful rather than superficial and extractive.

### *Extractive Logics*

Both data justice and design justice frameworks grapple with the legacies of extractive logics and epistemic violence. In data justice, extractive logics often manifest in environmental data practices, where the good intentions of researchers may inadvertently perpetuate colonial and racial biases due to the historical shaping of research institutions. This issue is compounded by industries like mining and fossil fuels, which influence how data is collected and utilized, reinforcing systemic oppression. In design justice, there is also the presence of epistemic violence where the experiences of a few marginalized individuals are incorrectly generalized to represent a marginalized group, informing incomplete and potentially harmful portrayals of the group (Vera et al., 2019; Poudyal, 2023).

### *Commodification and Tokenism*

Both frameworks face challenges related to the commodification and tokenism of diversity and inclusion. In data justice, the "charismatic and violent" nature of data can lead to marginalized groups being either exploited or rendered invisible, as their data is used without proper consideration of their control over representation. In design justice, the use of social justice rhetoric can sometimes become a superficial branding tool rather than a commitment to genuine equitable design practices. This commodification of diversity can exploit marginalized communities, particularly those from the Global South, while enabling privileged individuals to advance their careers under the guise of social justice (Chinn, 2022; Poudyal, 2023).

### *Practical Implementation Challenges*

The translation of theoretical principles into practical, actionable frameworks remains a significant limitation for both data justice and design justice. For data justice, there is a need for critical frameworks like Environmental Data Justice (EDJ) to address the political contexts embedded in data practices (Vera et al., 2019). However, the practical application of these frameworks often lacks clarity, leading to inconsistent results (Costanza-Chock, 2018a, 2018b). In design justice, despite a commitment to participatory design and equity, practical limitations include working with exploitative clients and organizations that perpetuate extractive practices. This disconnects between stated values and actual practices undermines the effectiveness of design justice approaches (Chinn, 2022).

### *Ambivalence of Legibility*

Both frameworks must address the challenges of "ambivalence of legibility" and persistent power imbalances. In data justice, marginalized populations risk losing control over how they are represented once they become visible through data initiatives, highlighting a struggle between visibility and control (Heeks & Shekhar, 2019. In design justice, power imbalances persist despite efforts to empower marginalized communities. Design practices may still reflect the power dynamics of privileged spaces, leading to tokenistic involvement rather than meaningful participation (Chinn, 2022).

## A Framework for Social Justice-Oriented Practices for Accessible and Inclusive AI

Based on our findings we advance the following framework for social justice-oriented practices for accessible and inclusive AI. A social justice-oriented AI framework should prioritize Data Sovereignty to give marginalized communities control over their data, fostering equitable outcomes. Community-Based Co-Design and Design Justice must involve communities from the outset to outcomes, ensuring their experiences shape design. Data Feminism and Data Justice should address systemic biases, ensuring fair representation and privacy. To combat tokenism and extractive practices, the framework should focus on genuine engagement and long-term partnerships. Finally, it must integrate self-reflection and accountability, ensuring theoretical principles translate into effective actions that challenge power imbalances. The detail of the proposed framework is below (Table 2):

## Conclusion

The data and design approaches discussed in this review reveal opportunities to support accessible and inclusive AI. Data Sovereignty, Community-Based Co-Design, and Design Probes focus on enhancing accessibility by affording marginalized communities the control over datasets and collection methods and influence over the design processes and outcomes. Data Justice, Data Feminism, and Design Justice seek to combat systemic inequities and power imbalances, by including marginalized communities in data and design processes.

However, these social justice-oriented approaches to data and design also involve challenges such as extractive logics, commodification, tokenism, and difficulties in practical implementation. The persistence of exploitative practices and the marketing of diversity compromises the integrity of these approaches. Practical implementation issues, including the ambivalence of legibility and persistent power imbalances, further complicate the translation of justice-oriented theoretical perspectives into transformative practice.

Addressing these limitations requires a critical and nuanced approach to both theory and practice, ensuring that efforts toward justice are both meaningful and impactful. By tackling these challenges reflexively, the field of AI can better realize its potential to create accessible, and inclusive AI systems that genuinely reflect and serve the needs of marginalized and underserved communities.

**Table 2** A framework for social justice-oriented practices for accessible and inclusive AI

| |
|---|
| **Co-researchers and co-designers must be afforded:** |
| 1. **Access to the control of processes from the outset to outcome** |
| To facilitate accessibility for marginalized and underserved communities in AI, access to governance and management of data and design processes must be supported. Accessibility must be understood as a process of negotiating power imbalances and not simply a product those with power (researchers) deliver to those who are disempowered in society (co-researchers and co-designers) |
| 2. **Inclusion to challenge power imbalances and systemic violence** |
| To facilitate inclusion for marginalized and underrepresented communities in AI, co-researchers and co-designers must be included to challenge systems of oppression and those in power, including the academic and industry researchers and designers. This objective can keep tokenizing forms of inclusion in check |
| 3. **Empowerment as a self-assessed outcome** |
| To facilitate meaningful accessibility and inclusion, co-designers, co-researchers, and communities most impacted by AI must be consulted for self-assessments of empowerment. Researchers must not assess the empowerment of communities on their behalf |
| **Academic and industry researchers and designers must undertake:** |
| 1. **Combat extractive logics** |
| To counter exploitative AI, researchers must fight the extractive logics of data and design in an ongoing way. Good intentions and aspirations for justice are empty promises if researchers do not actively fight the pervasive systems of injustice and extraction their research is embedded in |
| 2. **Combat the commodification of "diversity"** |
| To meaningfully support equity, researchers must be weary of co-opting the label of "diversity" to market themselves and their research |
| 3. **Address the practical challenges that arise from the gap in theory and practice** |
| To bring theories of accessible and inclusive AI to life, researchers address practical implementation challenges head-on. Researchers must also attend to contradictions between stated values and practices when developing social-justice oriented AI |
| 4. **Address the ambivalence of legibility** |
| To visibilize the marginalized and underrepresented communities to their benefit, researchers must ensure that those communities are afforded the power to shape their representation. Simply making communities experiencing oppression legible, without power to determine the nature of their visibility, can be detrimental to the communities concerned |

## Limitations and Directions for Future Research

While rapid reviews have their merits, they are limited by time constraints and a search strategy that is less rigorous than systematic reviews (Moons et al., 2021). As such, these limitations may have resulted in the exclusion of relevant studies and selection biases in this review. Future research should continue to explore and refine a comprehensive understanding of Data and Design Justice frameworks and practices, with particular attention to the limitations identified in this review, to create AI systems that are truly accessible and inclusive.

## References

Akbari, A. (2019). Spatial | data justice: Mapping and digitised strolling against moral police in Iran. *SSRN Electronic Journal*. Retrieved from https://doi.org/10.2139/ssrn.3460224

Albornoz, D., Reilly, K., & Flores, M. (2019). Community-based data justice: a model for data collection in informal urban settlements. SSRN Electronic Journal. Retrieved from https://doi.org/10.2139/ssrn.3460245

Arista, N., Costanza-Chock, S., Ghazavi, V., & Kite, S. (2021). *Against reduction: Designing a human future with machines*. MIT Press.

Barreneche, C., & Lombana-Bermudez, A. (2023). Civic participation in the Datafied society | Another infrastructure is possible: Grassroots citizen sensing and environmental data justice in Colombia. *International Journal of Communication, 17*, 3638–3659. Retrieved from https://ijoc.org/index.php/ijoc/article/view/18821.

Huffstetler, H.E., Boland, S. E., Williams, C. R., Rice, D. K., & Ramaswamy, R. (2022). Beyond virtue-signaling: Advancing Equity through Design Justice and Public Health Critical Race praxis. Health Equity, 6(1), 21–26. https://doi.org/10.1089/heq.2021.0075

Bray, K. E., Harrington, C., Parker, A. G., Diakhate, N., & Roberts, J. (2022). Radical futures: Supporting community-led design engagements through an Afrofuturist speculative design toolkit. In *CHI conference on human factors in computing systems* (pp. 1–13). https://doi.org/10.1145/3491102.3501945

C Collins, P. H. (1990). Black feminist thought in the matrix of domination. Black feminist thought: Knowledge, consciousness, and the politics of empowerment, 138(1990), 221–238.

Collins, P. H. (2002). What's going on? Black feminist thought and the politics of postmodernism. In Working the ruins (pp. 47–79). Routledge

Chinn, G. A. (2022). *Looking to labor: Supplementing design justice work with a labor analysis*. Georgetown University-Graduate School of Arts & Sciences, Communication, Culture & Technology.

Coombes, E., Wolf, A., Blunt, D., & Sparks, K. (2022). Disabled sex workers' fight for digital rights, platform accessibility, and design justice. *Disability Studies Quarterly, 42*(2), 2. https://doi.org/10.18061/dsq.v42i2.9097

Costanza-Chock, S. (2018a). Design justice, A.I., and escape from the matrix of domination. *Journal of Design and Science*. https://doi.org/10.21428/96c8d426

Costanza-Chock, S. (2018b). *Design justice: Towards an intersectional feminist framework for design theory and practice*. DRS biennial conference series. Retrieved from https://dl.designresearchsociety.org/drs-conference-papers/drs2018/researchpapers/38.

Costanza-Chock, S. (2020). *Design justice: Community-led practices to build the worlds we need*. The MIT Press. Retrieved from https://library.oapen.org/handle/20.500.12657/43542.

Dagne, T. W. (2021). Where copyright meet privacy in the big data era: Access to and control over user data in agriculture and the role of copyright. *Vanderbilt Journal of Entertainment & Technology Law, 24*, 675. Retrieved from https://heinonline.org/HOL/Page?handle=hein.journals/vanep24&id=715&div=&collection=.

Das, M., Ostrowski, A. K., Ben-David, S., Roeder, G. J., Kimura, K., D'Ignazio, C., Breazeal, C., & Verma, A. (2023). Auditing design justice: The impact of social movements on design pedagogy at a technology institution. *Design Studies, 86*, 101183. https://doi.org/10.1016/j.destud.2023.101183

Dencik, L., Hintz, A., & Cable, J. (2016). Towards data justice? the ambiguity of anti-surveillance resistance in political activism. Big Data & Society, 3(2). https://doi.org/10.1177/2053951716679678.

Dobbins, M. (2017). Rapid Review Guidebook. Hamilton, ON: National Collaborating Centre for Methods and Tools.

D'Ignazio, C., & Klein, L. F. (2020). Data feminism. The MIT Press.

Gitelman, L. (Ed.). (2013). Raw data is an oxymoron. MIT press.

Goldkind, L., Wolf, L., & LaMendola, W. (2021). Data justice: Social work and a more just future. *Journal of Community Practice, 29*(3), 237–256. Retrieved March 14, 2025, from https://www.tandfonline.com/doi/full/10.1080/10705422.2021.1984354?scroll=top&needAccess=true.

Leslie et al. (2022). Data Justice: Data Justice in Practice: A Guide for Developers, Report, November 2022, Global Partnership on AI.

Heeks, R., & Shekhar, S. (2019). Datafication, development and marginalised urban communities: An applied data justice framework. *Information, Communication & Society, 22*(7), 992–1011. https://doi.org/10.1080/1369118x.2019.1599039

Heeks, R., & Renken, J. (2016). Data Justice for development: What would it mean? SSRN Electronic Journal. https://doi.org/10.2139/ssrn.3431744

Hodgson, D. L., & Schroeder, R. A. (2002). Dilemmas of counter-mapping community resources in Tanzania. Development and Change, 33(1), 79–100. https://doi.org/10.1111/1467-7660.00241.

Hoefsloot, F. I., Richter, C., Martínez, J., & Pfeffer, K. (2023). The datafication of water infrastructure and its implications for (il)legible water consumers. *Urban Geography, 44*(4), 729–751. https://doi.org/10.1080/02723638.2021.2019499

Bhatia, A. (2020, September 16). How a community-led design initiative in Toronto is redefining neighborhood revitalization from the bottom-up . Brookings. https://www.brookings.edu/articles/how-a-community-led-design-initiative-in-toronto-is-redefining-neighborhood-revitalization-from-the-bottom-up/

Huffstetler, H. E., Boland, S. E., Williams, C. R., Rice, D. K., & Ramaswamy, R. (2022). Beyond virtue-signaling: Advancing equity through design justice and public health critical race praxis. *Health Equity, 6*(1), 21–26. https://doi.org/10.1089/heq.2021.0075

Khangura, S., Konnyu, K., Cushman, R., Grimshaw, J., & Moher, D. (2012). Evidence summaries: The evolution of a rapid review approach. Systematic Reviews, 1(1). https://doi.org/10.1186/2046-4053-1-10

Kinnula, M., Iivari, N., Sharma, S., Eden, G., Turunen, M., Achuthan, K., Nedungadi, P., Avellan, T., Thankachan, B., & Tulaskar, R. (2021). Researchers' toolbox for the future: Understanding and designing accessible and inclusive artificial intelligence (AIAI). *Academic Mindtrek* 2021:1–4. https://doi.org/10.1145/3464327.3464965

Krishna, S. (2019). Aadhaar-led identification and datafication among informal workers in South India: A data-justice perspective. *SSRN Electronic Journal*. https://doi.org/10.2139/ssrn.3460235

Masiero, S., & Das, S. (2019). Datafying anti-poverty programmes: Implications for data justice. *Information, Communication & Society, 22*(7), 916–933. https://doi.org/10.1080/1369118X.2019.1575448

Moon, M. J. (2023). Searching for inclusive artificial intelligence for social good: Participatory governance and policy recommendations for making AI more inclusive and benign for society. *Public Administration Review, 83*(6), 1496–1505. https://doi.org/10.1111/puar.13648

Moons, P., Goossens, E., & Thompson, D. R. (2021). Rapid reviews: the pros and cons of an accelerated review process. European Journal of Cardiovascular Nursing, 20(5), 515–519.

Murphy, M. (2022). Chemical futures and environmental data justice. *UnderCurrents: Journal of Critical Environmental Studies, 21*, 45–48. https://doi.org/10.25071/2292-4736/40349

Noble, S. U. (2018). Algorithms of oppression: How search engines reinforce racism. In Algorithms of oppression. New York university press.

Poudyal, B. (2023). *Re-rhetoricizing global souths contrapuntally: Borderless transnational feminist design justice.* Open access theses & dissertations. Retrieved from https://scholarworks.utep.edu/open_etd/3884.

Reyna, M. (2022). *Design justice in community-oriented engineering pedagogy and practice.* Master's theses. Retrieved from https://doi.org/10.15368/theses.2022.60

Roy, A., Oldfield, S., McElroy, E., Malson, H., Graziani, T., Nevarez Martinez, D., Rosenthal, T. J., Losier, T., Samara, T., Blomley, N., Goodling, E., DeFilippis, J., Bissell, E., Haas, G., Garcia-Lamarca, M., Kaika, M., Kurwa, R., Khan, H., Fields, D., … Perry, K.-K. (2019). *Housing justice in unequal cities*. Retrieved from https://escholarship.org/uc/item/4kq1j0df.

Shaw, J., & Sekalala, S. (2023). Health data justice: Building new norms for health data governance. *NPJ Digital Medicine, 6*, 30. https://doi.org/10.1038/s41746-023-00780-4

Sivajothy, S. (2019). With and against transparency: taking a critical look at how "transparency" is taken up in data justice discourses. *The iJournal: Student Journal of the Faculty of Information, 5*(1), 1. https://doi.org/10.33137/ijournal.v5i1.33474

Stanley, C. (2020). Community-based co-design of a crowdsourcing task management application for safeguarding indigenous knowledge.

Taylor, L. (2017). What is data justice? The case for connecting digital rights and freedoms globally. *Big Data & Society, 4*(2), 205395171773633. https://doi.org/10.1177/2053951717736335

Taylor, L. (2019). Global Data Justice. Communications of the ACM, 62(6), 22–24. https://doi.org/10.1145/3325279

Till, S., Farao, J., Coleman, T. L. Shandu, L. D., Khuzwayo, N., Muthelo, L., Mbombi, M. O., Bopane, M., Motlhatlhedi, M., Mabena, G., Van Heerden, A., Mothiba, T. M., Norris, S., Verdezoto Dias, N., & Densmore, M. (2022). Community-based co-design across geographic locations and cultures: Methodological lessons from co-design workshops in South Africa. In *Participatory design conference 2022* (Vol. 1, pp. 120–132). https://doi.org/10.1145/3536169.3537786.

Vera, L. A., Walker, D., Murphy, M., Mansfield, B., Siad, L. M., & Ogden, J. (2019). When data justice and environmental justice meet: Formulating a response to extractive logic through environmental data justice. *Information, Communication & Society, 22*(7), 1012–1028. https://doi.org/10.1080/1369118X.2019.1596293

# Part II
# Social Impact: Examining the Crossroads of AI and Disability

## 1.1 Introduction

In this section, we explore how AI is reshaping everyday experiences for disabled people across education, employment, accessibility, and healthcare. The authors offer empirical, theoretical, and design-based reflections that illuminate both the potential and the perils of AI technologies in these domains. Through a disability justice lens, these chapters interrogate where AI reinforces ableist norms and where it might be harnessed to support inclusion, empowerment, and meaningful participation.

# AI and the Disability Divide: Towards a Transdisciplinary Approach

**Sarah Taleghani**

## Introduction

Envision a world where artificial intelligence (AI) development is guided by a transdisciplinary approach, integrating disability justice principles from the initial design phase throughout implementation. Such an approach would not only enhance accessibility but also actively dismantle systemic inequities, ensuring that AI technologies serve as tools of empowerment rather than exclusion.

Disability and AI are often discussed in terms of potential, such as how new and emerging technologies can significantly improve accessibility or promote independence. However, AI's potential to enhance equity in accessibility often falls short due to deep-seated systemic biases and practices that marginalize groups (Gorman et al., 2024). Biases are not inevitable; they stem from decisions made throughout AI technologies' development, evaluation, management, and design features (Newman-Griffis et al., 2023). These biases reflect broader societal inequities, such as ableism, which can become embedded in AI systems if not actively addressed (Newman-Griffis et al., 2023).

Furthermore, the underrepresentation of marginalized groups, including Indigenous and Black people, within Canadian disability sector organizations is being noticed (Gorman et al., 2024). This lack of representation affects the development of equitable technologies and highlights the need for greater diversity in decision-making processes. In this chapter, I argue for a transdisciplinary approach to disability justice and AI that actively challenges exclusionary systems rather than simply adapting to them.

S. Taleghani (✉)
School of Health Policy and Management, York University, Toronto, ON, Canada
e-mail: saraht48@yorku.ca


C. El Morr et al. (eds.), *Beyond Tech Fixes*,
https://doi.org/10.1007/978-3-031-93022-5_3

According to Gorman et al. (2024), disability data justice is "an important aspect of Disability Justice, which centres critical race, anticolonial, feminist, and abolitionist disability politics" (p. 30). The author states that this framework challenges data ableism and emphasizes making data more accessible and enhancing digital literacy within diverse disability communities. Equitable AI adoption relies on technological progress and ensuring that marginalized communities, particularly those in institutional settings, have access to digital literacy and internet access and contribute to data collection and sharing processes (Gorman et al., 2024). In Canada, institutionalized individuals with developmental and intellectual disabilities are excluded from the Canadian Survey on Disability, making it challenging to advocate for their rights and needs (Gorman et al., 2024). The responsible collection and use of data to inform AI development is equally important. However, fully integrating insights from excluded communities and diverse fields into AI development processes is equally crucial for actively dismantling existing power structures. Incorporating multiple perspectives offers an alternative to traditional research frameworks, often reinforcing exclusion.

A similar challenge exists in AI and disability justice: ensuring that insights from diverse fields are brought together and fully integrated into frameworks that actively dismantle existing power structures. Transdisciplinary research (TDR) paves the way for AI development to move beyond surface-level inclusion and strive for meaningful, justice-driven transformation (Boger et al., 2017). This approach prioritizes accessibility from the start of the design process and encourages continuous adaptation, addressing the evolving nature of societal challenges often referred to as "wicked problems" (Boger et al., 2017). By embedding collaborative practices into AI development, we can ensure that technologies accommodate diverse needs and actively support and empower affected communities. Without this collaboration, algorithmic hiring systems, for example, can unintentionally create barriers for people with disabilities, limiting their access to employment opportunities and resulting in financial hardship (Newman-Griffis et al., 2023). As AI developers, disability justice advocates, healthcare providers, and researchers, we must adopt a transdisciplinary approach that balances personalized strategies and promotes solutions that protect the rights of individuals with disabilities. This commitment to equity requires ethical data collection and use management, identifying structural shortcomings, and working toward more equitable systems to ensure fairness throughout.

Building on the principles of TDR in healthcare and aging, this chapter extends these concepts into AI and disability justice. Justice-centred innovations must prioritize the voices of those directly affected, ensuring AI's benefits are accessible and equitable.

## Advancing Disability Justice Through TDR and Justice-Oriented AI

TDR is widely recognized for effectively bringing together various experts and stakeholders to address complex challenges (Grigorovich et al., 2019; Lawless et al., 2024; Lawrence et al., 2022; Pineo et al., 2021). This approach combines various areas of knowledge, encouraging collaborative problem-solving to address challenges too complex for any single discipline to solve alone (Pineo et al., 2021). To move beyond theoretical strategies and actively incorporate feedback, achieving equity and inclusivity in AI requires more than interdisciplinary collaboration.

Transdisciplinary approaches at The Interactive Media, Poetics, Aesthetics, Cognition, and Technology (IMPACT) lab at the University of Regina utilize transdisciplinary and interdisciplinary methods to integrate diverse perspectives into health and technology research and involve disability communities (Riegel & Robinson, 2023). This is evident in a project that uses eye-tracking technology for creative expression, demonstrating how disability, technology, and ableism intersect within an interdisciplinary and transdisciplinary framework (Riegel & Robinson, 2023). Transdisciplinary research is essential in disability justice, where traditional research methods have often treated disabled individuals as subjects rather than contributors. By working alongside disabled individuals and integrating their expertise, researchers can help ensure that AI systems are designed to be fairer and more accessible. However, achieving this level of collaboration requires fully integrating transdisciplinary perspectives, which remains a significant challenge. Riegel and Robinson (2023) present a compelling case for viewing TDR as an essential framework for changing our understanding of disability. The authors emphasize that TDR is more than just a research method; it is a way to reshape how disability is understood, stating:

> *As researchers, transdisciplinarity affords a way to conceive a project that relies on community participation to address the broader social challenge of how we perceive disability and how ableism pervades health research rather than of disability as a problem to be solved. (*Riegel & Robinson, 2023*, p. 188).*

This insightful perspective challenges traditional narratives that portray disability solely as an impairment that needs fixing. Instead, it invites us to recognize disability as a social reality shaped by systemic exclusion. Riegel and Robinson advocate for a paradigm shift, viewing disability not as a flaw to be fixed but as an aspect of human diversity impacted by social exclusion.

Boger et al. (2017) discuss the COACH project, which exemplifies a transdisciplinary approach to AI by combining expertise from computer science, engineering, healthcare, and human factors to create an assistive technology for individuals living with dementia (Boger et al., 2017). The system uses adaptive learning to personalize prompts for daily activities like handwashing and adjusting guidance based on users' evolving needs as their dementia progresses (Boger et al., 2017). The COACH project not only demonstrates how transdisciplinary collaboration can lead to transformative, real-world outcomes within a disability justice framework but also emphasizes its development process involving regular feedback loops with users and caregivers, ensuring the technology effectively meets real-world needs (Boger et al., 2017). Results showed that COACH enabled individuals to wash their hands independently, enhancing autonomy and improving quality of life (Boger et al., 2017).

Both the COACH project (Boger et al., 2017) and IMPACT Lab (Riegel & Robinson, 2023) highlight how TDR can drive meaningful change through AI and technology for disability justice. COACH enhances autonomy for individuals with dementia through personalized assistive technology, and the IMPACT Lab creates opportunities for art and creative expression for individuals with mobility limitations. These projects emphasize the importance of positioning disabled individuals as active collaborators and co-creators in technology development. As the AI field advances, integrating diverse expertise, lived experiences, and perspectives becomes essential to creating technologies that do more than address surface-level accessibility needs. Instead, we must ensure that AI systems embody equity, autonomy, and empowerment principles, which can only be achieved through sustained, inclusive, and justice-oriented collaboration across disciplines.

We must also consider the significant barrier to achieving effective transdisciplinary collaboration: researchers do not always share a common understanding of what TDR entails (Lawless et al., 2024). Lawless et al. (2024) found that nearly half of the participants in their study could not identify the difference between multidisciplinary, interdisciplinary, and TDR, using these terms synonymously (Lawless et al., 2024, p. 7). Such confusion can lead to projects where disciplines remain disconnected rather than fully integrated, limiting the potential for meaningful collaboration. One of the chief investigators in the Lawless et al. (2024) study explained:

> *Transdisciplinary is what you have to do to be able to manage complexity. And I think my experience in the team is about negotiating the movement of knowledge. And, in trying to do that, you have to understand the different paradigms that people are coming from. For me, transdisciplinarity is the ability to interpret and translate different ways of seeing the world into something that is more cohesive and integrative. And ultimately, the whole is greater than the sum of the parts. (*Lawless et al., 2024, *p. 7)*

This highlights the need to align approaches and aims and actively translate and incorporate various viewpoints. Embracing transdisciplinarity to manage complexity is not just about agreement but about integrating different ways of seeing the world to build AI systems that are accessible, fair, and supportive of all individuals. If we integrate TDR into the development of AI systems, it becomes an opportunity for more effective solutions. In the evolving field of AI, transdisciplinary approaches will be crucial for dismantling ableism, promoting fairness, and ensuring that technologies serve as tools of empowerment and inclusivity. By embedding these principles into AI development, we can shape a future where technology truly supports disability justice.

## User-Centred Design (UCD) and Its Role in Inclusive AI

To move beyond traditional accessibility frameworks in assistive technology, user-centred and transdisciplinary approaches must be integrated throughout the design and innovation process. This shift rebalances power in tech design, ensuring AI aligns with real user needs. User-centred design (UCD) ensures that assistive technologies effectively address users' needs (Boger et al., 2017).

According to Boger et al. (2017), integrating the expertise and lived experiences of disabled individuals into development processes leads to more inclusive assistive technologies. In other words, when disabled users are excluded from meaningful participation, assistive technologies risk perpetuating ableist assumptions, an outcome that user-centred frameworks aim to avoid (Gorman et al., 2024). Thoroughly examining disability-related AI technology development is essential for informing the creation of new technologies, evaluating the decisions that have shaped existing ones, and exploring alternative design options (Newman-Griffis et al., 2023). UCD insists that AI tools should be developed not just for disabled individuals but with them, integrating their lived experiences directly into the design process (Boger et al., 2017). This shift is needed because traditional tech design often overlooks important perspectives.

While AI can sometimes support disabled individuals, it often introduces new barriers, and accessibility challenges persist despite efforts to enhance fairness and inclusivity (Smith & Smith, 2021). These real-world experiences and narratives reveal the need for more effective, justice-oriented approaches to AI design. Effective co-design requires the inclusion of diverse perspectives, ensuring that individuals with various types of disabilities are part of every stage of development, especially the beginning (Smith & Smith, 2021).

Achieving true inclusivity in AI requires more than simply designing for accessibility; it necessitates ongoing collaboration, shared decision-making, and continuous enhancement. Pineo et al. (2021) emphasize that structured processes, such as co-learning and conceptualization, are essential in TDR through their six-phase model. Co-learning promotes continuous knowledge exchange among disciplines and communities, encouraging a shared language and emphasizing that true expertise emerges through collaboration, trust, mutual respect, and understanding (Pineo et al., 2021). These principles teach us the importance of integrating diverse perspectives as key contributors to system design, ensuring that real-life experiences directly influence the development process. The conceptualization phase is crucial in developing systems, incorporating a wide range of knowledge from the beginning (Pineo et al., 2021). The authors highlight the importance of establishing structured research frameworks through early-stage activities, such as setting governance processes and facilitating collaborative meetings to develop a shared understanding and clearly define research goals (Pineo et al., 2021). This phase also connects with the Reflection and Refinement phase, where initial frameworks are continuously revisited and adapted, enabling teams to identify and resolve emerging issues, such as conflicts, within projects (Pineo et al., 2021). From these principles, we learn that systems striving to support disability justice must be informed by direct engagement with disability communities, shaping research questions and technology. However, transdisciplinary collaboration is insufficient if AI development fails to address broader power structures deciding who controls technology.

An approach that aligns with these principles is user-centred and transdisciplinary design, which ensures that AI technologies are developed with the needs of disabled individuals at the forefront. Casado et al. (2024) showcase this approach by developing the *sonoUno* software, which was designed from the beginning with a user-centred and transdisciplinary framework. This software facilitates the conversion of first, second, and third-dimensional data into an accessible audio-visual format, incorporating contributions from sighted and blind individuals. The study emphasizes the importance of co-designing resources that adapt to individual needs (Casado et al., 2024). The authors clarify how assistive technologies can help dismantle barriers that people with disabilities face, stating:

> *In generic terms, people with disabilities see their chances of doing any job they set out to do drastically reduced. In this sense, assistive technologies allow the removal of certain barriers and the integration of people with disabilities into active society. (*Casado et al., 2024, *p. 2).*

To meet the needs and preferences of individuals with disabilities, AI-driven assistive technologies should adopt a user-centric design and undergo continuous development informed by user feedback (Almufareh et al., 2024). This approach ensures that AI technology goes beyond accommodation and actively supports autonomy and inclusion (Almufareh et al., 2024). Aside from addressing functional limitations, AI must empower users by prioritizing autonomy, control, and informed decision-making.

Therefore, user-centred design must be a fundamental part of AI oversight. To create real change, people with disabilities need to be included and positioned as leaders and decision-makers in AI development rather than testers. Disabled individuals should be involved in every stage, from dataset curation to the oversight of AI systems. This means every new AI project should begin with a diverse team that includes disabled individuals as core leadership members. Adopting a user-centred and collaborative approach to AI design is not simply about achieving improved technological outcomes, but also about shifting power distribution in the tech world.

## The Role of a Holistic Approach in Transdisciplinary AI for Disability Justice

When developing AI solutions to support and create meaningful opportunities for people with disabilities, a holistic approach is essential (Almufareh et al., 2024). This approach involves navigating the ethical landscape of AI-driven disability support, addressing practical implications and broader societal effects, especially how technology shapes the opportunities and outcomes for the individuals it impacts (Bennett & Keyes, 2020). This involves prioritizing fairness in algorithmic decision-making, safeguarding privacy, upholding autonomy, maintaining ethical accountability, and ensuring informed consent (Almufareh et al., 2024). Ongoing collaboration and oversight from researchers, policymakers, ethics experts, and people with disabilities is essential to ensure that AI solutions are developed in ways that respect societal values and protect individual rights (Almufareh et al., 2024).

Another significant part of this process requires recognizing the varied nature of disabilities, which affect neurological functions, mobility, sensory processing, and cognition, each presenting distinct challenges (Almufareh et al., 2024).

TDR moves beyond traditional disciplinary boundaries by integrating diverse forms of knowledge to tackle complex global challenges, including inequalities, chronic disease, and challenges that cannot be addressed by just one discipline (Pineo et al., 2021). This emphasis on integrating multiple perspectives offers valuable insights for AI oversight, particularly in ensuring disability justice through inclusive and participatory approaches.

A holistic approach to AI development involves addressing specific challenges while considering the broader scope of the innovation process, ensuring solutions move seamlessly from conceptualization to real-world impact (Boger et al., 2017). Transdisciplinary collaboration facilitates this holistic perspective by allowing teams to gain a well-rounded understanding of complex problems and identify practical solutions (Boger et al., 2017). Instead of narrowing the focus, this method embraces the nuances of each issue while striving to create long-lasting, positive change. By considering the end goals, technology developers can ensure that their work translates from research to practical, social, and economic benefits (Boger et al., 2017). Collaborative learning and the pooling of expertise allow transdisciplinary teams to drive innovation forward, promoting inclusivity and advancing disability justice. By integrating diverse expertise, transdisciplinary teams can develop AI solutions that drive innovation and promote disability justice, ensuring a more inclusive and equitable future.

A study by Whitehead et al. (2021) provides an example of how multidisciplinary collaboration in mental health services can improve care coordination and support for individuals with multifaced needs. Their study evaluated a community-based program designed to support young people aged 12–25 with intellectual disabilities (ID) and co-occurring mental illness (Whitehead et al., 2021). The program was built on a person-centred, multidisciplinary approach, incorporating specialists in psychiatry, psychology, and allied health professions to provide coordinated care (Whitehead et al., 2021). Parents reported feeling more included in decision-making and better prepared to navigate complex healthcare systems, as one parent stated:

> *From my perspective it's great to have a team of people who are understanding the situation … I think it just gives you some comfort that you have 8 specialists who will come up with some great ideas … to guide you and advise you on ways to manage some of the behaviours and situations that we have to deal with.* (Whitehead et al., 2021, *p. 11)*

The study's findings revealed the necessity of a holistic and collaborative approach, revealing that integrating multiple perspectives can create systems that are adaptable, inclusive, and truly supportive of diverse needs. We can see that the program was effective because it did not rely on a single specialization. Instead, it brought together professionals from areas like psychology, psychiatry, and speech pathology to provide coordinated, specialized care while addressing the needs of families (Whitehead et al., 2021).

This coordinated, multidisciplinary care model provides a valuable lesson for AI development: Just as effective healthcare for people with disabilities requires cross-disciplinary collaboration, so too must AI development integrate diverse perspectives through a transdisciplinary approach. A transdisciplinary approach requires the direct involvement of disabled individuals, community advocates, accessibility experts, and healthcare professionals. These collaborations can ensure that AI development is inclusive, equitable, and designed to create a just future.

## Conclusion: Transdisciplinary Pathway to Justice-Centred AI for People with Disabilities

This chapter has argued that achieving disability justice in AI requires more than just mitigating digital bias or improving accessibility. It necessitates a transdisciplinary approach that combines diverse perspectives from advocacy, technology, and social science to create inclusive systems that empower people with disabilities. It is essential to ensure that individuals with disabilities play a significant role in shaping the technologies of our future. By including disability communities as leaders in AI development discussions, AI systems can truly cater to their needs, elevate their voices, and achieve true disability justice. We must commit to making technology more inclusive by actively listening to voices that have long been unheard and marginalized and by raising awareness to ensure people with disabilities lead discussions on technological innovations and policymaking.

To create meaningful change, AI developers, healthcare providers, and policymakers must collaborate with disabled individuals, ensuring they have decision-making power in AI oversight. By utilizing TDR and UCD to achieve this transformation, we can reshape knowledge production by integrating diverse expertise, especially lived experiences, into AI development. This helps ensure that AI goes beyond quick tech fixes for accessibility and focuses on creating lasting, meaningful changes in our systems. Incorporating TDR principles into AI oversight can be crucial in breaking down systemic ableism. Embedding transdisciplinary principles throughout AI development transforms technology, not just as a tool for accessibility but as a means of advancing social change and broader equity goals.

Effective AI oversight requires transdisciplinary collaboration and participatory design that integrates disabled leaders into decision-making, policy design, and dataset curation. Empowering the voices of people with disabilities in AI development is a fundamental obligation and a crucial step toward creating a more inclusive and equitable technological landscape. Only through sustained commitment, transdisciplinary collaboration, and active inclusion can AI overcome barriers and become a powerful tool for empowerment, shaping a more just and inclusive society for all.

## References

Almufareh, M. F., Kausar, S., Humayun, M., & Tehsin, S. (2024). A conceptual model for inclusive technology: Advancing disability inclusion through artificial intelligence. *Journal of Disability Research, 3*(1). https://doi.org/10.57197/JDR-2023-0060

Bennett, C. L., & Keyes, O. (2020). What is the point of fairness?: Disability, AI and the complexity of justice. *ACM SIGACCESS Accessibility and Computing, 125*, 1. https://doi.org/10.1145/3386296.3386301

Boger, J., Jackson, P., Mulvenna, M., Sixsmith, J., Sixsmith, A., Mihailidis, A., Kontos, P., Miller Polgar, J., Grigorovich, A., & Martin, S. (2017). Principles for fostering the transdisciplinary development of assistive technologies. *Disability and Rehabilitation: Assistive Technology, 12*(5), 480–490. https://doi.org/10.3109/17483107.2016.1151953

Casado, J., García, B., & Lucero, N. M. M. B. (2024). *Transdisciplinary multi modal approach to knowledge* (version 1). arXiv. https://doi.org/10.48550/ARXIV.2402.00136

Gorman, R., Creighton, A., Dada, S., Maret, P., Mgwigwi, T., Muhlenbach, F., Kundi, B., & Tadesse, R. (2024). Disability data justice from the ground up: A practice-led, participatory co-design approach to building an AI search engine and data repository for local, national, and transnational disability organizations. *Critical Studies: An International and Interdisciplinary Journal, 18*(1), 28–43. https://doi.org/10.51357/cs.v18i1.229

Grigorovich, A., Fang, M. L., Sixsmith, J., & Kontos, P. (2019). Defining and evaluating transdisciplinary research: Implications for aging and technology. *Disability and Rehabilitation: Assistive Technology, 14*(6), 533–542. https://doi.org/10.1080/17483107.2018.1496361

Lawless, M. T., Tieu, M., Archibald, M. M., Pinero De Plaza, M. A., & Kitson, A. L. (2024). From promise to practice: How health researchers understand and promote transdisciplinary collaboration. *Qualitative Health Research, 35*(1), 3–16. https://doi.org/10.1177/10497323241235882

Lawrence, M. G., Williams, S., Nanz, P., & Renn, O. (2022). Characteristics, potentials, and challenges of transdisciplinary research. *One Earth, 5*(1), 44–61. https://doi.org/10.1016/j.oneear.2021.12.010

Newman-Griffis, D., Rauchberg, J. S., Alharbi, R., Hickman, L., & Hochheiser, H. (2023). Definition drives design: Disability models and mechanisms of bias in AI technologies. First Monday. https://doi.org/10.5210/fm.v28i1.12903

Pineo, H., Turnbull, E. R., Davies, M., Rowson, M., Hayward, A. C., Hart, G., Johnson, A. M., & Aldridge, R. W. (2021). A new transdisciplinary research model to investigate and improve the health of the public. *Health Promotion International, 36*(2), 481–492. https://doi.org/10.1093/heapro/daaa125

Riegel, C., & Robinson, K. M. (2023). Interdisciplinarity, transdisciplinarity, and health humanities: Eye tracking, ableism, disability, and art creation. In C. Riegel & K. M. Robinson (Eds.), *Health humanities in application* (pp. 175–193). Springer International Publishing. https://doi.org/10.1007/978-3-031-08360-0_8

Smith, P., & Smith, L. (2021). Artificial intelligence and disability: Too much promise, yet too little substance? *AI and Ethics, 1*(1), 81–86. https://doi.org/10.1007/s43681-020-00004-5

Whitehead, R., Hopkins, L., Hughes, E., Kehoe, M., & Pedwell, G. (2021). "Everyone on the same team, all working together": Implementing a co-ordinated multi-disciplinary approach to supporting young people with co-occurring intellectual disability and mental health issues. *Journal of Mental Health Research in Intellectual Disabilities, 14*(1), 1–22. https://doi.org/10.1080/19315864.2020.1864689

# Evaluating AI Assistive Technologies for Older Adults Living with Dementia Using a Disability Justice Framework

**Janna Zeid**

## Introduction

As the global population continues to age, it is likely that dementia will become a more prevalent concern in years to come (The Many Faces of Dementia, 2024). The Alzheimer's Society defines dementia as an umbrella term under which fall a variety of symptoms, often caused by a progressive and gradual deterioration of brain function and structure. It also underscores the diversity of the condition, its potential causes, risk factors, and lived experiences. In Canada alone, the number of people living with dementia is expected to increase by 187% over the next three decades (The Many Faces of Dementia, 2024).

Despite the daily obstacles that people living with dementia face, dementia is sometimes excluded from literature on disability justice (DJ), with disagreements on whether or not it should be classed as a disability (Shakespeare et al., 2017). Since dementia (apart from early-onset and traumatic brain injuries) primarily affects older adults, ageism is a factor to consider, as is the widespread misconception that dementia is a normal part of aging. Thus, the DJ principles of intersectionality and commitment to cross-disability solidarity are of vital importance here (Berne et al., 2018). Moreover, Astell et al. echoes the need for a more holistic approach to dementia that prioritizes the needs, interests, and voices of people living with it as opposed to a purely neurobiological approach (Astell et al., 2019).

Thus far, there is a gap in the literature surrounding the application of DJ frameworks to AI assistive technologies specifically for dementia. Dementia rates are projected to increase over the coming decades with the aging global population, as is the ubiquity of AI. The integration of AI into assistive technologies seems inevitable (and, in fact, has already begun), but, moving forward, it is important to

---

J. Zeid (✉)
Cognitive Systems, The University of British Columbia, Vancouver, BC, Canada


C. El Morr et al. (eds.), *Beyond Tech Fixes*,
https://doi.org/10.1007/978-3-031-93022-5_4

consider who it is helpful to, whose voices are leading the research and development processes, and whether it addresses inequities in care.

In a recent publication, older adults living with dementia (OALWD)'s use of technology was evaluated according to an application of Nancy Fraser's three-dimensional social justice framework (Wong et al., 2024). The study also suggested adopting this model in future studies regarding technology use in this population to offer a holistic and robust examination of areas for improvement. However, it's important to note that social justice and DJ models can sometimes diverge. Nonetheless, Wong et al. (2024) make a compelling case for the applications of Fraser's framework in this particular context that I believe overlaps with the ten guiding principles of DJ (Berne et al., 2018). Therefore, I will integrate both Nancy Fraser's three-dimensional framework and the DJ principles into my evaluation of AI assistive technologies for dementia.

## Objective

The objective of this paper is to evaluate emerging assistive technologies featuring AI for dementia based on DJ principles, with the aim of identifying gaps for further research. As per Astell et al. (2019), there are four primary areas of relevant technological development for dementia, spanning "(1) diagnosis, assessment and monitoring, (2) maintenance of functioning, (3) leisure and activity, (4) caregiving and management," and all of these are classed as "assistive technologies" for the purposes of this paper. I also class diagnostic, functional, and leisure technologies as subsets of caregiving and management technologies. Thus, I will select an emerging AI tool from each of the domains of diagnosis, maintenance of functioning, and leisure and evaluate it. Where Fraser's framework is inconsistent with the ten DJ principles, I will ground my evaluation primarily in the latter, adapting and applying Fraser's framework as a means of working towards the principles wherever appropriate (Berne et al., 2018). I will also note the interconnectedness of all three dimensions in Fraser's framework and how that might contribute to a more intersectional approach (Fraser, 2003; Wong et al., 2024).

## Disability Justice Principles

The DJ principles are fundamental guiding values that serve as a cornerstone of the field of DJ. They include intersectionality, leadership by those most impacted, anti-capitalist politics, cross-movement solidarity, recognizing wholeness, sustainability, commitment to cross-disability solidarity, interdependence, collective access, and collective liberation (Berne et al., 2018).

While all ten DJ principles are certainly applicable to dementia care, I believe intersectionality (the understanding that we have plural identities that interact and impact us and others in different ways) is especially salient, since dementia is a disability that exists primarily at the intersection with ageism. Moreover, when it comes to technology use, Wong et al. (2024) highlight important considerations regarding the "digital divide" that demonstrate the necessity of acknowledging intersectionality in further research. Specifically, they propose that there are three "levels" involved in the digital divide, namely access (physical and economic means to obtain resources), use (skills and knowledge needed to operate technological tools), and outcomes (how much people benefit from use of those tools). This also overlaps with the DJ principle of collective access (that accessibility needs vary and should be respected in all forms).

## The Three Dimensions of Fraser's Framework, Integration of DJ Principles, and Applications to Technology Use in Dementia

Fraser's framework is a prominent one in the field of social justice, and includes economic ("redistribution"), cultural ("recognition"), and political ("representation") dimensions (Fraser, 2003).

**Redistribution**. As the first dimension of the framework, redistribution traditionally refers to the economic aspects of social justice (i.e. a just reallocation of resources) (Fraser, 2003). On an individual level, this might look like ensuring emerging technologies are cost-friendly for caregivers of OALWD. However, this redistribution in the case of dementia is not limited to financial factors, but should also be guided by accessibility considerations (in line with the DJ principle of collective access) as a part of redistributing resources and their usability to address the other levels of the digital divide. For instance, to address "use", assistive technologies should require no steep learning curve, as OALWD may have less digital literacy, but even if they do not, cognitive impairments and emotional/ behavioral disturbances associated with dementia may lead to frustration or distress surrounding changes to one's daily routine. It is also worth noting that dementia symptoms can be unpredictable and inconsistent—a person might be able to utilize a tool on one day, but be unable to the next, and remembering that anti-capitalist politics of productivity and sustainability are central to DJ principles is important here; tools that allow for OALWD's frequent variation of capacity and facilitate sustainability by helping alleviate feelings of frustration and isolation should be prioritized.

Moreover, Wong et al. mention that a limitation they faced in introducing new technologies to care homes is that care aides had to be present to help operate them, and care homes were often short-staffed (Wong et al., 2024). In that case, a redistribution of usability, so to speak, is needed in the short-run to help OALWD utilize these technologies more independently, but increased funding to care homes, digital literacy education, and research and development of innovative assistive technologies as well as systemic change is needed in the long-run, in line with the anti-capitalist politics of DJ.

**Recognition**. To bring these changes about requires recognition of the needs of OALWD, as well as the diversity within that population (cultural, linguistic, socio-economic, etc.), in line with the DJ principles of collective access, intersectionality, and recognizing wholeness (Berne et al., 2018). Furthermore, where other social justice theories have leaned toward independence, I believe Fraser's dimension of recognition is more compatible with the DJ principle of interdependence. As the second and cultural dimension of Fraser's framework, recognition involves identifying a population's needs and interest, and emphasizes that equal respect is not contingent on assimilation to majority norms (in a capitalist, individualistic society, the majority norm would be "independence") (Fraser, 2003). In the context of dementia and technology, a "difference-friendly world" should be one that is flexible, reflecting the fluctuating nature of life with dementia. For instance, OALWD may not ascribe to the majority norms of a linear perception of time. They may combine or confuse events from the distant past with more current ones (or even fictional narratives from media they consume) (Li, 2022). This may lead to caregivers either trying to correct these recollections or overlooking them as nonsensical instead of recognizing the need for a sense of self through narrative power, which can contribute to feelings of frustration and isolation in OALWD (Li, 2022). There is an urgent need to recognize the wholeness of OALWD and the validity of their perceptions of the world.

**Representation**. This narrative power is also reflected in the third dimension of the framework (representation) and is particularly salient in the context of dementia. This is because the memory impairments associated with dementia may contribute to a loss of sense of self, and thereby feelings of frustration, isolation, and anxiety. Li (2022) argues that rejection of one's stories is also an invalidation of the self. Thus, there is an inherent interdependence between recognition and validation of one's stories and enrichment of one's sense of self. Acceptance of the self underlies DJ principles, which sheds light on an additional challenge when it comes to DJ and dementia—with rapid changes in sense of self (as well as cognitive and physiological changes), OALWD may struggle with self-advocacy and direct involvement in decision-making. Leadership and decision-making (DJ principle of leadership by those most impacted) are hallmarks of the representation dimension of Fraser's framework (Wong et al., 2024). Nonetheless, this participation can and should be adapted to OALWD's needs and capacities, ranging from involvement in their care/management plans where possible, from choice of daily activities to small-scale decisions, or, in a broader sense, being research partners for emerging assistive technologies.

## Evaluating the Tools

**AI for Diagnosis**. Since dementia is an umbrella term that encompasses Alzheimer's disease, dementia with Lewy bodies, vascular dementia, and frontotemporal dementia (among others) diagnosis can be an extensive and time-consuming process involving a battery of cognitive tests, brain scans, and specialist consultations. Although there are now biomarker tests available, they are costly and invasive. Diagnosis often occurs when a person presents with symptoms, which can be years, if not decades, after the disease has begun to develop. As well as early detection, an accurate diagnosis of the type of dementia a person has is essential to ensuring customized care (Xue et al., 2024).

An emerging diagnostic tool for dementia utilizes machine learning to integrate multiple factors including demographic data, medical and personal history, cognitive tests, and neuroimaging to reach an accurate and differential diagnosis (Xue et al., 2024). This yielded the best outcomes (i.e. most accurate diagnosis, verified by biomarker testing and postmortem analysis) when combined with (human) clinician evaluations.

While much further research is needed before use of this tool can become more widespread, its potential value can be evaluated through the principles of redistribution, recognition, and representation. Firstly, considering the nationwide shortage of clinicians (particularly specialists) in Canada and the time it can take patients to access them, investing in AI diagnostic tools could be a redistribution of resources toward AI tools to facilitate and expedite the diagnosis process. As for recognition and representation, this saved time affords patients the opportunity to process their diagnosis, acknowledge current needs and anticipate future ones (recognition/ DJ principle of collective access), and create a plan in which they are active participants that they may not have been able to otherwise contribute to as cognitive impairments progress (representation/ DJ principle of leadership by those most impacted).

**AI for Maintenance of Functioning & Leisure**. As cognitive and motor impairment progresses, OALWD may struggle with activities of daily living (ADLs) that they once performed with ease (Begum et al., 2013). These activities could include feeding a pet, for instance, or handwashing. While DJ embraces interdependence, it also acknowledges balancing autonomy and community support (Berne et al., 2018). Moreover, ADLs, regardless of magnitude, can help maintain a sense of self and leadership. This presents a potential avenue for assistive technologies, and there have been studies with robots to assist OALWD in performing ADLs. However, such robots were either tele-operated by a researcher, preprogrammed, or integrated sensors and Internet of Things but not AI (Arthanat et al., 2020; Begum et al., 2013; Wang et al., 2017). Thus, I exclude these from my evaluation.

Nonetheless, there is a plethora of socially assistive robots (SARs) that utilize AI in emotion and language processing to engage in more naturalistic interactions with OALWD (Wong et al., 2024). A review of the literature revealed that, of these, Paro was the most prominently used (Kelly et al., 2021). Paro is a therapeutic SAR that resembles a baby seal and can act as a more controlled substitute for animal therapy.

Equipped with multiple sensors, it can respond to a range of sensory stimuli, much as a pet would, and express emotion through non-speech vocalizations, movements, and facial expression. This can help alleviate some of the pressure on caregivers allowing for sustainability in caregiving (e.g. in short-staffed care homes), and improve mood and engagement in OALWD (Wong et al., 2024).

However, while SARs such as Paro can be useful, they are also very costly (and therefore most research on them has been in long-term care homes, where the facility obtains a few for resident use). This is certainly a limitation that falls under the redistribution dimension and the anti-capitalist politics of DJ, as well as sustainability. Even in long-term care homes, there were limitations such as a lack of "time, robots, infrastructure, and maintenance costs" (Wong et al., 2024). As mentioned before, accessibility considerations should include the learning curve (time, funds, and educational content) needed to operate the tool (whether that is facilitated by a caregiver or independently initiated by the older adult).

Because research on SARs for dementia has primarily been conducted in care homes, the needs of OALWD living at home, either alone or with family, are seldom included (Inoue et al., 2021). This could be a limitation, because those living at home, particularly alone, may lack the social stimulation that residents at a care home have. Even in the only study examining the role of Paro in supporting care for OALWD living at home, those living alone were excluded, since family and caregiver supervision and feedback were needed for research purposes (Inoue et al., 2021). While this population (OALWD living alone at home) could be most in need of this technology, not only is it less accessible to them, but they are less included and represented in the literature.

## Discussion

After evaluating a few emerging AI assistive technologies for diagnosis and maintenance of functioning and leisure in OALWD through an approach that integrates DJ principles with Fraser's three-dimensional framework, I find that AI diagnostic technologies could contribute to earlier diagnosis and more accurate detection in the future. On the redistribution front, redistributing resources toward diagnostic AI may offer ways to mitigate inequity in access due the shortage of clinicians and difficulty accessing them. This can then enable patients to be active actors in their own care and management plan (representation/DJ principle of leadership by those most impacted).

However, developers should be wary of perpetuating injustices with the introduction of AI diagnostic tools, from design and training to distribution and access. Current healthcare systems in many cases fail or under-serve the most vulnerable community members, which is why intersectionality should be a guiding principle in the development and training of AI diagnostic tools. Almost twice as many women than men are affected by Alzheimer's (The Many Faces of Dementia, 2024). Change is necessary at a fundamental level to ensure research includes social determinants of health and biopsychosocial risk factors for people of different backgrounds, and in the meantime, we should be cautious of biased training data, which is a prevalent issue in diagnostic AI. For instance, in a study that developed a neural network to classify skin cancer, less than 5% of the training data included images of dark skin, which could affect the performance of the model in a diagnostic setting (Esteva et al., 2017; Zou & Schiebinger, 2018). In this domain (diagnostic), there is a concern that AI tools might perpetuate existing injustices (e.g. sexism, racism, ageism) since the training data itself may have inherent bias due to inequities in research. There is an additional concern regarding accessibility (physical and economic) of diagnostic tools, since these tools fall under healthcare, the access to which is itself inequitable in many capitalist societies.

As for AI assistive technologies for maintenance of functioning and leisure, there were notably few assistive technologies for maintenance of functioning that incorporated AI rather than tele-operated systems used in research settings only. Nevertheless, there were many SARs, with Paro being the most popular. While these can enhance mood and engagement, and encourage emotional curiosity, they were very costly (contrary to redistribution/DJ principle of anti-capitalist politics), and research was mainly limited to long-term care homes (posing issues to representation).

Moreover, there are ethical concerns around safety, privacy, and surveillance pertaining to use of AI and robots with OALWD that warrant further research (Hung et al., 2022*; Wong et al., 2024). With regards to SARs like Paro that resemble plush toys, there are concerns of infantilizing OALWD and some reported embarrassment at interacting with Paro (Hung et al., 2022; Ienca et al., 2016*). These concerns indicate the possibility of SARs perpetuating ageism and stereotypes of older adults as child-like, which could impact their sense of selfhood and dignity, leading to feelings of frustration. Certain sensory aspects of Paro interactions didn't appeal to everyone, and recognizing individual needs, interests, and changing capacities for interaction with SARs should be further examined.

Furthermore, there are a few overarching limitations to these evaluations in part due to the available literature, and a deeply intersectional approach is needed to enhance robustness. Educational background and socioeconomic variables factor into the digital divide; an older adult with higher digital literacy and from a wealthier socioeconomic background may have greater access to assistive technologies, as well as the knowledge/skills needed to operate them (Wong et al., 2024). Secondly, there are several forms of dementia, with different etiologies. Within that, presentation of symptoms may vary greatly based on many factors (previous occupation, gender, temperament, etc.), including the stage of the condition (mild vs severe, for instance). Thirdly, most studies on AI assistive technologies (especially SARs) for OALWD are conducted in care homes, and care homes able to accommodate such research programs and experimental technologies could be better funded, which could indicate higher socioeconomic backgrounds of residents, which, in turn, can affect outcomes of technology use (Wong et al., 2024). This loop neglects the needs and voices (recognition and representation/DJ principle of leadership by those most impacted) of OALWD who do not fit in this category. This is especially concerning considering the projected stress on care homes as the number of people living with dementia increases.

Moving forward, assessing the strengths and shortcomings of AI assistive technologies for OALWD using a DJ-driven framework is important in recognizing both their strengths and areas in which they might perpetuate existing injustices. Identifying patterns and gaps when applying such frameworks can also help guide future research toward AI assistive technologies that are personalized, widely accessible to people of different backgrounds, and facilitate both a sense of agency and social connectedness.

## References


Alzheimer's Society Canada. (2024). *The many faces of dementia in Canada landmark study.* Retrieved from https://alzheimer.ca/en/the-many-faces-of-dementia-in-canada-landmark-study-volume-2.

Arthanat, S., Begum, M., Gu, T., LaRoche, D.P., Xu, D., Zhang, N.: Caregiver perspectives on a smart home-based socially assistive robot for individuals with Alzheimer's disease and related dementia. Disability and Rehabilitation: Assistive Technology. **15**(7), 789–798 (2020). https://doi.org/10.1080/17483107.2020.1753831

Astell, A.J., Bouranis, N., Hoey, J., Lindauer, A., Mihailidis, A., Nugent, C., Robillard, J.M.: Technology and dementia: The future is now. Dementia and Geriatric Cognitive Disorders. **47**(3), 131–139 (2019). https://doi.org/10.1159/000497800

Begum, M., Wang, R., Huq, R., & Mihailidis, A. (2013). Performance of daily activities by older adults with dementia: the role of an assistive robot. In *IEEE ... international conference on rehabilitation robotics: [proceedings], 2013*, 6650405. https://doi.org/10.1109/ICORR.2013.6650405

Berne, P., Morales, A.L., Langstaff, D., Invalid, S.: Ten principles of disability justice. WSQ: Women's Studies Quarterly. **46**(1), 227–230 (2018). https://doi.org/10.1353/wsq.2018.0003

Esteva, A., Kuprel, B., Novoa, R.A., Ko, J., Swetter, S.M., Blau, H.M., Thrun, S.: Dermatologist-level classification of skin cancer with deep neural networks. Nature. **542**(7639), 115–118 (2017). https://doi.org/10.1038/nature21056

Fraser, N.: Social justice in the age of identity politics. Redistribution, recognition and participation. In: Fraser, N., Honneth, A. (eds.) Redistribution or recognition. A political-philosophical exchange. Verso (2003)

Inoue, K., Wada, K., Shibata, T.: Exploring the applicability of the robotic seal Paro to support caring for older persons with dementia within the home context. Palliative Care and Social Practice. **15**, 26323524211030285 (2021). https://doi.org/10.1177/26323524211030285

Kelly, P.A., Cox, L.A., Petersen, S.F., Gilder, R.E., Blann, A., Autrey, A.E., MacDonell, K.: The effect of PARO robotic seals for hospitalized patients with dementia: A feasibility study. Geriatric Nursing. **42**(1), 37–45 (2021). https://doi.org/10.1016/j.gerinurse.2020.11.003

Li, B. (2022). Navigating through the narrative montages: Including voices of older adults with dementia through collaborative narrative inquiry. *International Journal of Qualitative Methods, 21*. https://doi.org/10.1177/16094069221083368

Shakespeare, T., Zeilig, H., Mittler, P.: Rights in mind: Thinking differently about dementia and disability. Dementia. **18**(3), 1075–1088 (2017). https://doi.org/10.1177/1471301217701506

Wang, R.H., Sudhama, A., Begum, M., Huq, R., Mihailidis, A.: Robots to assist daily activities: views of older adults with Alzheimer's disease and their caregivers. International Psychogeriatrics. **29**(1), 67–79 (2017). https://doi.org/10.1017/S1041610216001435

Wong, K.L., Hung, L., Wong, J., Park, J., Alfares, H., Zhao, Y., Mousavinejad, A., Soni, A., Zhao, H.: Adoption of artificial intelligence–enabled robots in long-term care homes by health care providers: Scoping review. JMIR Aging. **7**, e55257 (2024). https://doi.org/10.2196/55257

Wong, K.L.Y., Pan, D., Hung, L.: Applying Nancy Fraser's framework on three dimensions of justice in the understanding of justice in the use of technology with older adults with moderate to severe dementia in care settings: Closing the digital divide. Journal of Technology in Human Services. **42**, 215–235 (2024). https://doi.org/10.1080/15228835.2024.2376552

Xue, C., Kowshik, S.S., Lteif, D., Puducheri, S., Jasodanand, V.H., Zhou, O.T., Walia, A.S., Guney, O.B., Zhang, J.D., Pham, S.T., Kaliaev, A., Andreu-Arasa, V.C., Dwyer, B.C., Farris, C.W., Hao, H., Kedar, S., Mian, A.Z., Murman, D.L., O'Shea, S.A., et al.: AI-based differential diagnosis of dementia etiologies on multimodal data. Nature Medicine. **30**, 2977–2989 (2024). https://doi.org/10.1038/s41591-024-03118-z

Zou, J., Schiebinger, L.: AI can be sexist and racist—it's time to make it fair. Nature. **559**(7714), 324–326 (2018). https://doi.org/10.1038/d41586-018-05707-8

# An Opportunity to Use AI to Support Content Creators in Creating Born-Accessible Documents

**Jonathan Lazar, Abhinav Kannan, Garreth W. Tigwell, Rajiv Jain, Mary Ann Jawili MJ, Yalpi Shiva Prasad, Alexa Siu, and Rick Treitman**

## Introduction: What Is Born-Accessible Design?

Disability advocates have for years been asking that all digital technologies and content be born-accessible (Boll et al., 2023; Olsen et al., 2022; Wentz et al., 2011). Here's one example of that call:

> *It should not take any time to make new course content accessible because it should be accessible from the beginning…content would be born-accessible and would not need to involve the waste of time and energy for remediation that this exception requires [referring to an exception in a proposed regulation]. Students with disabilities should not have to bear the burden of a postsecondary institution's decision to delay accessibility. (*National Federation of the Blind of South Carolina, 2023*)*

People with disabilities (PWD) often face (1) the need to advocate for accessibility remediation, (2) if advocacy is successful, then the delay as the technology or content is remediated, or (3) if unsuccessful, the frequent reality that the technology or content is never remediated. This situation of "people without disabilities have access to the content and people with disabilities do not have access to the content" can be a form of ableism, as PWD are excluded even further from society (Harpur, 2013) and even sometimes themselves blamed for not having access (Lazar, 2022).

---

J. Lazar (✉) · A. Kannan
College of Information, University of Maryland, College Park, MD, USA
e-mail: jlazar@umd.edu; abhinavk@umd.edu

G. W. Tigwell
School of Information, Rochester Institute of Technology, Rochester, NY, USA
e-mail: garreth.w.tigwell@rit.edu

R. Jain · M. A. Jawili MJ · Y. S. Prasad · A. Siu · R. Treitman
Adobe, Inc., San Jose, CA, USA
e-mail: rajijain@adobe.com; mjawili@adobe.com; yprasad@adobe.com; asiu@adobe.com; treitman@adobe.com



C. El Morr et al. (eds.), *Beyond Tech Fixes*,
https://doi.org/10.1007/978-3-031-93022-5_5

A born-accessible model for documents would limit the need to advocate, eliminate the delay as a document is remediated for accessibility, and eliminate the need to find workarounds if the document is never remediated. Born-accessible approaches can, in theory, move the world of digital accessibility more toward disability justice. Yet it's more than just theory. The new U.S. regulation for website and mobile accessibility under Title II of the Americans with Disabilities Act moves U.S. legal rules more towards a model of born-accessible, since for instance, at universities that are a part of state and local government, under the new regulations those institutions must proactively make all course content accessible, regardless of whether they serve students with disabilities in a given class and regardless of whether the course content is behind a password wall (U.S. Department of Justice, 2024).

As policies and laws move more in the direction of born-accessible approaches, it is important to fully flesh out methods and models, since in many ways, born-accessible design at this point is more of a concept than a model (Lazar, 2023) because it is not yet fully defined in the research or practitioner literature. In 2023, Jonathan Lazar (first author of this chapter) interviewed disability rights organizations affiliated with the Maryland Initiative for Digital Accessibility (MIDA) about how they perceive born-accessible design, and based on the responses, sketched out a core set of four key concepts for born-accessible design: (1) **Set clear accessibility goals from the start of a project**, (2) **Include PWD from the start of the design process**, (3) **Code to accessibility standards, and** (4) **Involve PWD in user evaluations.** Born-accessible design reflects multiple shifts in power dynamics, one of which is that the born-accessible approach encourages the involvement of disability rights organizations, not only individual users. Furthermore, disability rights organizations may be the ones who determine which technologies are prioritized for the communities that they represent.

Why are we focusing on documents? Document accessibility remains a barrier for PWD, and existing tools for document creators are inadequate. Remediation (making documents accessible after their creation) is time-consuming, delays access for PWD, and requires scarce special knowledge and skills. Thus, PWD often cannot access the vast array of digital documents required for full participation. Electronic documents are a necessary part of our everyday lives, and every delay in a PWD accessing a document stops them from doing their work, advancing their education, accessing healthcare, taking part in commerce and banking, and/or accessing local, state, and national government information. Simply put—you cannot participate fully in society or employment without equal access to documents, and research data shows that within higher education, PDF accessibility is getting worse. Open access papers, in particular, have seen a reducing trend in accessibility compliance—exacerbated by the COVID-19 pandemic—which is concerning directly for the field of academic education (Kumar & Wang, 2024). In the past, a majority of digital documents have been inaccessible, and research efforts have focused on the remediation model–how to support either content creators or external actors in remediating existing, previously created documents for accessibility. Pradhan et al. describe some of the barriers and steps in document remediation (Pradhan et al., 2022):

> *First, when PDFs are created from source files, they often lose the tagging metadata present in the authoring application related to the content type and order (*Bigham et al., 2016*). Second, the complexity of the PDF format leads to only a few tools capable of adding the required metadata during remediation (*Bigham et al., 2016*). Third, many users do not understand what is needed to make a PDF accessible or how to use current tools such as PAVE (*Doblies et al., 2014*) or Acrobat Pro accurately, leading to the need for third-party remediators (*Jembu Rajkumar et al., 2020*). Fourth, the process of making a PDF accessible today is very time-consuming for an average user, especially when it comes to tagging elements, setting the reading order, and repairing tables (*Jembu Rajkumar et al., 2020*). These problems can be seen in a study where, even when authors of papers in the CHI 2014 conference were made aware of the specific accessibility barriers within their PDF document before submitting the camera-ready version, only 26.8% of the papers for the CHI 2014 conference contained all of the requested accessibility tagging. (*Lazar et al., 2017*)

That last part of the quote described how even when authors are made aware of the accessibility barriers in their paper before submitting their final version, only approximately a quarter of the papers were made accessible. Furthermore, a recent study published in 2022 by Menzies et al. reviewed 10 years of proceedings from an accessibility conference, focusing on visual content and layout, and then interviewed academic authors who conduct accessibility research to understand the combination of factors in the workflow and publication process that result in inaccessible content, and one recommended solution was to improve the available tools to authors (Menzies et al., 2022). Therefore, even with awareness, we must figure out ways to make the process of adding accessibility markup easier for content creators because being aware of document accessibility does not necessarily translate to authors making accessible documents.

We believe that AI can be used to support content creators in moving towards a born-accessible approach for documents. In line with the calls from disability rights groups for born-accessible design, this can usher in a shift in power dynamics since the content creators will become responsible for accessibility, rather than putting the demands of advocacy onto PWD. For this shift to be successful, content authors will need both (1) general guidance while they are making their document on how to make their documents accessible, and also (2) specific suggestions for what types of labels and markup may be more contextually appropriate. We believe that while UI approaches that can notify, coach, and educate the content creator in real-time solutions for the first issue, AI is a potential solution for the second issue, with the overall goal of moving towards born-accessible documents where PWD are not required to advocate or remediate. In addressing the second issue by introducing AI tools that support creation workflows, it will be crucial to ensure these tools are designed with proper guardrails against bias and that users are aware of the limitations of AI.

## Document/Design Authoring Tools

We ground our exploration of born-accessible document authoring by considering the tool Adobe Express (https://www.adobe.com/express/). Express is a web-based authoring tool that allows users to create creative documents with workflows often starting from templates. This type of design tool poses unique challenges for accessibility since authors often create aesthetically pleasing, visually rich documents such as menus, flyers, posters, and social media posts composed of layers of graphics, media, and text in creative layouts. Additionally, the tool is targeted towards users with any level of design experience with many of the users being novices who are unfamiliar with document design or the core concepts needed for document accessibility. The beta versions of Adobe Express were neither accessible as a tool nor created accessible content. Adobe engineers were already working on making the tool itself accessible, and Adobe and the University of Maryland decided to collaborate on making Express a tool that could support content creators in making born-accessible content.

Our project entailed the following high-level goals:

Goal 1. Providing supportive ways (or "supports") to help authors of all skill levels to apply accessibility markup seamlessly during the process of authoring;

Goal 2. Identifying ways in which we can incentivize these authors to apply such markup; and

Goal 3. Creating benefits for all stakeholders as a result of born-accessible authoring.

## Listening Sessions with Disability Rights Groups

Born-accessible design has a primary goal of involving PWD from the start of the process and making full accessibility a primary design goal from the start. To initialize this project, we conducted listening sessions involving disability rights groups (DRGs) in Fall 2023 to obtain their perspectives on supporting content creators during authoring. We invited all of the disability rights groups affiliated with MIDA, and five groups (National Federation of the Blind, National Association of the Deaf, Maryland Department of Disabilities, Maryland Library for the Blind and Print Disabled, and Melwood) chose to attend the sessions. We discussed ideas and feedback, using low-fidelity prototypes in the form of pen-and-paper sketches, as a starting point.

Over the course of these sessions, we obtained several key takeaways from the disability rights groups:

1. *Enable accessibility features by default ("opt-out"):* Accessibility support should automatically be enabled by default unless authors specifically choose to opt out of it. Doing so would enable more content authors to follow these

prompts, increase accessibility awareness, and save time that is otherwise spent in remediating a document later on.

2. *Explain the "why" in the messaging:* Our initial feedback from disability rights groups highlighted that providing clearer messaging up-front about the impact of accessibility would motivate authors to invest their effort in making content more accessible. Not just saying, "please make it accessible" but noting how it increases the potential user base for the content. For example, a meaningful message could be "adding an alt-text caption for this image would make it readable for 30% more users". Prompts that provide communication about increasing potential market share can be a novel and impactful way to make an impact. Such a suggestion is not only meaningful but also action-oriented.
3. *Time-savings:* Adding accessibility markup should benefit authors and enable them to make bulk edits in one go. For example, grouping similar headings as heading levels can allow authors to edit their font and style simultaneously. Bulk edits are not the only potential time-savings using AI. Part of the time savings could come from the AI-generated recommendations for instance, for alt text, that could assist authors in making images accessible. The quality of AI-generated recommendations has certainly improved over time, and this can benefit authors in terms of the ability to just confirm or make a quick modification rather than to come up with text markup from scratch.
4. *No coding language requirement*: Authors should not require programming knowledge in order to create accessible content.
5. *Fewer dialog boxes*: Continuous interruptions to the flow of content created can lead to distraction and loss of focus. This can be frustrating for authors who are in the mental state of highest engagement, focus, and creativity (Csikszentmihalyi et al., 2016). Since pop-up dialog boxes can contribute to interrupting the state of flow, and our goal is to assist the content creators in accessibility while ensuring maximum cognitive flow, an idea discussed with DRGs was to provide a significant proportion of notifications in the ribbon bar and side panel, as opposed to having an increased number of dialog boxes which might impede cognitive flow.

## Understanding How to Create Born-Accessible Documents and How AI Can Support that Goal

Standards such as WCAG (W3C Web Accessibility Initiative (WAI), 2024) and PDF/UA (PDF/UA Foundation, n.d.) outline the requirements of additional markup needed to make documents accessible to users with disabilities. Examples that we explore include: (1) Setting semantic tagging for document elements (i.e. Headings, Lists, Tables, Paragraphs), (2), Setting heading levels (i.e. H1-H6) to allow for efficient navigation of document sections, (3) Setting alt text for images, (4) Providing the reading order of the content, and (5) Ensuring color contrast of the text from complex backgrounds.

However, even with these technical standards, few digital documents are accessible at the time they are authored, requiring remediation after-the-fact (Pradhan et al., 2022). Our work explores how the combination of AI tools with intelligent user interfaces can better support content creators in adding accessibility markup seamlessly. In this context, we have identified interventions that can be made broadly across 4 stages of authoring:

- Stage 1:Starting from accessible templates
- Stage 2: Authoring with accessibility
- Stage 3: Autotagging soon after content is authored
- Stage 4: Exporting

## *Stage 1: Starting from Accessible Templates*

Having a template that is already marked up with accessibility tags can provide a head-start for authors, especially if they are unaware of accessibility. Not only does this improve the user experience of adding accessibility markup (since it means less work for the author), but also reduces the likelihood of exporting an inaccessible document (meaning that it increases the likelihood of exporting an accessible document!).

Recently a number of generative AI algorithms have been published that can automatically create document layouts and, in some cases, even content from simple user text prompts to automatically generate simple templates for users (Adobe, 2024; Biswas et al., 2024; Feng et al., 2023; Zheng et al., 2023). However, a limitation of these tools is that many of them do not contain the necessary semantic markup needed for accessibility. They only produce layout designs or directly predict the content without noting if it's part of a list, table, or heading. Additionally, other WCAG or PDF / UA guidelines are not optimized by these algorithms, potentially resulting in issues such as poor color contrast. So at this point, these templates cannot be generated via AI.

## *Stage 2: Authoring with Accessibility*

As authors increasingly turn toward AI tools to generate their text and media content, it provides an opportunity to incorporate accessibility tagging into the generation process. Tools like chatGPT are already capable of producing many of the required HTML markup tags as evident by their ability to generate full HTML pages from text-prompts.

- **Image alt text/captions**: When a user uploads an image, an alternative text caption describing the image can be automatically generated and added to the document. The system could also use the image generation prompt as the basis for the ALT text with some modifications to match specific details that have appeared in the image. At this point, human confirmation that the ALT text is appropriate is still required. As AI text-to-image generation such as Firefly or Dall-E becomes more popular, we imagine that the alt text could be used to suggest improved generated images and could act as a motivator for users to provide more detailed descriptions.
- **Lists**: We can assist authors with creating more accessible ordered, unordered, and nested lists—by auto-aligning them and enabling smart addition of new list items.
- **Heading level**: In the event where a user increases the font size and font weight for a single line of text, we can automatically markup such a line as a heading. This enables better document navigation, readability and AI-based style suggestions for text. At this point, the AI in the tool can accurately identify that text is a heading, but not accurately identify the level of the heading, which requires human intervention. Given this discrepancy, we asked our disability rights partners to weigh in on whether this would be useful, either to auto-tag or to suggest headings without knowing the heading level (keeping in mind the ongoing call of "nothing about us without us") from the disability rights groups. The responses we heard varied from "yes, it would be useful even to know it's a heading without a level assigned" to "it's better than nothing but only barely, you still need to have humans mark up the heading level."
- **Color**: We can assist authors in making text color choices that are more accessible to people with color vision deficiencies (CVD). Whenever an author places text against a backdrop that results in low contrast, we provide smarter high-contrast recommendations (see Fig. 1).

**Fig. 1** Higher contrast recommendations for text

## *Stage 3: Autotagging Soon After Content Is Authored*

Similar to a stage where we can help authors automatically apply markup *before* they go into Stage 2 (i.e. authoring with accessibility), we propose a stage for applying markup *after* Stage 2. Compared to Stage 2, the context for accessibility supports would be based on authoring changes made over longer intervals of time. We have not yet investigated this idea further, but we believe that AI could identify opportunities for suggesting accessibility markup to content authors when patterns appear over time as authors are creating content.

## *Stage 4: Exporting*

As a user gets ready to complete their document and export it to a different format such as PDF, it becomes both a natural intervention point and the final chance in the document journey to make the document accessible. Here the goal would be to automatically insert any missing accessibility markup and only alert the users for areas where the AI is uncertain and human confirmation still is needed. This shares many similarities with the workflow of remediation-based approaches, with the key distinction that this is being done at the time of file conversation by the content creator rather than after a document is converted and distributed to others.

Advancements in AI for document understanding make it possible to auto-tag a document for semantic tags (Gu et al., 2021; Huang et al., 2022; Pfitzmann et al., 2022), reading order (Nguyen et al., 2024; Qiao et al., 2024; Wang et al., 2021), table structure (Kayal et al., 2023; Tensmeyer et al., 2019), and form fields. Many of these features are available through commercial AI solutions such as the Azure AI Document Intelligence (Microsoft, n.d.) or the Adobe Document Cloud Extract API (Adobe, 2023). While these approaches are not perfect, they can significantly reduce the effort needed for an author to manually tag the document. This style of approach has been explored by previous tools (Pradhan et al., 2022; Wang et al., 2021) used for making PDFs of scientific papers accessible.

## *Considerations for Interaction Between the AI and Author*

We observed some UI dimensions in our work; one of them being the tension between forcing the content creator to make it accessible and suggesting to the content creator some accessible options. Our research identifies the following user interface (UI) dimensions in enabling born-accessible authoring:

D1. Suggesting vs Forcing
D2. Automatic markup vs prompted markup
D3. Immediate vs delayed

Dimension 1. Suggesting vs Forcing

We suggest accessibility markup in the form of design recommendations that an author can utilize. For example, if there is an issue with text contrast, then we provide high-contrast recommendations (Fig. 1). In other instances, we force the user into accessibility, such as when an author is creating a list. This can apply to ordered (numbered), or unordered (bulleted), icon-based, or nested lists. (There are actually benefits to this enforcement – alignment, "+" button with "smart" list item additions.)

Dimension 2. Automatic markup vs prompted markup

For some document elements, markup can be added automatically, while for others, authors would be *required* to add markup or confirm AI-generated suggestions.

For example, if an author uploads an image into the document, then they would be *prompted* to edit its alt text (see Fig. 2). Similarly, an author would be required to either create table headers or confirm AI-generated table headers. On the other hand, when a user adds a list, it is automatically turned into a list, without any additional

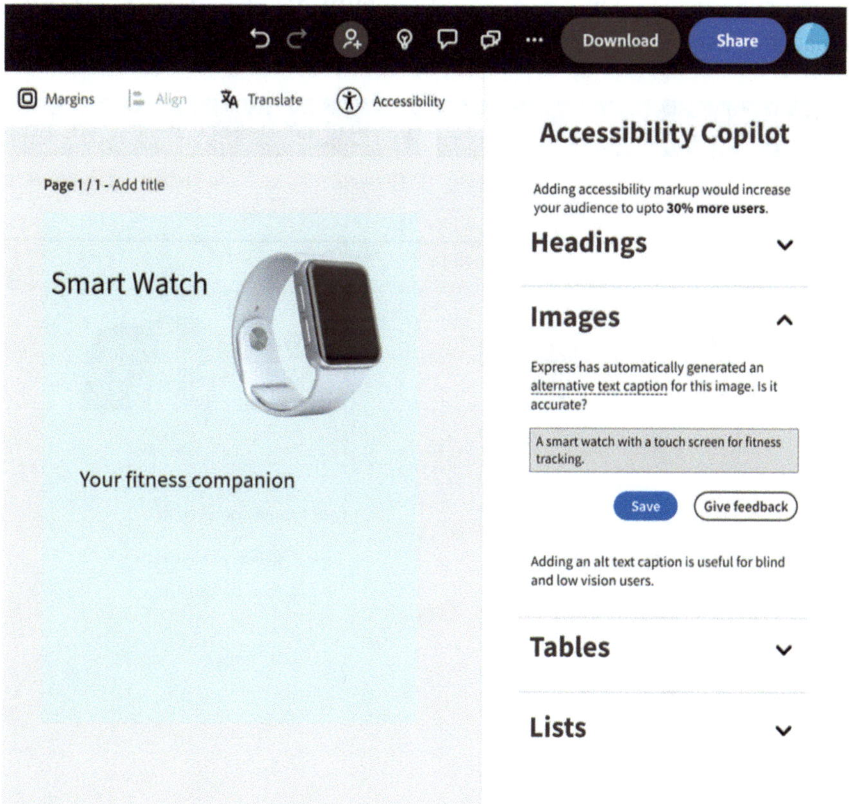


**Fig. 2** Automatic captioning of image alt-text

feedback needed. This applies not only to numbered and bulleted lists but also to nested and icon-based ones.

Dimension 3. Immediate vs delayed

Some markup can be added instantly, while some can only be added later.

For example, a color contrast issue is detected immediately, while lists are detected only after a certain number of items are created (see Fig. 3).

## Summary and Next Steps

We believe that document accessibility broadly does not receive the attention it merits, given the daily impact of inaccessible documents as barriers to the employment and education of PWD. In this chapter, we present our progress toward understanding how to use AI to support content creators in creating born-accessible documents. We are obviously at the early stages of creation, and will be usability testing some of our designs during this Fall. Usability testing for a content creation tool such as this one requires a balancing act. Typically in born-accessible design, we are focused on usability testing involving PWD. Yet since the end goal in this situation is that we have a tool that both people with and without disabilities can use

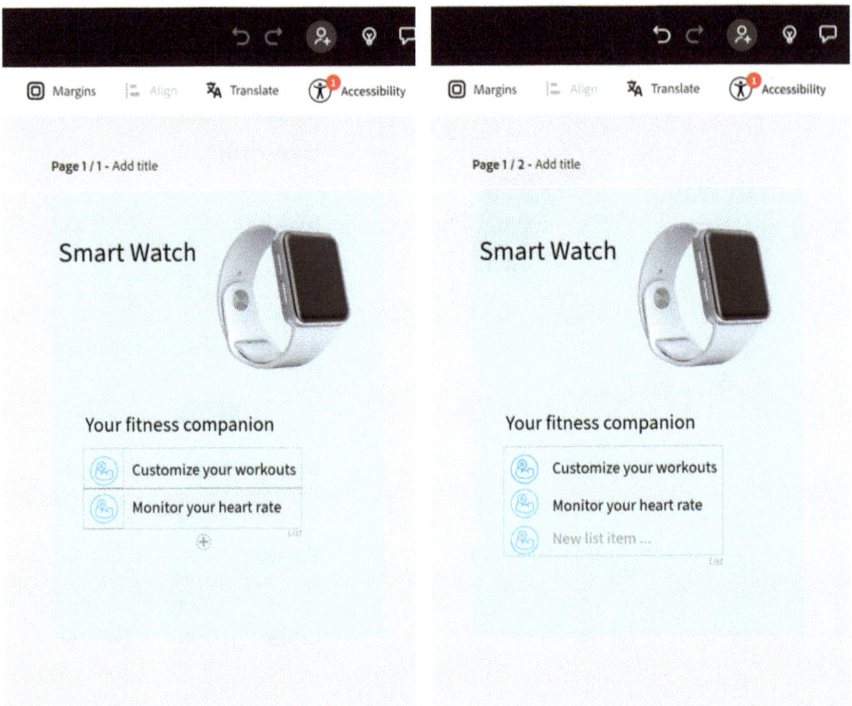


**Fig. 3** List editing: 2-step flow

to create accessible content, it is equally important to have people without disabilities involved. As discussed, some aspects of born-accessible documents require UI features to help content creators understand where accessibility is needed, while other aspects can utilize AI to provide content creators with suggested markup. We hope that usability testing on prototypes of our initial designs can help identify which features might be effective and which ones require improvement in the journey toward creating accessible content.

Given the enormous pressure on PWD to advocate for digital accessibility, we believe that by putting the responsibility on the content creator, and giving the content creator more powerful tools to assist them in the accessibility journey for their document, we can alleviate some of the responsibilities that PWD have to fight for document accessibility, changing the existing dynamics of power and responsibility, and moving the world towards disability justice. At the same time, we acknowledge that there are still trillions of documents that already exist in an inaccessible format, where remediation approaches are needed, and such a born-accessible approach will not solve the problem for already-existing documents.

What are the next steps forward? Given that the born-accessible approach has the potential for empowering PWD and changing some of the ableist existing power dynamics, we encourage others to investigate various ways that AI can be used to support content creators in taking responsibility for creating accessible content. Furthermore, policymakers are already taking notice and starting to incorporate born-accessible concepts into policies and potential legal rules. For instance, new policies put out by the White House Office of Management and Budget (policies at a federal level) (U.S. Executive Office of the President, 2023), and the state of Maryland (Maryland Department of Information Technology, 2024) encourage the use of born-accessible concepts, while a bill currently pending in the US Congress, the Section 508 Refresh Bill, would encode into law some born-accessible concepts: "*The acquisition or development of information and communications technology in a manner that incorporates accessibility for people with disabilities from the beginning to the end of the acquisition or development process*" (U.S. Senate, 2024).

## References

Adobe. (2023). *PDF extract API*. Retrieved from https://developer.adobe.com/document-services/docs/overview/pdf-extract-api/.

Adobe. (2024, October 16). *Adobe express: Create editable templates with generative AI*. Retrieved from https://helpx.adobe.com/express/create-with-templates/create-templates/text-to-template.html.

Bigham, J. P., Brady, E. L., Gleason, C., Guo, A., & Shamma, D. A. (2016). *An uninteresting tour through why our research papers aren't accessible*. In Proceedings of the 2016 CHI conference extended abstracts on human factors in computing systems (pp. 621–631). https://doi.org/10.1145/2851581.2892588

Biswas, S., Jain, R., Morariu, V. I., Gu, J., Mathur, P., Wigington, C., Sun, T., & Lladós, J. (2024). *DocSynthv2: A practical autoregressive modeling for document generation (version 1)*. arXiv. https://doi.org/10.48550/ARXIV.2406.08354

Boll, R., Mahajan, S., Burke, T., Alkhudaidi, K., Henriques, B., Cordova, I., Walker, Z., Solovey, E., & Reis, J. (2023). *User perceptions and preferences for online surveys in American sign language: An exploratory study*. In The 25th international ACM SIGACCESS conference on computers and accessibility (pp. 1–17). https://doi.org/10.1145/3597638.3608444

Csikszentmihalyi, M., Khosla, S., & Nakamura, J. (2016). Flow at work. In L. G. Oades, M. F. Steger, A. D. Fave, & J. Passmore (Eds.), *The Wiley Blackwell handbook of the psychology of positivity and strengths-based approaches at work* (pp. 99–109). Wiley. https://doi.org/10.1002/9781118977620.ch7

Doblies, L., Stolz, D., Darvishy, A., & Hutter, H.-P. (2014). *PAVE: A web application to identify and correct accessibility problems in PDF documents* (pp. 185–192). In ICCHP 2014, 14th international conference on computers helping people with special needs, Paris, France, 9–11 July 2014. Springer. https://doi.org/10.1007/978-3-319-08596-8

Feng, W., Zhu, W., Fu, T., Jampani, V., Akula, A., He, X., Basu, S., Wang, X. E., & Wang, W. Y. (2023). *LayoutGPT: Compositional visual planning and generation with large language models (version 2)*. arXiv. https://doi.org/10.48550/ARXIV.2305.15393

Gu, J., Kuen, J., Morariu, V. I., Zhao, H., Jain, R., Barmpalios, N., Nenkova, A., & Sun, T. (2021). UniDoc: Unified pretraining framework for document understanding. *Advances in Neural Information Processing Systems, 34*, 39–50. Retrieved from https://proceedings.neurips.cc/paper/2021/hash/0084ae4bc24c0795d1e6a4f58444d39b-Abstract.html.

Harpur, P. (2013). From universal exclusion to universal quality: Regulating ableism in a digital age. *Northern Kentucky Law Review, 40*(3), 529–565.

Huang, Y., Lv, T., Cui, L., Lu, Y., & Wei, F. (2022). *LayoutLMv3: Pre-training for document AI with unified text and image masking*. In Proceedings of the 30th ACM international conference on multimedia (pp. 4083–4091). https://doi.org/10.1145/3503161.3548112

Jembu Rajkumar, A., Jordan, J. B., & Lazar, J. (2020). Improving PDF accessibility tools for content developers: Looking towards the future. In P. Langdon, J. Lazar, A. Heylighen, & H. Dong (Eds.), *Designing for inclusion* (pp. 173–181). Springer International Publishing. https://doi.org/10.1007/978-3-030-43865-4_18

Jembu Rajkumar, A., Lazar, J., Jordan, J. B., Darvishy, A., & Hutter, H.-P. (2020). *PDF accessibility of research papers: What tools are needed for assessment and remediation?* Retrieved from http://hdl.handle.net/10125/64254.

Kayal, P., Anand, M., Desai, H., & Singh, M. (2023). Tables to LaTeX: Structure and content extraction from scientific tables. *International Journal on Document Analysis and Recognition (IJDAR), 26*(2), 121–130. https://doi.org/10.1007/s10032-022-00420-9

Kumar, A., & Wang, L. L. (2024). *Uncovering the new accessibility crisis in scholarly PDFs* (no. arXiv:2410.03022). arXiv. Retrieved from http://arxiv.org/abs/2410.03022.

Lazar, J. (2022). Ableist language in the web accessibility case of Robles v. Domino's Pizza LLC: When "everyone" doesn't include people with disabilities. *Including Disability, 2*. https://doi.org/10.51357/id.vi2.197

Lazar, J. (2023). *A framework for born-accessible development of software and digital content*. In IFIP conference on human-computer interaction (pp. 333–338).

Lazar, J., Churchill, E. F., Grossman, T., Van Der Veer, G., Palanque, P., Morris, J., & Mankoff, J. (2017). Making the field of computing more inclusive. *Communications of the ACM, 60*(3), 50–59. https://doi.org/10.1145/2993420

Maryland Department of Information Technology. (2024). *State of Maryland digital accessibility policy*. Retrieved from https://doit.maryland.gov/policies/Pages/DigitalAccessibilityPolicy.aspx.

Menzies, R., Tigwell, G. W., & Crabb, M. (2022). Author reflections on creating accessible academic papers. *ACM Transactions on Accessible Computing, 15*(4), 1–36. https://doi.org/10.1145/3546195

Microsoft. (n.d.). *Azure AI document intelligence*. Retrieved November 3, 2024, from https://azure.microsoft.com/en-us/products/ai-services/ai-document-intelligence.

National Federation of the Blind of South Carolina. (2023). *Comments on the ADA title II website and mobile app notice of proposed rulemaking*. Retrieved from https://nfbofsc.org/comments-ada-title-ii-website-and-mobile-app-notice-proposed-rulemaking-september-19-2023.

Nguyen, L., Piwowarski, B., Laborde, J., & Moyse, G. (2024). Learning reading order via document layout with Layout2Pos. In *Linking theory and practice of digital libraries* (Vol. 15177, pp. 3–19). Springer Nature Switzerland. https://doi.org/10.1007/978-3-031-72437-4_1

Olsen, S. H., Cork, S., Anders, P., Padrón, R., Peterson, A., Strausser, A., & Jaeger, P. T. (2022). The disability tax and the accessibility tax: The extra intellectual, emotional, and technological labor and financial expenditures required of disabled people in a world gone wrong...and mostly online. *Including Disability, 1*, 51–86. https://doi.org/10.51357/id.vi1.170

PDF/UA Foundation. (n.d.). *Why PDF/UA*. Retrieved November 3, 2024, from https://pdfua.foundation/en/why-pdf-ua/.

Pfitzmann, B., Auer, C., Dolfi, M., Nassar, A. S., & Staar, P. (2022). *DocLayNet: A large human-annotated dataset for document-layout segmentation*. In Proceedings of the 28th ACM SIGKDD conference on knowledge discovery and data mining (pp. 3743–3751). https://doi.org/10.1145/3534678.3539043

Pradhan, D., Rajput, T., Rajkumar, A. J., Lazar, J., Jain, R., Morariu, V. I., & Manjunatha, V. (2022). Development and evaluation of a tool for assisting content creators in making PDF files more accessible. *ACM Transactions on Accessible Computing, 15*(1), 1–52. https://doi.org/10.1145/3507661

Qiao, L., Li, C., Cheng, Z., Xu, Y., Niu, Y., & Li, X. (2024). Reading order detection in visually-rich documents with multi-modal layout-aware relation prediction. *Pattern Recognition, 150*, 110314. https://doi.org/10.1016/j.patcog.2024.110314

Tensmeyer, C., Morariu, V. I., Price, B., Cohen, S., & Martinez, T. (2019). *Deep splitting and merging for table structure decomposition*. In 2019 international conference on document analysis and recognition (ICDAR) (pp. 114–121). https://doi.org/10.1109/ICDAR.2019.00027

U.S. Department of Justice. (2024). *Nondiscrimination on the basis of disability; Accessibility of Web Information and Services of State and Local Government Entities*. Retrieved from https://www.federalregister.gov/documents/2024/04/24/2024-07758/nondiscrimination-on-the-basis-of-disability-accessibility-of-web-information-and-services-of-state.

U.S. Executive Office of the President. (2023). *Memorandum for the heads of executive departments and agencies: Strengthening digital accessibility and the management of section 508 of the Rehabilitation Act*. Retrieved from https://www.whitehouse.gov/wp-content/uploads/2023/12/M-24-08-Strengthening-Digital-Accessibility-and-the-Management-of-Section-508-of-the-Rehabilitation-Act.pdf.

U.S. Senate. (2024). *Section 508 Refresh Act of 2024 (S.4766) (2024-07-24)*. Retrieved from https://www.congress.gov/bill/118th-congress/senate-bill/4766/cosponsors.

W3C Web Accessibility Initiative (WAI). (2024). *WCAG 2 overview*. Retrieved from https://www.w3.org/WAI/standards-guidelines/wcag/.

Wang, L. L., Cachola, I., Bragg, J., Cheng, E. Y.-Y., Haupt, C., Latzke, M., Kuehl, B., Van Zuylen, M. N., Wagner, L., & Weld, D. (2021). *SciA11y: Converting scientific papers to accessible HTML*. In The 23rd international ACM SIGACCESS conference on computers and accessibility (pp. 1–4). https://doi.org/10.1145/3441852.3476545

Wang, Z., Xu, Y., Cui, L., Shang, J., & Wei, F. (2021). *LayoutReader: Pre-training of text and layout for reading order detection*. In Proceedings of the 2021 conference on empirical methods in natural language processing (pp. 4735–4744). https://doi.org/10.18653/v1/2021.emnlp-main.389

Wentz, B., Jaeger, P. T., & Lazar, J. (2011). Retrofitting accessibility: The legal inequality of after-the-fact online access for persons with disabilities in the United States. *First Monday, 16.* Retrieved from https://firstmonday.org/ojs/index.php/fm/article/download/3666/3077.

Zheng, G., Zhou, X., Li, X., Qi, Z., Shan, Y., & Li, X. (2023). *LayoutDiffusion: Controllable diffusion model for layout-to-image generation (version 2).* arXiv. https://doi.org/10.48550/ARXIV.2303.17189

# Understanding the Digital Disability Creation Process and Bridging the Gap Between Responsible AI Design and Disability Frameworks

**Nadia Metoui**

## Introduction

AI systems used in the context of disability (including but not limited to assistive technologies) have the potential to fight stigmas, empower, and enable healthy, productive, independent, and dignified living for PWD. However, many risks are associated with using ill-designed AI, e.g., privacy breaches, safety and security threats, harmful biases, etc. PWD are often targets of discrimination when prescriptive AI is used as a technology supporting or automating decision-making (Nugent & Scott-Parker, 2022; Sabatello, 2022). This unfairness adds to the social and economic precarity historically imposed upon these individuals in the offline world. Furthermore, assistive and human-augmenting AI's efficiency, inclusiveness, security, and safety have raised many controversies. Very often, these AI systems are designed by non-PWD designers with limited, wrong or prejudiced perceptions and understanding of disability and without the participation or involvement of users and technology makers with disability (Blanchard, 2022; Shew, 2020).

Disability studies is the field concerned with understanding disability and improving the lives of PWD. Conceptual, ethical and legal frameworks (e.g., the social models of disability (Oliver, 1990), the Human Development Model and Disability Creation Process HDM-DCP (Fougeyrollas et al., 2019; Fougeyrollas & Grenier, 2018), the capabilities approach (Harnacke, 2013; Nussbaum, 2003), and The United Nations Convention on the Rights of Persons with Disabilities CRPD (UN, 2006) stemming from -or inspired by- disability studies have been integrated into -and positively influenced several fields including urbanism and the built

N. Metoui (✉)
Faculty of Technology, Policy, and Management, Delft University of Technology, Delft, The Netherlands
e-mail: n.metoui@tudelft.nl


C. El Morr et al. (eds.), *Beyond Tech Fixes*,
https://doi.org/10.1007/978-3-031-93022-5_6

environment (Gharebaghi et al., 2018), media (Greco, 2016), welfare and social services (Priestley, 2000), healthcare (Berghs et al., 2016; St-Germain et al., 2011) etc. In the responsible AI communities, many scholars and activists used several tools from disability studies to identify and analyse risks and harms related to using AI in the context of disability (see Bennett & Keyes, 2019; Blanchard, 2022; Buyl et al., 2022; Sabatello, 2022; Shew, 2020; Tilmes, 2022; Whittaker et al., 2019). However, very few efforts have been made to explore leveraging and integrating these theories and frameworks to improve AI systems' design, implementation and assessment in this context. This paper is an attempt to bridge this gap.

More specifically, the contributions of this paper are: (1) Shifting the focus of responsible AI design for PWD from "quantifying" data bias to understanding and alleviating disabling situations created or exacerbated by AI systems (section "Understanding the Digital Disability Creation Process"). (2) Identifying and defining the digital (AI-related) environment factors creating or exacerbating disability (section "Digital Environment Factors in D-DCP"). (3) Categorising and analysing PWD-AI interactions (and subjection) models and their implications in disability created or exacerbation (section "Interactions with and Subjection to AI"). (4) Proposing a conceptualisation of fairness assessment based on the capabilities approach to justice as an alternative to the resourcist approaches (section "Quality of Life Through the Lenses of the Capabilities Approach to Justice"). (5) Mapping personal factors, Digital factors, interactions and fairness measures within a comprehensive design framework inspired by the HDM-DCP framework. We will refer to this framework as the Digital Disability Creation Process framework or D-DCP.

## Understanding the Digital Disability Creation Process

The D-DCP framework is inspired by HDM-DCP (Fougeyrollas et al., 2015, 2019). The HDM-DCP conceptualises disability as the Interactions between a set of "Personal" and "Environment" factors. These interactions create contextual and temporal disabling situations that impact individuals' "Life Habits" and prevent them from carrying out "Daily Activities" or fulfilling "Social Roles". The broad framing of HDM-DCP allows it to support and adapt to new understandings of disability brought by new generations of activists and new disciplines. For instance, the first version of HDM-DCP was based on the individual medical model of disability and then adopted the social model (for an overview of disability models, see Berghs et al., 2016; Retief & Letšosa, 2018) (Fig. 1).

Our framework aims to extend this conceptualisation further and take into consideration the risks of intersecting oppressions resulting from the usage of AI. Another powerful aspect of HDM-DCP is its ability to adapt to many contexts with reasonable contextualisation efforts.[1] In 2018, Gharebaghi et al. apply

[1] We define *contextualisation* as understanding, interpreting and adapting the abstract components of the framework in a given context.

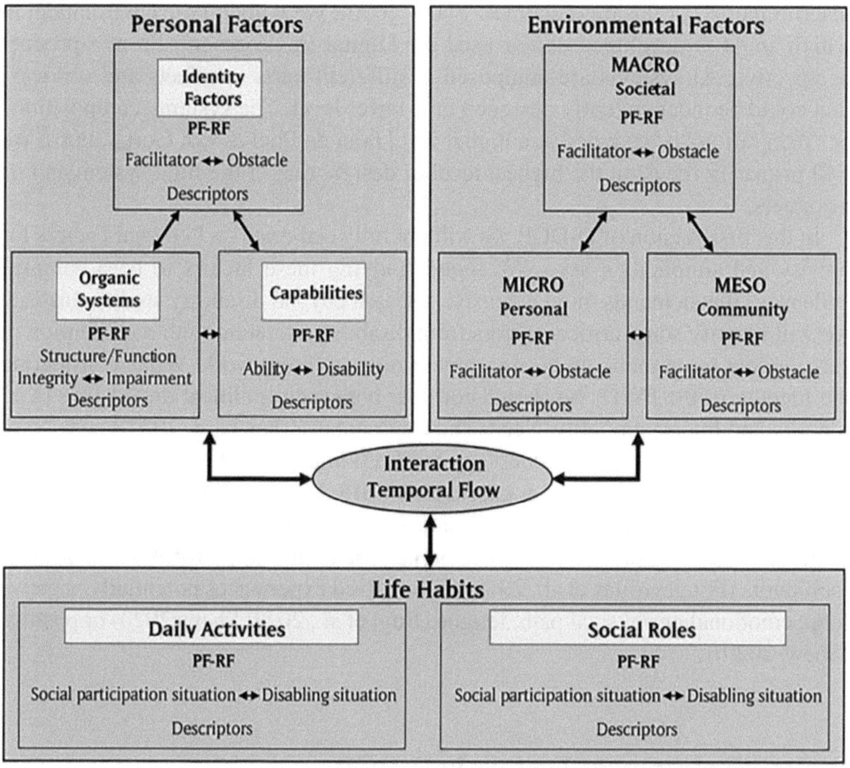


**Fig. 1** Human Development Model and Disability Creation Process (HDM-DCP). *PF-RF* Protective Factor—Risk Factor. (Source: Fougeyrollas et al., 2019)

HDM-DCP to urban design, focusing on facilitating mobility for PWD. To do so, they contextualised different components of the framework to fit the urban mobility context. In 2011, St-Germain et al. engaged in the same exercise of contextualising HDM-DCP in healthcare and nursing to improve quality of services for PWD. AI, however, is a disruptive technology that brings new forms of interactions and risks. Emergent risks can participate in the creation of new disability and injustice situations. These injustices can have profound impacts on PWD beyond hindering their life habits (understood as the capacity "to do" and "to participate"). Therefore, our framework will both leverage the flexibility of HDM-DCP and extend it to fit the complexity and challenges of the AI context and the principles of disability justice.

Understanding the impacts of AI Systems requires analysing all aspects of these systems, including socio-technical, socio-political and socio-economic dimensions. It also requires mapping and understanding all stakeholders involved. We will make some abstractions to delimit the scope of this first exploration. We will start from the assumption that disabling situations arise when PWD "interact" with ill-designed or misused AI systems, resulting in exclusionary, stigmatising, discriminatory, or unsafe outcomes (Shew, 2020). We will call the environment in which an AI is developed and/or used the Digital Environment. From a product perspective, AI systems are composed of different parts (artefacts and services) that could be independently designed on a lower level. The system "composition" or "integration" is designed at a higher level (van de Poel & van Gorp, 2006). We will primarily focus on the highest level of design, that of the final system and its designers.

In this first version of D-DCP, we will not fully elaborate on Personal Factors for brevity and simplicity's sake. We found studying these factors to be a complex endeavour that demands more extensive research beyond disability studies. Instead, we will identify some critical factors from disability literature with the intention of carrying out more meticulous conceptualisation in future work. When considering the Identity of the PWD, we should consider both socio-political dimensions (e.g., Identity and Intersectionality, Needs and Aspirations (Blanchard, 2022)) and socio-technical dimensions (e.g., Technology Skills (Whittaker et al., 2019) and Attitudes towards Technology (Bigham & Carrington, 2018; Smith & Smith, 2021)). Instead of focusing on the integrity of the Organic System or lack of it, we plan to focus on Impairment as a hindrance to capacities (i.e., the ability to perform a task without facilitators (Fougeyrollas et al., 2019)) and as lived experiences potentially negative (e.g., emotional or physical pain, fatigue (Buyl et al., 2022; Shew, 2020) or positive (Shew, 2020)).

## Digital Environment Factors in D-DCP

AI development and deployment environments can be influenced by a large number of factors, including sociocultural aspects, technological factors, business decisions, regional and sector-specific policies, practices and regulations, etc. The aim of this section is not to enumerate each and every Digital Environment Factor. Instead, we will present two factors we find to be common to most AI environments used in the context of disability. The first is related to the Conceptualisation of disability, and the second to the Operationalisation of Disability.

### *Conceptualisation of Disability*

Many responsible AI scholars argue that one of the most critical issues in design and usage of AI in the context of disability are of a conceptual nature. Negative or uninformed perceptions of disability and PWD create ableist technological imaginary (Shew, 2020). This can have very harmful effects, especially when PWD are excluded from the design processes and debates and have no choosing power over the developed AI systems (Buyl et al., 2022). It is, therefore, essential to establish a deliberate, adequate, inclusive and empowering Conceptualisation of Disability and PWD in AI projects.

Disability studies include an important number of theoretical frameworks attempting to understand and conceptualise disability as a phenomenon and a human experience based on assumptions, concerns, positioning, or disciplinary framing (Beaudry, 2016; Lawson & Beckett, 2020; Smart, 2004). These frameworks are referred to as Models of Disability. These models also attempt to explain the causes of disability and guide the formulation and implementation of a response to disability (Retief & Letšosa, 2018). They can shape the identity of PWD and society's perceptions and discourses. When consciously or unconsciously adopted in technology design and narratives, they contribute to exacerbating or reducing prejudices and discrimination against PWD (Shew, 2020). Despite the important number of models of disability (see Berghs et al. (2016); Retief and Letšosa (2018) for an overview), most of these models can be categorised into two categories: the Individual Models and the Social Models (Fig. 2).

**Individual Models of Disability**: following the terminology and definition from Lawson and Beckett (2020), these models situate disability as a "problem" located within the individual (i.e., the PWD) impacting their ability to function "normally" in society. The cause of disability is attributed to an impairment, i.e., a physiological and or psychological deficit, defect, disease, or abnormality (Devlieger, 2005; Smart, 2004; Whittaker et al., 2019). The response of society

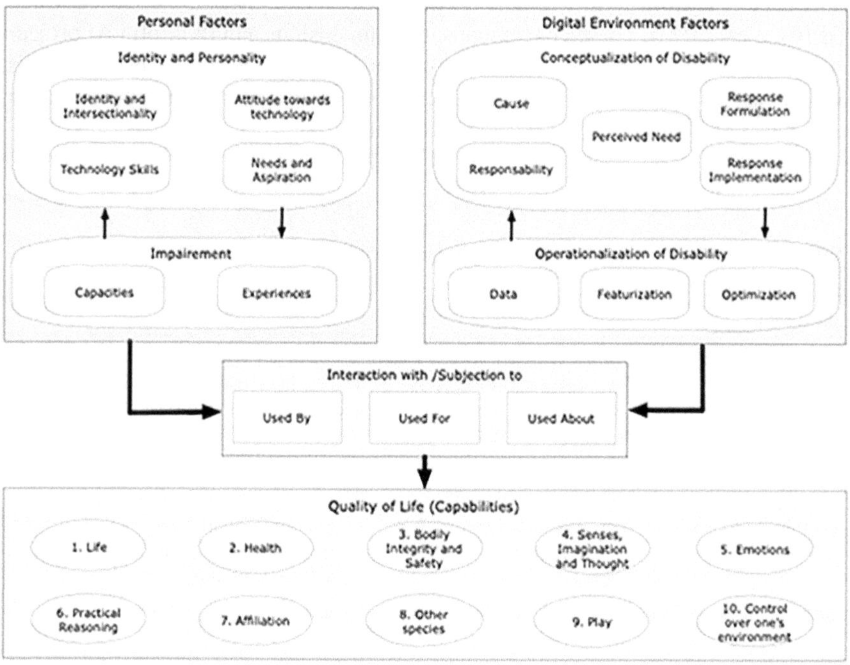


**Fig. 2** D-DCP: The Digital Disability Creation Process Framework

should be to medically fix this abnormality (Berghs et al., 2016) and rehabilitate the PWD IOM (, 1997) to help them regain "normal" abilities and have a "normal" life. The society also perceives the PWD as in need of pity and charity (Retief & Letšosa, 2018).

**Social Models of Disability**: emerged from criticism and rejection of the individual models in disability activism circles (Beaudry, 2016; Blanchard, 2022; Oliver, 2013). There are many versions of disability models said "social". These versions differ in many regards. There is, however, an underlying agreement on making a conceptual and terminological distinction between "impairment" and "disability". Disability, according to social models, is socially created marginalisation, disadvantages, or oppressions exercised on PWD through barriers of different natures (Beaudry, 2016). These barriers can be in the environment (natural, built, digital) (Fougeyrollas & Grenier, 2018), political barriers (Berghs et al., 2016; Byrne, 2018; Newman-Griffis et al., 2023), or cultural barriers (Whittaker et al., 2019), etc. In these models, the response to disability should be alleviating these social barriers and abolishing injustices towards PWD. Social models also advocate for putting the PWD at the centre of response design and implementation and raise the activist motto "nothing about us without us".

Table 1 summarises the most important conceptual differences between models of disability using five high-level conceptualisation dimensions. Our aim here is not to demonstrate which model is best or which one should be adopted in an AI project. In fact, many argue that each model has advantages and shortcomings when operationalised in a given context to achieve a given goal (Berghs et al., 2016; Newman-Griffis et al., 2023). These conceptualisation dimensions aim to inform AI projects and steer them towards a deliberate and context-adequate conceptualisation of disability instead of unconsciously perpetuating a biased and harmful conceptualisation based on ableist tropes or lack of information.

**Table 1** High-level conceptual differences between models of disability

| Conceptualization dimension | Individual models | Social models |
|---|---|---|
| Causal attribution | Impairment or abnormality | Socially erected barriers |
| Responsibility attribution | The problem is inherent to PWD (bodies, minds, or attitudes) | The problem is related to social, institutional, and political settings |
| Perceived need | Medical interventions, rehabilitation and charity | Inclusion, representation, participation, decision-making power, etc. |
| Formulation of a response | Interventions at the level of the PWD who needs "fixing" | Interventions to alleviate barriers at the level of the socio-political, cultural, or physical environment |
| Implementation of a response | By experts (medical or other fields) | By and with PWD |

## *Operationalisation of Disability*

We mean by this all ways in which disability (and PWD) is represented (or not) in Data, modelled through Featurisation, processed through predictions and classifications (we refer to this as Optimisation, not of disability itself but of the task the AI was developed for). These three operations are iteratively performed throughout an AI product lifecycle. In the following, we will take a closer look at each operation and some of its potential impacts on PWD.

**Data**: PWD are often absent, under-represented or misrepresented in the data collected by or to serve as bases for AI systems. Besides, as mentioned earlier, PWD are not a monolith. On the contrary, they are among the most internally diverse historically marginalised groups. It is, therefore, essential to consider all aspects in which data can become a factor in creating disabling situations starting from the design phase while keeping in mind the subgroup(s) of PWD that might be the most impacted by a system (Trewin et al., 2019). When preprocessing (or cleaning) data, PWD are often considered as "outliers" for a variety of reasons, including "non-conformity" to mainstream patterns considered as "normal" (Whittaker et al., 2019), missing information about PWD when aggregating data sources (Trewin, 2018), etc. Outliers' data is then considered as "noise" and removed to "homogenise" and "improve" data quality. This represents tremendous risks for PWD. Researchers and designers should explore new approaches to better handle data from groups considered so far as outliers.

**Featurisation**: aims to model or approximate real-life, sometimes socially constructed, sometimes very complex, concepts through selecting proxies present in the data or engineering new abstractions via analysis and combinations of thesis proxies. These features will then be used to achieve a particular goal, often in the form of predicting phenomena, identifying or classifying different kinds of entities, etc. The choices and abstractions necessary for featurisation are neither inevitable (i.e., not the only possibility) nor objective (i.e., value neutral). They are design choices driven by design priorities and influenced by the values and perceptions of designers. Therefore, responsible design should scrutinise featurisation. In many fields, removing sensitive features and proxies (or adding statistical perturbation) is a common practice to ensure the model does not learn and perpetuate bias. This approach received mixed reactions in the responsible AI community and faced many limitations (Whittaker et al., 2019). In the context of disability, many more aspects should be considered. In some cases, including features that abstract or explicitly represent disability can be beneficial (Trewin et al., 2019). More importantly, these considerations should be taken with the participation of impacted stakeholders, especially PWD.

**Optimisation**: The usage of AI systems is often linked to some form of optimisation (i.e., carrying a task while lowering the costs, human involvement, execution time, errors and other risks). This often demands making trade-offs and can have harmful externalities, especially when these trade-offs are not responsibly and fairly assessed. In the context of disability, optimisation can reinforce exclusionary norms of normalcy and classify PWD as "risks", "misfits", and "abnormal" (Trewin, 2018; Whittaker et al., 2019). It is, therefore, vital to understand what the AI system is optimising for and how that is done. i.e., what does the system as the optimisation criteria and parameters? For example, if we consider an AI system used in recruitment. The goal of such a system is to identify the candidates most likely to succeed in the workplace. The challenge in this case is to select inclusive disability-friendly indicators and predictors of employment success (Buyl et al., 2022; Tilmes, 2022).

## Interactions with and Subjection to AI

Studies tackling AI usage in the context of disability often refer to the PWD as a user of AI systems. Although this is correct in some cases, it is not valid for all cases. This amalgamation hinders our capacity to analyse interactions between the PWD and the AI system and accurately assess and address their impacts. In some of these cases, we argue that PWDs do not interact with the AI system; they are subjected to decisions made about them based on outputs and results of AI predictions or classifications. Following this logic, we propose three categories of AI systems according to a PWD-centric perspective. We will make a distinction between AI "used by" PWD, AI used by a third party and is "used for" PWD and AI used by a third party and is (fully or partially) "about" PWD.

**AI used by PWD**: In this first category, we will examine AI systems directly used by PWD to communicate, socialise, and interact with (or navigate) physical and virtual environments. In this category, we will include AI-powered Assistive technologies and Human-Augmenting technologies. Assistive technologies developed in the context of disability pre-date AI both in the digital and physical world. Some examples of very common pre-AI assistive technologies are wheelchairs or portable digital magnifiers. However, AI brings the promise to both significantly improve and democratise assistive technologies (by making them cheaper or easier to access (Hashemi et al., 2014)). AI can also push the boundaries of the possible and augment the abilities of everyone, not only persons with disability. Human-augmenting technologies can help to supplement, enhance, restore, replicate, and stimulate peoples' abilities and senses. Prominent examples of these technologies are prosthetics and bionics, Robots and autonomous avatars (e.g. operation of exoskeletons to help move the body), brain-computer interfaces (Bonci et al., 2021) and augmentations using biotechnology (Raisamo et al., 2019). Ill-designed AI products in this category can create or exacerbate disabling situations by, for example, increasing pain or discomfort or creating security and safety risks. They can also have negative impacts on the autonomy and dignity of PWD when prioritising the "practical" goal over PWD individual aspirations (Blanchard, 2022) (e.g., prioritising tools that help PWD with commuting to/from work over tools that allow PWD to enjoy nature).

**AI used for PWD**: Accessibility tools of mainstream technologies are tools used by digital platforms, content, and products (websites, video streaming, games, social media, etc.) creators to allow access and navigate these products (e.g., subtitling, close caption, screen readers, screen magnifiers). These tools also pre-date AI, yet, here as well, AI can drastically improve exciting practices and approaches used to enhance the accessibility of mainstream technologies, e.g., the design for all, inclusive design, and user interface adaptation and personalisation (see Burzagli et al. (2022) for an overview). In this category, AI products often act as intermediaries or gateways to the environment (physical or digital) for PWD. As such, these AIs bear the risk of forcing the designers' (and technology companies') world views, ideologies or agendas on PWD (Scheuerman et al., 2020) (e.g., exposing the PWD to miss-information, to harmful views on disability or other marginalised groups, to racism, misogyny, homophobia, etc.).

**AI used about PWD**: This third category can also be referred to as Prescriptive AI and includes all AI systems used in supporting or automating decision-making. A plethora of prescriptive AI is being developed and used in all fields and sectors, including very sensitive fields such as healthcare (diagnosis and clinical decision support systems (CDSS), treatment and therapy planning, hospital workflow management, insurance policies, etc.), school and university admission, job recruitment, job performance evaluation, social media, energy, transportation, and mobility, etc. As hinted earlier, PWD are not really users of these systems. PWD are often subject to outputs and decisions of these systems used by third parties to produce predictions about PWD. Prescriptive AI systems can have huge impacts on individuals and society at large. PWD are often targets of discrimination when prescriptive AI is used as a technology supporting or automating decision-making (see Nugent and Scott-Parker (2022); Sabatello (2022)).

## Quality of Life Through the Lenses of the Capabilities Approach to Justice

AI systems usages often influence the distribution and access to benefits of different natures: material (e.g., resources, loans, salaries, housing), services (e.g., healthcare, entertainment, education), or opportunities (e.g., jobs, political participation) etc. It also influences the distribution of burdens such as barriers, duties, taxes, sanctions, and punishments. This influence can create disparities and injustices if not measured and monitored. Responsible AI scholars called for applying principles from a theory of justice called distributive justice (Lamont & Favor, 2017) to assess fairness in AI. Despite the many approaches to distributive justice, most operationalisations of AI fairness are based on the resourcist approach proposed by Rawls Lamont and Favor (2017). Other approaches, such as Sen and Nussbaum's capabilities approach (Nussbaum, 2003; Sen, 1993), have yet to be explored in this context.

Although each approach has merits and downfalls, we argue that Sen and Nussbaum's capabilities approach better suits the context of PWD for the following reasons: First, resources are important to improve the quality of life. However, the availability of resources does not always guarantee access and inclusion for many historically marginalised groups, including PWD. There are differences between individuals (e.g., in physiological, psychological, social and political conditions) that influence their quality of life and well-being beyond the resources they possess. Therefore, Sen and Nussbaum argue that a measure of justice should be sensitive to these differences and conditions. Second, the capabilities approach is compatible with CRPD (UN, 2006), a groundbreaking legal framework that addresses the rights of PWD. The capabilities approach not only gives CRPD a normative grounding but also provides a way to facilitate its implementation (Harnacke, 2013).

Based on this understanding of the capabilities approach, Nussbaum presents a list of ten capabilities as minimum fundamental entitlements all humans should enjoy for a just society to be made: (1) "Life", (2) "Bodily Health", (3) "Bodily Integrity", (4) "Senses, Imagination, and Thought", (5) "Emotions", (6) "Practical Reason", (7) "Affiliation, (8) "Other Species", (9) "Play", (10) "Control Over One's Environment (Political and Material)". We will adopt these ten capabilities as defined by Nussbaum in Nussbaum (2003). In the same article, Nussbaum explains that this list was purposefully specified in a somewhat abstract and general way and can and should be objected to deliberation, rethinking and revision to suit different contexts and respect plurality and diversity. As such and for simplicity, we will provide this list as a guiding example for capabilities to assess and leave the colossal task of specification out of the scope of this paper and to future work.

## Conclusions

This paper endeavours to bridge gaps between disability studies and responsible AI design. It aims to provide scientific, practical and activist ground for designing better AI for PWD. On a scientific level, we proposed a transdisciplinary conceptualisation of "Disability Creation" in the AI environment. On a practical level, D-DCP is a flexible and robust framework easily adapted to different contexts and AI products. It situates AI for PWD in its socio-technical context. It provides a comprehensive overview of factors (personal, environmental, and interactions) to be considered in designing an AI that improves quality of life and contributes to social justice of PWD. As a future, we propose to: (1) Empirically validate the framework against real-life AI systems and use cases. (2) Develop scales for different factors and quality of life metrics to facilitate the use of the framework and ensure uniformity of its results.

## References

Beaudry, J. S. (2016). Beyond (Models of) disability? *Journal of Medicine and Philosophy (United Kingdom), 41*(2), 210–228.

Bennett, C.L., & Keyes, O. (2019, Aug). What is the point of fairness? Disability, AI and the complexity of justice. *ACM SIGACCESS Accessibility and Computing*, 1.

Berghs, M., Atkin, K., Graham, H., Hatton, C., Thomas, C. (2016, Jul). Implications for public health research of models and theories of disability: A scoping study and evidence synthesis. *Public Health Research, 4*(8), 1–166.

Bigham, J.P., & Carrington, P. (2018). *Learning from the front: People with disabilities as early adopters of AI*. HCIC.

Blanchard, E. (2022). Cripping assistive tech design: How the current disability framework limits our ability to create emancipatory technology. In *Service oriented, holonic and multi-agent manufacturing systems for industry of the future* (pp. 377–388). Springer International Publishing.

Bonci, A., Fiori, S., Higashi, H., Tanaka, T., & Verdini, F. (2021, Feb). An introductory tutorial on brain-computer interfaces and their applications. *Electronics, 10*(5):560.

Burzagli, L., Emiliani, P. L., Antona, M., & Stephanidis, C. (2022). Intelligent environments for all: a path towards technology-enhanced human well-being. *Universal Access in the Information Society, 21*(2), 437–456.

Buyl, M., Cociancig, C., Frattone, C., & Roekens, N. (2022, June). *Tackling algorithmic disability discrimination in the hiring process: An ethical, legal and technical analysis*. In 2022 ACM conference on fairness, accountability, and transparency (pp. 1071–1082). New York.

Byrne, B. (2018). Dis-equality: Exploring the juxtaposition of disability and equality. *Social Inclusion, 6*(1), 9–17.

Devlieger, P. J. (2005). *Generating a cultural model of disability*. In 19th congress of the European Federation of Associations of Teachers of the Deaf (pp. 1–15).

Fougeyrollas, P., Boucher, N., Edwards, G., Grenier, Y., Noreau, L. (2019, Feb). The disability creation process model: A comprehensive explanation of disabling situations as a guide to developing policy and service programs. *Scandinavian Journal of Disability Research, 21*(1):25–37.

Fougeyrollas, P., Boucher, N., Fiset, D., Grenier, Y., Noreau, L., Philibert, M., Gascon, H., Morales, E., & Charrier, F. (2015). Handicap, environnement, participation sociale et droits humains: du concept d'accès à sa mesure. Développement Humain, Handicap et Changement Social, 5.

Fougeyrollas, P., & Grenier, Y. (2018). Monitoring disability policies and legislation towards effective exercise of rights to equality and inclusive access for persons with disabilities: The case of the Quebec model. *Societies, 8*(2), 41.

Gharebaghi, A., Mostafavi, M.-A., Edwards, G., Fougeyrollas, P., Gamache, S., & Grenier, Y. (2018, Aug). Integration of the social environment in a mobility ontology for people with motor disabilities. *Disability and Rehabilitation: Assistive Technology, 13*(6):540–551.

Greco, G. M. (2016). On accessibility as a human right, with an application to media accessibility. In *Researching audio description* (pp. 11–33). Palgrave Macmillan UK.

Harnacke, C. (2013, Jan). Disability and capability: Exploring the usefulness of Martha Nussbaum's capabilities approach for the UN disability rights convention. *Journal of Law, Medicine & Ethics, 41*(4):768–780.

Hashemi, J., Tepper, M., Vallin Spina, T., Esler, A., Morellas, V., Papanikolopoulos, N., & Sapiro, G. (2014). Computer vision tools for low-cost and noninvasive measurement of autism-related behaviors in infants. *Autism Research and Treatment, 2014*, 1–12.

IOM: Institute of Medicine (US)—Committee on Assessing Rehabilitation Science and Engineering (1997, Aug). Models of disability and rehabilitation. In E. N. J. Brandt, & A. M. Pope (Eds.), *Enabling America: Assessing the role of rehabilitation science and engineering*. National Academies Press (US).

Lamont, J., & Favor, C. (2017). Distributive justice. In E. N. Zalta (Ed.), *The Stanford Encyclopedia of Philosophy* (Winter 2017 ed.). Metaphysics Research Lab, Stanford University.

Lawson, A., & Beckett, A. E. (2020). The social and human rights models of disability: towards a complementarity thesis. *International Journal of Human Rights, 25*(2), 1–32.

Newman-Griffis, D., Rauchberg, J.S., Alharbi, R., Hickman, L., Hochheiser, H. (2023, Jan). Definition drives design: Disability models and mechanisms of bias in AI technologies. *First Monday*.

Nugent, S. E., & Scott-Parker, S. (2022). Recruitment ai has a disability problem: Anticipating and mitigating unfair automated hiring decisions. In *Towards trustworthy artificial intelligent systems* (pp. 85–96). Springer International Publishing.

Nussbaum, M. C. (2003). Capabilities as fundamental entitlements: Sen and social justice. *Feminist Economics, 9*(2–3), 33–59.
Oliver, M. (1990). *The politics of disablement: A sociological approach.* Palgrave Macmillan.
Oliver, M. (2013). The social model of disability: Thirty years on. *Disability and Society, 28*(7), 1024–1026.
Priestley, M. (2000, Jul). Adults only: Disability, social policy and the life course. *Journal of Social Policy*, *29*(3):421–439.
Raisamo, R., Rakkolainen, I., Majaranta, P., Salminen, K., Rantala, J., & Farooq, A. (2019, Nov). Human augmentation: Past, present and future. *International Journal of Human-Computer Studies*, *131*(May):131–143.
Retief, M., & Letšosa, R. (2018, Mar). Models of disability: A brief overview. *HTS Teologiese Studies*, *74*(1):1–8.
Sabatello, M. (2022, July). Wrongful birth: AI-tools for moral decisions in clinical care in the absence of disability ethics. *The American Journal of Bioethics*, *22*(7):43–46.
Scheuerman, M. K., Wade, K., Lustig, C., & Brubaker, J. R. (2020, May). How we've taught algorithms to see identity: Constructing race and gender in image databases for facial analysis. In *Proceedings of the ACM on human-computer interaction*, *4*(CSCW1):1–35.
Sen, A. (1993, Mar). *Capability and well-being. The quality of life* (pp. 30–53). Oxford University Press.
Shew, A. (2020). Ableism, technoableism, and future AI. *IEEE Technology and Society Magazine, 39*(1), 40–85.
Smart, J. (2004). Models of disability: The juxtaposition of biology and social construction. In *Handbook of rehabilitation counselling* (pp. 25–49).
Smith, P., & Smith, L. (2021). Artificial intelligence and disability: too much promise, yet too little substance? *AI and Ethics, 1*(1), 81–86.
St-Germain, D., Boivin, B., & Fougeyrollas, P. (2011). The caring-disability creation process model: A new way of combining 'care' in nursing and 'rehabilitation' for better quality of services and patient safety. *Disability and Rehabilitation, 33*(21–22), 2105–2113.
Tilmes, N. (2022, Jun). Disability, fairness, and algorithmic bias in AI recruitment. *Ethics and Information Technology*, *24*(2):21.
Trewin, S. (2018). *AI fairness for people with disabilities: Point of view.* CoRR, abs/1811.10670, Retrieved from http://arxiv.org/abs/1811.10670.
Trewin, S., Basson, S., Muller, M., Branham, S., Treviranus, J., Gruen, D., Hebert, D., Lyckowski, N., & Manser, E. (2019). Considerations for AI fairness for people with disabilities. *AI Matters, 5*(3), 40–63.
UN (2006). *United Nations convention on the rights of persons with disabilities.*
van de Poel, I., & van Gorp, A. C. (2006). The need for ethical reflection in engineering design: The relevance of type of design and design hierarchy. *Science, Technology, & Human Values, 31*(3), 333–360.
Whittaker, M., Alper, M., Bennett, C.L., Hendren, S., Kaziunas, E., Mills, M., Ringel Morris, M., Rankin, J.L., Rogers, E., Salas, M., Myers West, S. (2019, November 20). *Disability, bias, and AI.* AI Now Institute.

# Assessing AI's Role in Digital Accessibility

**Tlamelo Makati**

## Introduction

Digital accessibility involves designing and developing online platforms to ensure individuals with disabilities can interact meaningfully with digital content (W3C Web Accessibility Initiative, 2023a). With the rise of Artificial Intelligence (AI), a wide range of tools and techniques have emerged to assist in improving digital accessibility features. From the generation of automatic alternative text (alt text) for images to AI-powered screen readers, the landscape of digital accessibility is rapidly evolving (Yuksel et al., 2020). While technical innovations in AI have shown promise in addressing accessibility challenges, it is crucial to view these innovations through a disability studies lens. Historically, accessibility efforts have often centered on technical fixes, without fully considering how societal structures, such as ableism and power dynamics, shape disabled individuals' experiences. By adopting frameworks like the Social Model of Disability (Oliver, 1990) and Disability Justice (Sins Invalid, 2019), this study assesses AI-driven tools and explores how they can better address the diverse and intersectional needs of disabled communities (Smith & Smith, 2021).

The chapter investigates how AI technologies, particularly machine learning algorithms, have been applied to enhance digital accessibility. It explores key areas where AI has improved accessibility, as well as the limitations and challenges that persist. The study also seeks to highlight gaps in existing research and identifies opportunities for improving AI-driven solutions. By examining AI's current role in accessibility, this research aims to offer strategic recommendations to guide future developments in this field. The chapter is structured as follows: it begins with a

T. Makati (✉)
School of Computer Science, Technological University Dublin, Dublin, Ireland
e-mail: D21124389@mytudublin.ie



C. El Morr et al. (eds.), *Beyond Tech Fixes*,
https://doi.org/10.1007/978-3-031-93022-5_7

literature review that provides context for AI's role in digital accessibility, followed by an analysis of key AI technologies. Two case studies are then presented, focusing on the practical application of reinforcement learning and supervised learning in enhancing accessibility. Finally, the chapter discusses the implications of these findings and proposes future directions for research and practice in AI-driven accessibility.

## Literature Review

### *What Is Digital Accessibility?*

According to the World Wide Web Consortium (W3C), digital accessibility ensures that websites, tools, and technologies are designed to accommodate the diverse needs of individuals with disabilities (W3C Web Accessibility Initiative, 2023b). Accessibility plays a critical role in enabling equitable participation in the digital society, particularly for the 16% of the global population living with disabilities (World Health Organization, 2022). Beyond a technical requirement, digital accessibility is also a human rights issue, as emphasized by the UN Convention on the Rights of Persons with Disabilities (UNCRPD) and other international bodies (Accessible EU Report, 2023). The failure to provide accessible digital services can lead to the exclusion of people with disabilities from essential aspects of life, including education, employment, and social engagement, reinforcing existing inequalities (Dobransky and Hargittai 2006).

From a disability studies perspective, particularly the social model of disability (Oliver, 1990), accessibility is viewed not as a matter of individual impairment but as an issue created by barriers within society. This model suggests that digital platforms that fail to remove accessibility barriers contribute to the disablement of individuals rather than empowering them. By viewing accessibility as a structural issue, the social model advocates for inclusive designs that address societal biases and assumptions. Disability justice (Sins Invalid, 2019) extends this perspective by emphasizing intersectionality and addressing how race, gender, and class intersect with disability, underscoring the need for digital accessibility solutions that are sensitive to diverse experiences and vulnerabilities.

Historically, digital accessibility focused on design elements like color contrast, font size, and text alternatives for non-text content (Botelho, 2021). Yet, as the digital landscape has evolved, multimedia content, interactive platforms, and AI-driven technologies have introduced new, complex accessibility challenges. Accessibility must now account for a variety of user experiences, accommodating those with visual, auditory, motor, and cognitive impairments (Gilbert, 2019). Incorporating the perspectives of disabled users in developing these solutions is essential for overcoming limitations in conventional designs and understanding the lived realities of individuals with disabilities.

## *AI in Digital Accessibility*

AI has emerged as a promising tool to improve digital accessibility by automating tasks that were previously labor-intensive or unscalable. For instance, technologies such as automatic alternative text generation (Yuksel et al., 2020), real-time captioning for video content (Bragg et al., 2019), and text simplification algorithms (Alarcon et al., 2021) significantly enhance accessibility for disabled users. AI-powered assistive technologies facilitate navigation for individuals with visual impairments, allow deaf users to engage with multimedia content, and enable people with motor impairments to interact with digital platforms via voice commands or gesture recognition (Chemnad and Othman 2024).

However, the application of AI in accessibility raises concerns from a disability studies perspective. Ableism, which is the assumption that non-disabled experiences are the norm, can be embedded within AI algorithms, especially if disabled voices are absent from the design process. For example, automatic alt text generation often lacks context or fails to capture the full meaning of an image, providing a suboptimal experience for visually impaired users (Smith & Smith, 2021). Disability Justice advocates argue that such limitations reflect a broader societal failure to prioritize the experiences and agency of disabled people, particularly those from intersecting marginalized groups (Sins Invalid, 2019). This oversight may deepen digital exclusion and perpetuate inequalities.

Additionally, accessibility overlays, which are AI tools designed to "fix" accessibility issues on the fly, are criticized for providing superficial fixes that rarely meet the Web Content Accessibility Guidelines (WCAG) comprehensively (Law et al., 2020). Critics argue that such tools exemplify the medical model of disability, which seeks to "fix" the individual or their immediate environment without addressing the larger societal barriers that contribute to exclusion (Garland-Thomson, 2005). This approach contrasts with the social model, which advocates for systems designed with accessibility in mind from the outset, rather than relying on after-the-fact solutions that may lack nuance and depth.

The risks of overreliance on AI-driven tools without adequate human oversight and input from the disability community have been raised by disability advocates, as these tools often fail to account for the diversity within disabled communities (European Accessibility Resource Centre, 2023). From a disability justice perspective, this critique highlights the importance of inclusive design processes that center the experiences of disabled people throughout the development of accessibility solutions, ensuring that technologies address real-world needs rather than theoretical or idealized versions of accessibility.

## Theoretical Framework

The literature on AI's role in digital accessibility reveals both the potential and challenges of implementing AI-driven solutions to enhance the inclusivity of digital platforms. From assistive technologies like automated captioning to AI's application in accessibility auditing, it is clear that while AI offers significant advancements, there remain inherent limitations and biases that affect its efficacy. These issues underscore the need for a more thoughtful and inclusive approach to designing AI systems for accessibility, one that not only addresses technical challenges but also incorporates the lived experiences of individuals with disabilities.

To address these challenges, this study draws on the social model of disability, which shifts the focus from individual impairments to societal barriers, arguing that it is society's responsibility to remove these barriers in both physical and digital spaces (Oliver, 1990). By viewing disability as a social construct, this model suggests that accessibility efforts, including AI-driven solutions, must work to dismantle societal barriers rather than focusing solely on "fixing" the individual. Building on the social model, the disability justice model further expands this perspective by incorporating an intersectional approach. Developed by disabled activists, this model highlights how race, gender, sexuality, and class intersect with disability, underscoring that AI systems must address these multiple layers of oppression to create truly inclusive solutions (Sins Invalid, 2019). By incorporating both frameworks, this study suggests that AI-driven solutions must go beyond technical fixes to address deeper structural inequalities.

Grounded in both the social model of disability and disability justice, this human-centered AI framework emphasizes that involving diverse stakeholders, particularly disabled individuals, throughout the design process is essential to create solutions that are not only accessible but also equitable (Heitmeier et al., 2023). By directly engaging end-users, AI systems can better align with the actual needs and preferences of people with disabilities, addressing structural barriers rather than merely offering superficial fixes.

A critical concept underpinning this framework is the recognition that AI, while powerful, cannot fully replace human judgment, particularly in context-specific situations where individual needs vary. For example, while an AI model may excel at generating captions for pre-recorded content, it might struggle with real-time interactions or nuanced language that requires human interpretation (Bird et al., 2020). Furthermore, biases in AI systems, stemming from incomplete or unrepresentative training data, can perpetuate exclusion if not addressed (Pereira & Duarte, 2023).

By applying these disability studies frameworks, this study calls for an integrated approach to AI development that combines technical capabilities with a nuanced understanding of human experiences, particularly those of marginalized disabled communities. This inclusive design process aims to ensure that AI solutions address both accessibility and broader societal equity issues. To operationalize this framework, it is essential to adopt a structured methodology that not only examines the existing AI technologies and their applications but also actively engages stakeholders to provide insight into user needs and design requirements. The following methodology section outlines the mixed-methods approach used in this study.

## Methodology

This research employs a mixed-methods approach, combining a narrative literature review, case studies, and qualitative stakeholder engagement to assess the role of AI in digital accessibility. The methodology is designed to evaluate both the technical capabilities of AI-driven systems and the perceptions of stakeholders, including people with disabilities, developers, and accessibility experts.

### *Phase One: Narrative Literature Review*

The research explored AI's application in digital accessibility, focusing on assistive technologies, auditing, and remediation tools. The review focused on peer-reviewed articles, conference papers, and reports from databases like the ACM Digital Library, Google Scholar, and IEEE Xplore. The goal was to identify the main themes, challenges, and opportunities associated with AI-driven accessibility solutions.

The review revealed that while AI technologies have made significant contributions to improving accessibility, particularly in areas like alt text generation and real-time captioning, they also present challenges. These include the need for continuous human oversight, the risk of perpetuating biases, and technical limitations in understanding complex user needs.

### *Phase Two: Case Studies*

Building on the insights from the literature review, two case studies were conducted to assess the practical application of machine learning techniques in digital accessibility. The first case study explored reinforcement learning for web navigation, examining how personalized and adaptive user interfaces can enhance accessibility. The second case study focused on supervised learning for content block classification, analyzing how AI can be used to improve website structure and navigation for users with disabilities.

Both case studies highlighted the potential of AI to improve digital accessibility but also underscored the importance of user involvement and human oversight in the development and deployment of AI systems.

### *Phase Three: Stakeholder Engagement*

In the third phase, the research will engage directly with stakeholders through focus groups and semi-structured interviews. This phase aims to capture the diverse perspectives of individuals with disabilities, developers, and policymakers. This is because stakeholder input is essential for understanding the practical requirements and design considerations needed to develop effective AI-driven accessibility tools. The qualitative data gathered from these interactions will provide valuable insights into the design preferences, concerns, and unmet needs of users, which will then be used to inform the development of strategic recommendations.

### *Phase Four: Action Research*

The final phase of the research will employ an action research methodology. Based on the findings from the previous phases, a collaborative design process will be developed. This process aims to emphasise the co-creation of AI-based accessibility tools with direct input from users. The goal is to create a sustainable development model that could be used to refine existing AI systems and ensure they are both effective and ethical in addressing the needs of users with disabilities.

## Work Done

### *Phase One: Exploration of AI in Digital Accessibility*

The role of AI in digital accessibility has brought forward numerous insights, particularly in areas like assistive technology, accessibility auditing, remediation, and usability. AI applications such as adaptive interfaces and automated content recognition have been instrumental in enhancing interaction for users with visual and motor impairments (Krishnamurthi et al., 2019; Sarwar & Eika, 2020). These technologies allow users to navigate digital spaces more efficiently, offering alternatives to traditional input methods through adaptive designs and machine learning-powered recognition systems.

However, the exploration also identified critical challenges with AI-driven accessibility. One major issue is the necessity for human oversight, as AI alone struggles to fully comprehend complex user needs and context-specific accessibility challenges (Pereira & Duarte, 2023). AI systems, while powerful, often lack the nuanced understanding required to cater to the highly individualized needs of people with disabilities (Smith & Smith, 2021). This limitation poses risks when these technologies are applied without adequate human involvement, as they may fail to provide the level of accessibility required.

Furthermore, the risk of perpetuating biases is significant. AI systems, trained on data that may not fully represent diverse populations, can unintentionally marginalize user groups. These biases may manifest in AI's decision-making, causing further exclusion for people with disabilities. Thus, AI technologies must be integrated cautiously, ensuring they do not inadvertently exacerbate the very barriers they aim to dismantle (Henry, 2023). While AI holds immense potential in making digital environments more inclusive, ongoing research, inclusive design, and stakeholder engagement remain critical to overcoming these inherent challenges (Bird et al., 2020).

In summary, AI-driven advancements must be complemented by inclusive design practices and active stakeholder participation to ensure their effectiveness. Continued research and collaboration between AI developers and individuals with disabilities are necessary to create sustainable, accessible digital environments that meet the complex needs of all users (Bragg et al., 2021).

## *Phase Two: Analysis of Machine Learning Techniques in Digital Accessibility*

The analysis of machine learning (ML) techniques applied to digital accessibility reveals both the potential and limitations of these technologies. While ML has shown promise in improving accessibility, challenges related to the inherent design of websites and the quality of training data remain significant barriers (Smith & Smith, 2021).

The first case study explored reinforcement learning (RL) for web navigation, focusing on personalization and adaptive interfaces in line with the Web Content Accessibility Guidelines (WCAG) 2.1. Despite the potential for RL to enhance accessibility, the models faced challenges such as data collection and content mismatches. RL models were most effective with text-based websites but struggled with dynamic content and complex structures, limiting their generalizability across web environments (Gur et al., 2019). This limitation reduces user autonomy when the models are applied without sufficient human involvement.

The second case study examined supervised learning techniques for classifying web content blocks to improve navigation for users with disabilities. Manual classification methods using DOM Trees and ARIA landmarks showed promising results, but limitations arose due to the diverse nature of web content (Chiou et al., 2023) and a lack of well-annotated datasets. This study underscored the importance of engaging users in the development process and the complexity of developing accurate and adaptable AI models.

Both case studies emphasize the need for collaboration, user-centric design, and careful consideration of data quality. In the RL case, the models' limitations in addressing inaccessible starting points suggest that these technologies cannot function independently. Similarly, supervised learning approaches, such as leveraging ARIA landmarks, offer potential but require substantial improvements in data quality and system design (Watanabe et al., 2022) .

In conclusion, these ML approaches highlight both the potential and challenges of AI in digital accessibility. While they can improve certain aspects of navigation and content interaction, their limitations show that an inclusiec approach; one that involves human oversight and continual refinement, is necessary. The findings suggest that future research should focus on resolving these challenges and exploring further AI innovations in accessibility (Bragg et al., 2021).

## Discussion and Analysis

This research explores AI's role in digital accessibility, addressing key challenges and opportunities through case studies and a literature review. Digital accessibility is the practice of making content and services usable by people with diverse abilities, combining technical and human components (Gilbert, 2019). AI technologies, such as text-to-speech, gesture recognition, and adaptive interfaces, have enhanced user interaction. However, challenges like human oversight, biases, and technical limitations persist (Smith & Smith, 2021).

Furthemore, in analyzing machine learning techniques like reinforcement learning, results showed a high accuracy (90%) in task completion of this techinque but that it faced limitations with dynamic content (Liu et al., 2018). Challenges include users' understanding of system performance and the need for more annotated data (Gur et al., 2019). Autonomy in RL systems also raised questions about user involvement (Bragg et al., 2021).

In examining supervised learning for web content classification, results highlighted the need for user input in data labeling and accessibility strategies (Power et al., 2013). Performance varied, with accuracies from 80 to 95% (Adar et al., 2009; Watanabe et al., 2022). Both studies emphasize the importance of stakeholder engagement in developing effective AI solutions. Future work will therefore focus on qualitative methods, involving stakeholders to ensure AI systems align with user needs and ethical standards.

While AI-driven accessibility solutions have demonstrated technical capabilities, their design processes often reflect ableist assumptions, where the focus is on "fixing" the individual's limitations rather than addressing systemic barriers (Oliver, 1990). This approach not only diminishes user agency but also overlooks how power dynamics shape the effectiveness of these solutions. For instance, the widespread reliance on accessibility overlays ignores the lived experiences of disabled users and their call for deeper engagement in the design and deployment of AI systems (Law et al., 2020). Applying the Disability Justice Model further emphasizes the necessity of centering disabled voices in AI development, particularly those from marginalized communities, to create tools that are not only accessible but also equitable (Sins Invalid, 2019).

## Conclusion

This research has highlighted both the potential and limitations of AI technologies in enhancing digital accessibility. While AI-driven solutions like reinforcement learning and supervised learning have demonstrated their ability to improve web navigation, content interaction, and assistive technologies for individuals with disabilities, significant challenges remain. The need for human oversight, the risk of perpetuating biases, and technical limitations in handling complex user needs underscore the importance of a cautious approach to AI integration in digital accessibility.

The findings emphasize the critical role of inclusive design practices and stakeholder involvement, particularly the engagement of individuals with disabilities in the development process. By incorporating the perspectives of diverse user groups, AI systems can be more effective and ethically aligned with accessibility goals. Furthermore, the research stresses that AI cannot fully replace human judgment in context-specific scenarios, where individual user needs vary greatly.

Future research should prioritize the co-design of AI-driven accessibility tools with disabled individuals, drawing on participatory research methods that center their lived experiences. Moreover, AI developers must engage with diverse disabled communities, including those facing intersecting oppressions related to race, gender, and class, as outlined in the Disability Justice Model (Sins Invalid, 2019). Such an approach will ensure that AI solutions are not only technically robust but also socially just and representative of the diverse needs of all disabled individuals.

## References


Adar, E., Teevan, J., Dumais, S. T., & Elsas, J. L. (2009). The web changes everything: understanding the dynamics of web content. In Proceedings of the Second ACM International Conference on Web Search and Data Mining (pp. 282-291).

Alarcon, R., Moreno, L., & Martínez, P. (2021). Lexical simplification system to improve web accessibility. *IEEE Access, 9*, 58755–58767.

Bird, E., Fox-Skelly, J., Jenner, N., Larbey, R., Weitkamp, E., & Winfield, A. (2020, March). *The ethics of artificial intelligence: Issues and initiatives*. European Sources Online. Retrieved from https://www.europeansources.info/record/the-ethics-of-artificial-intelligence-issues-and-initiatives/.

Botelho, F. H. (2021). Accessibility to digital technology: virtual barriers, real opportunities. *Assistive Technology, 33*(sup1), 27–34.

Bragg, D., Caselli, N., Hochgesang, J. A., Huenerfauth, M., Katz-Hernandez, L., Koller, O., et al. (2021). The fate landscape of sign language AI datasets: an interdisciplinary perspective. *ACM Transactions on Accessible Computing (TACCESS), 14*(2), 1–45.

Bragg, D., Koller, O., Bellard, M., Berke, L., Boudreault, P., Braffort, A., … & Ringel Morris, M. (2019, October). *Sign language recognition, generation, and translation: An interdisciplinary perspective*. In Proceedings of the 21st international ACM SIGACCESS conference on computers and accessibility (pp. 16–31)

Chemnad, K., & Othman, A. (2024). Digital accessibility in the era of artificial intelligence—Bibliometric analysis and systematic review. In Frontiers in Artificial Intelligence (Vol. 7). Frontiers Media SA. https://doi.org/10.3389/frai.2024.1349668.

Chiou, P. T., Alotaibi, A. S., & Halfond, W. G. J. (2023). BAGEL: An Approach to Automatically Detect Navigation-Based Web Accessibility Barriers for Keyboard Users. Proceedings of the 2023 CHI Conference on Human Factors in Computing Systems, 1–17. https://doi.org/10.1145/3544548.3580749

Dobransky, K., & Hargittai, E. (2006). The disability divide in internet access and use. Information, Communication & Society, 9(3), 313–334.

European Accessibility Resource Centre. (2023). Accessible EU Report Digital Accessibility.

Garland-Thomson, R. (2005). Disability and representation. *PMLA, 120*(2), 522–527.

Gilbert, R. M. (2019). *Inclusive design for a digital world: designing with accessibility in mind.* Apress.

Gur, I., Rueckert, U., Faust, A., & Google, H.-T. (2019). *Learning to navigate the web.*

Heitmeier, K. A., Kersken, V., Piskorek, P., Böhm, A. K., Egger, N., Lang, M., & Zimmermann, G. (2023, April). *Persona co-design for improving digital accessibility.* In Extended abstracts of the 2023 CHI conference on human factors in computing systems (pp. 1–7).

Henry, S. L. (Ed.) (2023, August 1). *Conformance evaluation and reports.* Web Accessibility Initiative (WAI). Retrieved from https://www.w3.org/WAI/test-evaluate/conformance/#:~:text=Conformance%20evaluation%20determines%20how%20well,Content%20Accessibility%20Guidelines%20(WCAG).

Invalid, S. (2019). *Skin, tooth, and bone: The basis of movement is our people: A disability justice primer.* Sins Invalid.

Krishnamurthi, R., Patan, R., & Gandomi, A. H. (2019). Assistive pointer device for limb impaired people: A novel Frontier Point Method for hand movement recognition. Future Generation Computer Systems, 98, 650–659.

Law, C. M., Groves, K., Hoffman, A., Lewis, A., O'Neill, D., & Rowland, C. (2020). *Panel: Accessibility overlays.* In Proceedings of the 2020 ICT accessibility testing symposium: Time for testing in testing times (Remote Work, Commerce, Education, Support…) (pp. 25–27).

Liu, E. Z., Guu, K., Pasupat, P., Shi, T., & Liang, P. (2018). REINFORCEMENT LEARNING ON WEB INTERFACES USING WORKFLOW-GUIDED EXPLORATION.

Oliver, M., (1990), The Politics of Disablement, 1st edn., London: Macmillan Press.

Pereira, L. S., & Duarte, C. (Eds.). (2023, August 30). *Artificial intelligence (AI) and accessibility research symposium 2023.* Web Accessibility Initiative (WAI). Retrieved from https://www.w3.org/WAI/research/ai2023/.

Power, C., Petrie, H., Swallow, D., Murphy, E., Gallagher, B., & Velasco, C. A. (2013). *Navigating, discovering, and exploring the web: Strategies used by people with print disabilities on interactive websites.* Lecture notes in computer science (including subseries lecture notes in artificial intelligence and lecture notes in bioinformatics), 8117 LNCS (PART 1) (pp. 667–684).

Sarwar, U., & Eika, E. (2020). *Towards more efficient screen reader web access with automatic summary generation and text tagging.* In Computers helping people with special needs: 17th international conference, ICCHP 2020, Proceedings Part I (pp. 303–313). Springer International Publishing.

Smith, P., & Smith, L. (2021). Artificial intelligence and disability: too much promise, yet too little substance? *AI and Ethics, 1*(1), 81–86.

W3C Web Accessibility Initiative (2023a, November 20). *Introduction to web accessibility.* Web Accessibility Initiative (WAI). Retrieved from https://www.w3.org/WAI/fundamentals/accessibility-intro/.

W3C Web Accessibility Initiative (2023b, August 1). *Evaluating web accessibility overview.* Web Accessibility Initiative (WAI). . Retrieved from https://www.w3.org/WAI/test-evaluate/.

Watanabe, W. M., de Lemos, G., & Nascimento, R. W. (2022). Accessibility landmarks identification in web applications based on DOM elements classification. *Universal Access in the Information Society, 23*, 765–777. https://doi.org/10.1007/s10209-022-00959-8

World Health Organization (2022). Global Report on Health Equity for Persons With Disabilities. Geneva: World Health Organization.

Yuksel, B. F., Fazli, P., Mathur, U., Bisht, V., Kim, S. J., Lee, J. J., & Yoon, I. (2020, July). *Human-in-the-loop machine learning to increase video accessibility for visually impaired and blind users.* In Proceedings of the 2020 ACM designing interactive systems conference (pp. 47–60).

# Empowering Voices: The Role of Emerging Technologies in Workplace Inclusion for Individuals with Speech Impairments

T. Claire Davies and Shital Desai

## Introduction

The Accessible Canada Act (ACA) mandates new standards in equity, diversity, inclusion, and accessibility for persons with disabilities, recognizing access to communication as a priority area (Bill C-81, 2019). The employment rate of Canadians with disabilities was 47% in 2023 (Vergara & Hardy, 2024), yet people with speech impairments face employment rates as low as 14% (Blackstone, 1993 as cited in (McNaughton & Bryen, 2002)). If an individual cannot effectively communicate in employment settings, they are discounted as lacking in performance and unable to meet the workplace performance metrics, setting them up for failure.

Augmentative and alternative communication strategies can enable persons with speech impairment to effectively interact. Persons with speech impairment may require unaided (gestures), non-electronic, or electronic methods of interaction. Electronic means can vary from low-tech systems that include switch access to higher technology forms such as brain-computer interfaces or eye-tracking. Technologies must cater to neurophysiological differences that differ from the typically developed population.

Persons with disabilities have found devices to be extremely useful within social and home settings (Welker, 2023). However, there are many barriers to effective

T. C. Davies (✉)
Department of Mechanical and Materials Engineering, Queen's University, Kingston, ON, Canada
e-mail: claire.davies@queensu.ca

S. Desai
Social and Technological Systems (SaTS) Lab, School of Arts Media Performance and Design, York University, Toronto, ON, Canada
e-mail: desais@yorku.ca



C. El Morr et al. (eds.), *Beyond Tech Fixes*,
https://doi.org/10.1007/978-3-031-93022-5_8

integration within employment environments: they are undeniably slow as they require typed input or significant training by and with the individual, and they lack the ability for effective real-time interaction such that colleagues interrupt the persons with speech impairment and discount their expertise (Kochan et al., 2024). Even with higher-level postgraduate degrees, person with speech impairment have extreme difficulty with retention in employment situations (Dujay, 2023). There is a need for research into approaches that can enable effective integration within an employment setting. Accessible washrooms, ramps, and even braille ATMs are commonplace, but employers must also recognize the very real need to accommodate by integrating the acceptance of differing forms of speech to enable persons with speech impairments to be empowered employees within society.

This chapter will discuss the current literature and research around understanding barriers to employment by persons with speech impairments, followed by the results of a hybrid co-creation workshop that involved persons with speech impairments, clinicians, academics, and industrial collaborators who sought to better understand gaps that must be addressed to enhance future employment.

## Literature Review

Research evidence indicates that augmentative and alternative communication (AAC) systems support interaction and communication in diverse settings and can enable participation in employment [see for example (Batorowicz et al., 2014; Smith & Murray, 2016)]. Augmentative communication includes those methods that can supplement impaired speech for improving transmission and message understanding and thus enhancing communication itself. Alternative communication relates to methods and means of communication used to completely replace speech when it cannot be produced (Augmentative and Alternative Communication (AAC), 1991).

High-tech AAC devices have been designed to improve the lives of persons with disabilities. However, there is little evidence that these systems are effective for the intended population of users (Choi et al., 2017; Moghimi et al., 2013; Orlandi et al., 2021; Taherian et al., 2016, 2017). There has been a move towards more sophisticated means of interpreting intent using these systems, but many engineers *neglect to consult the client* throughout the design of the device, leading to preconfigured signal processing systems that do not account for neurophysiological differences among populations (Daly et al., 2009, 2013; Daly & Wolpaw, 2008; Kinney-Lang et al., 2020; Lazarou et al., 2018; Noyek et al., 2022; Perfect et al., 2020). The purpose of our workshop was to engage persons with speech impairments, academics, healthcare practitioners, and employers to understand perceptions around speech impairments, identify systemic barriers, and propose research topics that can enhance the employment of persons with speech impairments.

A systematic review (Lackey et al., 2023) identified both personal factors and environmental factors as contributors to the effective integration of persons with speech impairment in employment. Personal factors included level of education, previous and current experience, character, skills and knowledge, and psychosocial contributors. Environmental factors included products and technology, natural environment and human-made changes to the environment, temporal nature of accessibility, support and relationships, attitudes, services, systems and policies. The purpose of this workshop was to identify research objectives and approaches to fill the gaps in current research to enhance employment for persons with speech impairment.

## Methodology

A co-creation hybrid workshop was undertaken with 31 participants for two half days (October 21, 2024 and October 22, 2024) at York University, Keele Campus in Toronto, Canada. Involving multiple stakeholders in the discussions at the same time provided an ideal platform to collect information about the use of technology within employment settings.

### *Workshop Participants*

A total of 31 participants were involved (some of whom identified with more than one group): six persons with lived experience (four with cerebral palsy, one with multiple sclerosis, and one with autism), four therapists, a neurologist, eleven academics, two caregivers, one employer, two community-based researchers, two service providers, and two postgraduate students.

### *Equity Through Technology: Instructions for Workshop Participants*

To ensure equity through technology, each participant was required to use a phone, tablet, or computer connected to Zoom to participate and it was requested that all participants had cameras turned on throughout, as though they were all "in-person". On-site participants were required to turn off the volume on their systems and mute throughout the sessions to enable a more typical workshop environment with a central screen and audio, but cameras were to be left on. This enabled a more equitable approach to hybrid integration as the gallery and pinned views for all those on-site and in-person were equivalent.

### *Conduct of Workshop*

The workshop included a podcast presentation by participants with lived experience, followed by a research presentation from a prior study (https://carleton.ca/readi/action-team-projects/, 2023 cohort with CCRW) and group discussions in Zoom breakout rooms. All breakout rooms were recorded via Zoom for analysis.

## Podcast

The workshop began with a podcast in which five persons with lived experience were interviewed to answer the following questions:

(a) How do you use technology to communicate, if you use any? What works and what does not work when you use these technologies? What are the advantages and disadvantages of these technologies?
(b) What social change has enhanced your communication with others?
(c) If a family approached you to ask about how to enhance communication with non-familiar partners (new people), what recommendations would you provide?

## Research Presentation

This research presentation was based on a study conducted by a researcher with lived experience. They were supported and mentored by a community partner who has a doctorate in social science and is the manager of research and engagement at a community organization that seeks to increase meaningful and equitable employment of persons with disabilities. The presentation discussed the results of qualitative interviews with ten persons with speech impairment who were either engaged or had been engaged in active employment in either a paid or volunteer capacity.

## Breakout Sessions

Five breakout group sessions were undertaken in which interdisciplinary teams consisted of at least one person with speech impairment in addition to a mix of clinicians, employment advisors, family members of persons with speech impairment, and academics. The following questions were discussed:

(a) Where can technology intervene to support persons with speech impairment in seeking better employment prospects?
(b) What technology must be designed to better engage persons with speech impairment?
(c) What social frameworks around effective integration of technology during employment settings must be developed to enable persons with speech impairment?
(d) How can we increase knowledge-sharing to increase community engagement?

The study received ethics approval from the Research Ethics Boards of Queen's University and York University.

## Analysis

The recordings from the Zoom breakout room discussions were transcribed. The transcripts were then imported into a qualitative analysis software - ATLAS ti (version 24.0) to identify themes that were common across the five groups in the breakout room discussions. The thematic analysis helped us draw out meaningful insights and patterns from the transcripts. Atlas ti version 24.0 has built-in Generative AI tools (Open AI), in addition to a manual coding option, to assist with thematic analysis of qualitative data. Summaries of the transcripts were generated using the AI Summary tool. The summary of the transcripts gave broad insights into breakout discussions and provided a means for future accuracy checking after the use of Generative AI tools in analysis to fix the errors in the process.

The 'AI coding' tool was used on the transcripts to generate themes representative of the topics discussed in the breakout session. This resulted in 10 themes and 660 codes, a total of 6600 codes. There were overlaps and similarities in the meaning of the themes and codes, and thus, re-grouping of the codes was necessary. Some themes and codes were not relevant to the topic of discussion, and the quotations for some codes were not relevant to the codes defined. Manual coding was required to fix the errors.

In the next iteration of thematic coding, the 'Intentional AI' tool in Atlas ti was used. The specific questions from the breakout session were provided as prompts or research questions to explore in thematic analysis. This resulted in 10 themes and 1592 codes, a total of 15920 codes.

Finally, in the third iteration, 'Conversational AI' was used to generate themes for the data. The prompt for the tool was "Provide the emerging themes from the data?". This resulted in six themes. A follow-up prompt to the tool: "generate QDA codes for the themes," resulted in links in the data for each of the themes, which were checked for correctness and further coded manually. Using the 'Conversational AI' tool was more reliable than the 'AI coding tool' and 'Intentional AI' as errors could be identified and new themes and codes added during manual coding.

## Results

The thematic analysis of the transcripts using 'Conversational AI' and manual coding in Atlas ti from the breakout sessions revealed six themes, the heuristics for which with quotations are given in Table 1:

## Discussion

Themes generally revolved around societal acceptance. There was a strong belief that if society was more accepting, equitable employment would result from less stigma. Solutions around enhancing the experiences of people with speech

**Table 1** Heuristics table for the six themes from the analysis

| # | Theme | Description | Quotations |
|---|---|---|---|
| 1 | Technological Accommodations in Employment | Accessibility in job application and interviews | "If the job application requires a video submission... PowerPoint presentations and/or reels with text and/or voiceovers" |
| | | | "Interviews can be coordinated via email... written responses" |
| 2 | Inclusive Policies and Training | Sensitivity training and inclusive policies | "Train hiring managers to accommodate candidates with speech impairments" |
| | | | "Including diversity and inclusion in the organization's values" |
| 3 | Design and Ethics | Personalization and ethical concerns | "AAC can operate as an extension of oneself... to characterize a voice that feels like oneself" |
| | | | "If I want to have real-time captioning... ask people for permission to record them under privacy laws" |
| 4 | Barriers and Challenges | AI biases and societal attitudes | "One of the biggest barriers even to get into the process... you might not even get to that stage of being interviewed" |
| | | | "Our society is so ableist... we're talking about ableism to some extent" |
| 5 | Community and Social Engagement | Awareness and empathy | "We can increase the social awareness and these two can improve each other" |
| | | | "It's about both sides understanding each other" |
| 6 | Vision for Future Technologies | Future tech and adaptive solutions | "A device could use their camera to survey the environment... populate the vocabulary into the device" |
| | | | "Technology that doesn't just assist but actively learns and evolves alongside the user" |

impairments included offering accommodations to candidates with disability and educating employers and hiring managers about the needs of the candidates. The need for ethical and responsible adaptive technologies was echoed unanimously by all participants. Figure 1 shows a word cloud of prominent topics of discussion in the breakout sessions.

## *Technological Accommodations in Employment*

Participants suggested that specific adaptations to equipment and technologies are needed to make the job application and hiring process more accessible for individuals with speech impairments. Three main phases during the journey of obtaining and maintaining employment were outlined:

**Fig. 1** Word cloud based on the frequency of prominent words in the transcripts

## Pre-Employment Phase

The participants expressed the need for accessible job application processes, recognizing that traditional methods can present barriers for individuals with speech impairments. The solutions involve alternative formats that make the process more inclusive. The participants made the following suggestions to support people with speech impairments in applying for jobs:

Participants suggested that the format of video submissions could be modified to allow candidates to present their qualifications creatively and accessibly, leveraging visual aids and text to convey their message, which can be tailored to showcase their strengths without relying solely on speech.

> *If the job application requires a video submission, candidates with speech impairments should be permitted to submit PowerPoint presentations and/or reels with text and/or voiceovers.*

The participants emphasized the use of email and written responses for interviews. There are diverse communication needs of candidates with speech impairments and flexibility allows the expression of ideas more effectively and comfortably, reducing the anxiety associated with traditional spoken interviews.

> *Interviews can be coordinated via email and candidates with speech impairments can be provided the option to submit written responses.*

## Interview Phase

During the interview stage, technology is highlighted as a useful means to ensure equity in participation. Participants suggested the use of digital tools such as Zoom or Teams to minimize the barriers experienced by candidates with speech impairments.

*I sometimes wonder if interviews should be performed via text chat so that the HR staff never even see the person.*

This suggestion is practical for real-time communication in digital settings. By using chat features, individuals with speech impairments can engage in conversations and express their thoughts at their own pace, ensuring that their input is clear and precise. This was also evident in the way participants with speech impairments communicated at the hybrid workshop.

## Post-hiring Communication

The participants discussed the communication barriers experienced at work once an individual with a speech impairment is hired. They recommend continued use of assistive technology such as text-to-speech assistive software for daily interactions to support everyday communication needs. These applications convert written text into auditory speech, which can be especially useful in meetings or when employees need to contribute verbally. This technology bridges the communication gap, ensuring that their voices are 'heard' without the physical need for speech.

*Employers can encourage employees with speech impairments to use technology such as text-to-speech applications and the chat feature during Zoom or Teams meetings to better communicate with their colleagues.*

Participants suggested integrating AI-driven tools to help with formal communication tasks. AI Voice Generators could be personalized to reflect the user's preferred speaking style and accent, making their presentations more engaging and reducing the stress associated with speaking (Jreige et al., 2009). This technology could also allow for the expression of emotions and nuances that may be difficult to convey otherwise.

*For presentations, employers can allow employees with speech impairments to use AI Voice Generators.*

People with speech impairments described how assigning tasks that predominantly use email can be a valuable accommodation provided by employers at little to no cost to the company.

*Delegating them tasks for which email is the primary mode of communication.*

This approach would ensure that employees are not disadvantaged due to communication barriers, promoting a more productive and inclusive work environment.

## *Inclusive Policies and Training*

This theme emphasizes the need for organizations to implement structured policies and training initiatives that foster inclusivity. Inclusive policies set the foundation for equitable hiring, while sensitivity training for hiring managers and staff ensures that workplace interactions are respectful and accommodating (Glade et al., 2020). Together, they help create a workplace culture that values diversity and actively supports employees with different communication needs.

### Development of Inclusive Policies

Inclusive policies are formal commitments by an organization to support diversity and accessibility in all aspects of the workplace. These policies shape the company's values and provide a framework for creating an environment where employees with disabilities can thrive (Shore et al., 2018). By making diversity and inclusion a core part of its values, an organization signals its commitment to supporting all employees. This approach goes beyond surface-level inclusion, creating a deeper, structural change where policies actively promote fairness and accessibility for individuals with speech impairments (Barak, 2022).

> *The effective integration of technology in employment should entail including diversity and inclusion in the organization's values.*

Employees are more likely to stay with an organization that demonstrates a genuine commitment to inclusivity. When policies are aligned with values, they can improve morale, reduce turnover, and increase the sense of belonging for all employees including employees with disabilities.

Participants emphasized the need for inclusive recruitment practices that eliminate barriers from the very beginning of the hiring process.

> *What really needs to happen is a massive recalibration in how we hire people.*

Training hiring managers specifically in accommodating speech impairments can be an effective step toward eliminating biases and ensuring a fair recruitment process. This involves understanding alternative ways candidates can demonstrate their skills, such as through written answers or video submissions with text overlays.

Policies could include accessible interview options, alternative communication methods, and clear guidelines that discourage the use of AI screening tools that might unintentionally exclude candidates with disabilities (Richardson & Bissell, 2019). By setting up these policies, companies proactively reduce discrimination and create equal opportunities for all applicants.

### Sensitivity and Accessibility Training for Hiring Managers and Staff

Training programs are essential for building an inclusive workplace, especially when it comes to understanding and supporting employees with specific communication needs. Such training should focus on reducing unconscious bias, improving awareness, and teaching practical ways to support colleagues with speech impairments.

***Sensitivity Training for Hiring Managers***: Sensitivity training helps hiring managers understand the challenges faced by candidates with speech impairments and how best to accommodate them. Training sessions can cover topics such as adaptive communication methods, assistive technologies, and fostering patience and empathy in interviews (Vornholt et al., 2018). This training ensures that the hiring process does not inadvertently exclude qualified candidates due to biases or a lack of awareness.

> *Train hiring managers to accommodate candidates with speech impairments.*

Training might include role-playing exercises to help hiring managers learn how to effectively communicate with candidates who use alternative communication methods (Lengnick-Hall et al., 2008). It could also cover best practices for interviews conducted via email or other text-based formats, ensuring that hiring managers are well-equipped to assess all candidates fairly.

***Ongoing Accessibility Training for Employees***: To foster a supportive environment for employees with speech impairments, all employees should receive training on inclusivity and accessibility.

> *So each employee, if they can go through some sort of training as to how to address their unconcious bias.*

Accessibility training for all staff ensures that employees understand the specific needs of their colleagues with speech impairments and know how to interact respectfully. This training helps normalize the use of assistive technology in the workplace, reducing potential stigma and encouraging open communication among employees (Vaughan, 2019).

Accessibility training may include education on various assistive technologies, such as text-to-speech software and AI voice generators, and guidance on supporting colleagues using these tools. Training can also focus on the importance of clear written communication and the effective use of digital chat features to facilitate interactions, for examples, see Basiron et al. (2021), and Duval (2017).

## Leadership Accountability and Implementation

Creating a culture of inclusivity requires commitment from all levels of the organization, especially leadership. Accountability measures for leadership ensure that policies and training initiatives are upheld and evaluated consistently.

***Setting Clear Diversity Goals and Accountability Measures***: When leaders are held accountable for diversity and inclusion goals, it establishes a top-down commitment to inclusivity. This accountability might include regular reviews of recruitment data, employee feedback, and the effectiveness of accommodations for employees with speech impairments (Jacob et al., 2024).

> *Holding leaders accountable to ensure that the organization's diversity and inclusion goals are being met.*

Accountability also involves ongoing assessments of existing policies and their impact. Leaders can ensure that policies are adjusted based on feedback from employees with speech impairments, making the workplace progressively more accessible and supportive.

***Creating a Supportive Environment Through Leadership Advocacy***: Leadership can foster inclusivity by actively advocating for accessibility improvements and encouraging open dialogue about accommodations (Simmons & Yawson, 2022). For example, leaders could host regular forums where employees with disabilities can share their experiences and suggest improvements. When leaders openly discuss inclusivity and accessibility, it normalizes these conversations within the company. This visibility and commitment from the leadership team promotes a culture where all employees feel valued and supported, encouraging a more inclusive workplace.

## *Design and Ethics*

Assistive technologies aim to enhance accessibility and inclusion, but they also raise ethical concerns around privacy, data security, consent, and the balance between assistance and autonomy. This theme emphasizes the importance of designing tools that are both functional and respectful of users' rights and individuality.

### Personalization and Customization in Assistive Technology Design

Assistive technology designed for individuals with speech impairments must be highly customizable to meet the communication needs of each person. The participants highlighted the importance of creating tools that allow users to express themselves in a way that feels authentic and aligns with their communication style.

***Customized Communication***: The concept of "extension of self" is crucial in assistive technology for speech. By allowing people with speech impairments to customize aspects like tone, modulation, and pacing, these tools help them communicate in a way that feels personal and genuine. This level of customization can empower people, helping them convey not only words but also emotions, personality, and identity through technology.

> *If technology could capture tone, better nuances and speech... Be set up so you feel more like this is what you would like to be sounding like.*

Personalized communication tools can significantly enhance the confidence and social engagement of individuals with speech impairments. When the technology reflects their individual communication style, users are more likely to feel comfortable using it in professional and social settings, which supports workplace inclusion and broader societal engagement.

## Ethical Concerns: Privacy and Consent

As assistive technologies increasingly use AI and real-time data processing, the ethical implications of privacy, data security, and user consent become paramount. These issues are particularly relevant in settings where technology needs to record or analyze speech patterns to offer effective assistance.

***Consent for Real-Time Captioning and Recording***: Real-time captioning and other AI-driven tools require consent when they involve recording or processing conversations. This raises questions about the extent to which technology can monitor and store data, as well as how consent should be managed in workplaces or public environments. Ensuring user consent is obtained and maintained ethically is essential to respecting the privacy rights of both users and those with whom they interact.

> *If I want to have real-time captioning, I am technically supposed to ask people for permission to record them in order to do that, right under privacy laws.*

***Distinction Between Assistance and Surveillance***: This distinction reflects the need to use user data responsibly (Verhulst, 2021). Technologies designed to support individuals with speech impairments must avoid crossing the line into intrusive data collection. The use of AI that "listens" to assist in real-time communication should be limited to the task at hand, with transparent policies about what is recorded, stored, or shared. Avoiding data misuse is critical to maintaining trust in assistive technologies and preventing ethical conflicts around data ownership and surveillance.

> *There's a very big difference between recording somebody with the intent of understanding them... versus recording them and putting that in the cloud.*

## Balancing Assistance with Autonomy and Control

One risk of assistive technologies is that they can sometimes take over the communication process rather than support it. This raises ethical questions about user autonomy and how technology should support rather than override a person's natural ability to communicate.

***User Control and Autonomy in Technology Use***: An ideal assistive technology would adapt to the user's preferences and needs over time, supporting autonomy rather than dictating how communication should occur. Such technology would allow users to remain in control, with options to customize how it responds and learns (Hamidi et al., 2018). This approach ensures that users are active participants in their communication rather than passive recipients of technology-driven solutions.

> *Technology that doesn't just assist but actively learns and evolves alongside the user, making daily interactions more seamless.*

***Ethics of Adaptive AI in Assistive Devices***: Adaptive AI raises questions about the ethical implications of machines "learning" from users. If an assistive device adapts to a user's behaviour, it must do so transparently, with options to reset or modify learning patterns. Ensuring that users have full control over how their data is used and stored and the ability to "teach" or "retrain" the device is essential for preserving autonomy.

## Inclusivity versus Standardization in Design

While some users benefit from customizable technology, others may find highly personalized tools too complex or inaccessible. Striking a balance between individualized solutions and broadly accessible designs is an ongoing challenge in assistive technology design.

***Challenges of a One-Size-Fits-All Approach***: Many conditions affecting speech are unique, and each individual may have distinct needs and preferences for communication. A standardized solution may inadvertently exclude some users or fail to meet their specific requirements (Pedersen et al., 2021). However, creating highly individualized technology can increase costs and complexity. Ethical design in this context involves finding a balance and offering enough customization to suit individual needs while remaining user-friendly and accessible.

> *It's difficult to have a one-size-fits-all solution, because… there are different conditions and different communication needs.*

Inclusive design means considering the varying degrees of technology access among users, including cost and ease of use. Developers must address equity issues by ensuring that assistive technologies are affordable and available to those who need them most. Offering adaptable, cost-effective solutions is an ethical imperative in making technology a true equalizer for individuals with disabilities.

## Future Implications: AI, Data Ethics, and Accountability

With advances in AI and machine learning, the potential for assistive technology to transform communication for individuals with speech impairments is vast. However, these advances bring ethical considerations, including data handling, accountability, and future societal impacts.

***Transparency in Data Use and Ownership***: Users need full transparency about how and when their data is used. Clear information on data ownership, options to control data collection, and simple interfaces to enable or disable data-sharing features are essential. Providing control over data sharing is crucial to prevent misuse while empowering users to safeguard their privacy.

> *People just want to know when it's on and when it's off and be able to easily turn it on and off.*

***Long-term Ethical Considerations for Society***: The ethical implications of AI extend beyond individual use; they shape broader societal norms and values. As assistive technologies become more sophisticated, developers must address questions about the potential for over-reliance on AI, the societal impact of data surveillance, and the ethical responsibility of technology companies to uphold user privacy.

## *Barriers and Challenges*

The participants had an empathetic conversation about the technological, social, and systemic barriers that hinder the employment and workplace integration of individuals with speech impairments. The discussion covered challenges ranging from biases in AI systems used in recruitment, to physical and social barriers that exist due to societal ableism and lack of awareness. By understanding these barriers, we gain insight into the changes required to create a more inclusive workforce.

### Technological Barriers in Recruitment and Hiring

One of the primary technological challenges discussed is the role of AI in recruitment and hiring processes. AI is increasingly used to filter job candidates, but it can introduce biases, often unintentionally, that disproportionately affect individuals with disabilities, including those with speech impairments.

***Biases in AI Screening***: AI-driven recruitment tools often screen candidates based on standardized criteria that may not consider the potential contributions of individuals with speech impairments. For example, if an AI system favours candidates with verbal communication skills, it may unjustly screen out those who prefer or require written communication methods. Candidates with speech impairments may not have the opportunity to demonstrate their skills or qualifications if an AI system filters them out early in the hiring process. This barrier underscores the need for AI models that are trained with accessibility in mind or that incorporate alternative assessment methods.

***Lack of Adaptation in Application Processes***: Participants with speech impairments suggested that many application processes are not adapted to accommodate different communication styles.

> *The decision-making is pretty hidden… you don't know what it's using, it's using something, but we don't know what it's using.*

When AI and other screening tools lack transparency, candidates have no way of knowing why they may have been disqualified. This opacity prevents applicants from addressing potential misinterpretations of their qualifications and may reinforce structural biases against candidates with speech impairments. This issue highlights the need for transparency in recruitment algorithms and processes that allow for flexibility in communication.

## Social and Cultural Barriers: Ableism and Misconceptions

The participants discussed the pervasiveness of ableism and misconceptions about disabilities as major barriers. Ableism—prejudices in favour of able-bodied people—can influence both recruitment decisions and day-to-day interactions in the workplace.

***Societal Ableism and Stigma***: Ableism in society often leads to assumptions that individuals with disabilities are less capable or productive, which can affect hiring practices and limit career advancement opportunities for those with speech impairments (Erickson et al., 2014). This social bias is reflected in workplaces that fail to implement adaptive communication technologies or inclusive policies. These ableist attitudes can lead to the isolation and exclusion of employees with speech impairments. They may feel undervalued or overlooked when colleagues assume they cannot fully participate in certain tasks, even when assistive technology is available.

***Misconceptions about Communication Abilities***: There are often misunderstandings about the communication needs and preferences of individuals with speech impairments, leading to incorrect assumptions about their abilities.

> *Inclusion is not just about checking a box… It's about active participation or participation as per one's abilities.*

Simply providing minimal accommodations without genuine understanding can be a barrier to meaningful inclusion. For example, some employers may believe they are meeting inclusive standards by offering superficial adjustments rather than by fostering an environment where diverse communication methods are encouraged and respected. This misunderstanding highlights the importance of educating all employees about communication diversity and ensuring that inclusivity goes beyond mere compliance.

## Physical and Structural Barriers in the Workplace

Participants noted that physical and structural barriers also play a role in limiting access and inclusivity for employees with speech impairments.

***Lack of Accessible Communication Tools***: The lack of accessible communication tools or willingness to adopt them can significantly impact employees with speech impairments. For example, not providing access to chat features or text-to-speech applications in digital platforms can limit the ability of these employees to participate fully.

> *There are a lot more challenging things to accommodate like physical building renovations… but communicating by text or email… we just need to be willing to do them.*

Some companies may resist implementing these tools due to perceived costs or logistical challenges. However, the quote suggests that implementing accessible communication methods is simpler and often less costly than other physical accommodations, indicating that resistance may stem more from reluctance or lack of awareness than physical environmental barriers.

***Challenges with Meetings***: The participants also highlighted challenges in meeting settings, where employees with speech impairments may find it difficult to interject or participate on an equal footing.

*Big meetings with many people... this space needs to be created for me to be able to jump in.*

Large, fast-paced meetings can create barriers for employees with speech impairments, especially if an employee relies on assistive technology to communicate (Kelly et al., 2022). They may need additional time to type or use text-to-speech software, which can be challenging when conversations move quickly. Requiring all participants to raise their hand in a meeting, and encouraging virtual meeting environments, provides the opportunity to type out an answer while waiting for one's turn. Meeting protocols must allow everyone an equal opportunity to contribute.

## Privacy and Ethical Concerns with Assistive Technology

The participants raised important concerns about the privacy and ethics of using assistive technology, especially when it involves recording or AI-driven speech adaptations.

***Privacy Concerns with Recording and AI***: Employees with speech impairments may need real-time captioning or recording to participate fully in meetings, yet these solutions introduce privacy issues. For example, obtaining consent for recording each meeting may be impractical, and employees may feel uncomfortable sharing that they need such accommodations. Additionally, there is a general concern about how recorded data might be stored, used, or potentially misused, especially if sensitive company information is involved.

*Voiceitt stores voice files in the cloud, which Voiceitt employees can access, and security can be breached.*

***Ethical Use of AI Voice Generators and Text-to-Speech***: While AI tools like voice generators can be instrumental in helping employees with speech impairments, they bring up ethical concerns about data storage and consent. Colleagues may worry about their voice patterns or personal data being stored or used without consent.

*There's a very big difference between recording somebody with the intent of understanding them... versus recording them and putting that in the cloud.*

Ethical usage policies and transparency in data handling are necessary to ensure all employees feel safe using these tools.

## Psychological Barriers and Self-advocacy

Beyond the technological and social barriers, individuals with speech impairments may face psychological challenges in advocating for their needs due to fear of stigma or being perceived as less capable.

***Fear of Stigma and Exclusion***: The participants reflected on the difficulty employees may have in advocating for themselves if they feel that requesting accommodations will lead to negative perceptions.

> *It's like such a metaphor, not being able to speak. It can get so frustrating… and people are not listening.*

Employees with speech impairments may fear that advocating for their needs will lead others to view them as high-maintenance or less competent. This barrier is compounded by ableist attitudes in society that assume verbal communication is a default standard. The frustration of not being heard is both literal and metaphorical, as individuals often feel excluded from full participation when their communication preferences are not respected.

***Limited Support for Self-Advocacy***: Without strong policies and support systems, employees may struggle to advocate for necessary accommodations. This underscores the importance of organizations fostering a culture where self-advocacy is encouraged and supported by management and leadership.

## *Community and Social Engagement*

This theme focuses on building a supportive social infrastructure that goes beyond policies and workplace initiatives. This theme suggests that societal attitudes toward disabilities, including speech impairments, need to shift to create a truly inclusive environment. Community engagement, social awareness campaigns, and storytelling are highlighted as effective strategies to combat ableism, raise empathy, and foster acceptance.

### Community-Based Awareness and Education

Awareness and education initiatives should target the broader community to address biases and misconceptions about disabilities. This approach aims to reduce the stigma associated with speech impairments and create a more inclusive society.

***Increasing Social Awareness***: Social awareness campaigns can educate people on the daily challenges faced by individuals with speech impairments, as well as the strengths and contributions these individuals bring to society. By increasing community understanding, these initiatives help to break down stereotypes and promote empathy.

> *We can increase the social awareness and these [two can improve each other]*

Community-based awareness programs could include public workshops, school curricula, and campaigns across social media that celebrate diversity in communication and highlight successful role models with speech impairments. These efforts not only inform but also inspire people to embrace inclusivity in their communities.

***Role of Educational Institutions***: Educational settings can play a pivotal role in shaping inclusive attitudes from a young age. Schools can introduce students to the concepts of accessibility and diversity, particularly in communication styles. Schools and universities can incorporate discussions on disabilities and accessibility into their curricula, helping young people understand and appreciate different communication methods. This early education helps instill inclusive values that carry over into adulthood, creating a society more receptive to diversity.

## Empathy and Understanding through Storytelling

Storytelling is a powerful tool for bridging gaps in understanding and building empathy. By sharing personal stories and lived experiences, individuals with speech impairments can foster deeper connections with others and dispel common misconceptions.

***Using Stories to Build Empathy***: Storytelling is presented as a two-way process that allows individuals with speech impairments to share their unique experiences while also encouraging listeners to reflect on their own communication and interaction habits. This mutual understanding promotes a culture where differences are respected and valued.

> *It is not about just one side understanding the other side. It's about both sides understanding each other.*

Stories can be shared in various formats—videos, podcasts, articles, or live events—to reach different audiences. Companies, non-profits, and community organizations can collaborate to amplify these voices. For instance, podcasts or social media series focused on the lives of people with speech impairments can help the public appreciate the diverse ways individuals contribute to society.

Recognizing and celebrating the experiences of individuals with speech impairments contributes to a more inclusive community narrative (Johnson et al., 2009). Highlighting stories of success, challenges overcome, and personal growth, showcases resilience, and shifts focus from disability to ability. For example, organizations can host events such as "storytelling nights" or digital exhibitions where people with speech impairments share their journeys. Such events foster connection and understanding within the community and provide a supportive platform for people with disabilities to share their voices.

## Advocating for Systemic Changes and Addressing Ableism

Participants suggested that addressing ableism and promoting accessibility in broader societal structures is essential for a genuinely inclusive community. Changing societal attitudes requires tackling deeply ingrained biases and advocating for systemic improvements.

***Confronting Societal Ableism***: The acknowledgment of ableism reflects a broader need to reshape how society views and interacts with people with disabilities. Ableism creates invisible barriers that prevent full inclusion, and by addressing it, communities can foster environments that welcome diverse abilities.

> *Our society is so ableist, whether we like it or not. The fact that we're having this conversation about employment, we're talking about ableism to some extent.*

Community leaders, educators, and activists can work together to address ableism through public policy, representation in media, and inclusive infrastructure (Jansens et al., 2023; Paramita et al., 2024). For example, local governments could launch initiatives to promote accessibility in public spaces and workplaces, while media platforms could feature more stories of individuals with disabilities in mainstream content.

Advocacy efforts are essential for ensuring that the rights of individuals with speech impairments are protected and respected. Legislative changes and public policies can drive inclusion and provide tangible support for individuals who face communication challenges. For example, organizations can partner with advocacy groups to campaign for policies that support accessibility, such as improved speech-to-text services in public places, accessible online services, and inclusive hiring policies. These legislative measures reinforce a community-wide commitment to accessibility and can help create sustainable change.

## Social Networks and Peer Support

Participants in the breakout sessions suggested the creation of social networks and peer support groups to provide vital resources and emotional support for individuals with speech impairments. These groups can allow individuals to connect, share experiences and information, and find support in facing similar challenges.

***Building Supportive Social Networks***: Support groups and social networks provide a safe space where individuals with speech impairments can share their experiences and seek advice from others who understand their challenges. Peer networks create a sense of belonging and reduce isolation by connecting individuals with similar experiences. This mutual support fosters resilience and can lead to the sharing of useful resources, such as information on assistive technology or accessibility services (Cui et al., 2018; Newman & Dale, 2005; Worton, 2020).

Organizing local events where individuals with disabilities and their families can connect with others in the community promotes an inclusive environment. For example, community centers could host monthly meetings or workshops for people with speech impairments and their families, allowing them to build connections and share coping strategies. Similarly, online forums or virtual support groups could serve as accessible alternatives for those who prefer digital communication.

## *Vision for Future Technologies*

This theme imagines how advanced technologies—particularly AI, augmented reality (AR), and adaptive tools—could support individuals with speech impairments in a highly personalized and responsive way. These potential technologies could allow for more seamless, natural, and effective communication because they can be programmed, trained and reconfigured, if designed responsibly and ethically, to align with the needs of people with disabilities.

### Adaptive and Context-Aware Technologies

One of the key ideas that participants expressed in the breakout session is the development of context-aware and adaptive technologies that can respond dynamically to the environment or the specific needs of the user. These technologies are envisioned as a means to enhance communication by anticipating needs and making real-time adjustments.

***Contextual Awareness through AI***: This type of technology would allow communication devices to identify and respond to contextual cues, such as recognizing objects or locations in the user's environment. For instance, if an employee with a speech impairment enters a meeting room, the device could automatically prepare relevant vocabulary for that setting, making communication more efficient and seamless.

> *A device could use their camera to survey the environment and then populate the vocabulary into the device based on what they see.*

In a workplace setting, this technology could support employees by streamlining conversations and minimizing preparation time. For example, a device that recognizes objects (like a laptop or a projector) or locations (such as a specific meeting room) could present vocabulary tailored to those items, allowing the employee to communicate more effectively with minimal manual input.

***GPS-Based Vocabulary Customization***: GPS-enabled devices could pre-load vocabulary and phrases that are relevant to a user's physical location. This feature would be particularly valuable in situations where quick, location-specific responses are required. By reducing the need for manual entry, this technology saves time and enhances the spontaneity of communication, which is crucial in dynamic workplace environments.

> *The GPS in a device can know where the individual is and then populate the device with vocabulary based on, for example, being in Tim Hortons.*

### Personalization and Emotional Expression in Communication

Another focal point for future technologies is the customization of voice and tone to reflect individual personalities, emotions, and preferences. This personalization is crucial for creating a more human and relatable interaction style for individuals with speech impairments.

***Emotion and Intonation in Computer-Generated Speech***: The ability to express emotions in synthesized speech represents a significant step forward in making communication feel authentic and expressive. Advanced AI could enable individuals to convey tones like enthusiasm, urgency, or empathy, which are often critical in professional communication.

> *To be able to show emotion with some of these computer voices… they can change pitch somewhat, but a lot more needs to be done to be able to show emotion.*

Emotionally expressive voice synthesis could enhance relationships between employees and colleagues by allowing for more nuanced and relatable conversations. For instance, an employee presenting an idea could emphasize enthusiasm or caution, thus conveying subtleties that are ideal for clear, persuasive communication.

***Customization as an Extension of Self***: Creating a personalized voice that matches the user's identity and preferred style of communication can significantly boost confidence and reduce the sense of alienation.

> *AAC can operate as an extension of oneself… with specificity to affect like the modulation and the pacing… to characterize a voice that feels like oneself.*

This idea of communication tools being an "extension of self" highlights the importance of individuality in future technologies, where devices not only serve functional roles but also represent the user's personality and communication preferences.

## Brain-Computer Interfaces (BCIs) and Direct Thought Communication

For users with more severe speech impairments, the potential for brain-computer interfaces (BCIs) is imagined that can interpret thoughts and transform them into text or spoken language. This futuristic technology represents a paradigm shift in how communication might be facilitated.

***Direct Communication through Brain-Computer Interfaces***: BCIs have the potential to bypass physical speech and allow direct communication through thought alone. Although current BCI technology is still in its infancy, future iterations could provide an almost seamless means for individuals with severe impairments to communicate complex ideas quickly and accurately. BCIs would be particularly useful in high-stakes, fast-paced environments, such as board meetings, where clear and immediate communication is essential.

> *I don't know if there are some EEG methods that I was reading about that can actually read the thoughts and convert it to text.*

This technology raises significant privacy and ethical concerns, particularly around the potential for unintended or unauthorized access to thoughts. For BCIs to be viable, robust privacy safeguards would be essential, including user control over when the device is "listening" and how data is stored or transmitted.

## Ethical and Privacy Concerns with Advanced Technology

Participants discussed the need for ethical frameworks to guide the development of advanced assistive technologies. Issues such as privacy, data security, and user consent are paramount, especially as these technologies become more personalized and contextually aware.

***Recording and Privacy Control***: Real-time captioning and adaptive technologies often require constant recording or data collection, which can pose privacy risks. For instance, a device that records speech or scans the environment could inadvertently capture sensitive information, potentially violating privacy laws. Ensuring user control and transparency about data usage is essential for building trust and protecting user rights.

> *Ethical implications of who owns what I say if everything I say and do is being factored into large language models and used to train the AI, where is my privacy of ideas and communication?*

Future technologies could integrate clear, user-friendly options to toggle recording functions on and off. Additionally, devices could incorporate on-device processing (instead of cloud-based storage) to enhance privacy and security. Building robust consent mechanisms will also be essential, ensuring that users have full control over when and how data is collected.

***Balancing Innovation with Ethical Responsibility***: Participants suggested the use of emerging technologies to facilitate autonomy and communication in the workplace for people with speech impairments. However, they also heeded caution that innovation should be balanced with ethical responsibility. As technology advances, developers and companies must proactively consider the ethical implications of their tools. This includes establishing guidelines for data use, addressing potential biases, and ensuring equitable access to technology.

> *We need to be ahead of those ethics and privacy issues rather than chasing them.*

Balancing rapid innovation with ethical foresight is key to creating tools that truly empower users without compromising their privacy or autonomy.

## Imagining Futuristic Communication Assistant

Participants discussed how technology might be designed to function intuitively as a personal communication assistant, combining multiple functions like listening, speaking, recording, and projecting. This concept of a "personalized AI assistant" goes beyond current technology by integrating multiple assistive features into a single, user-friendly device. Such a tool could enhance both accessibility and autonomy for employees with speech impairments, acting as a real-time interpreter, note-taker, and communicator. For instance, in a business presentation, the assistant could project captions or provide instant translations, adapting to the user's needs on the fly.

*Imagine an AI… like a little balloon that floats around in the sky… can see things, take pictures, speak on my behalf, listen on my behalf, project captions.*

This futuristic assistant would make workplaces more accessible and collaborative, empowering employees to engage fully with their teams. By offering functions like real-time captioning, voice recognition, and situational awareness, it would enable smoother, more integrated interactions in diverse workplace settings.

## Conclusion

This research highlights the significant opportunities and challenges associated with enhancing workplace inclusion for individuals with speech impairments. Through a participatory design approach that involved co-creating with individuals with lived experiences, researchers, and practitioners, the study explored themes including technological accommodations, inclusive policies, design and ethics, barriers and challenges, social engagement, and the future of assistive technology. The findings underscore the necessity of tailored technological solutions and adaptive workplace policies to bridge existing gaps, allowing individuals with speech impairments to participate fully in the workforce.

As the demand for inclusivity grows, the development of assistive technologies—particularly those that integrate AI and adaptive interfaces—offers promising solutions. However, ethical considerations, including privacy, data security, and the personalization of assistive devices, remain critical to ensuring that these advancements empower rather than marginalize people with disabilities. The results from this study advocate for a workplace culture where diverse communication methods are normalized, and structural changes are prioritized to address ableism and biases that hinder access to employment opportunities for individuals with speech impairments.

Future research should continue to focus on refining these assistive technologies while fostering partnerships across sectors to ensure that the solutions are inclusive, adaptable, and reflective of users' needs.

## References

Augmentative and Alternative Communication (AAC). (1991). American Speech-Language-Hearing Association; American Speech-Language-Hearing Association. Retrieved November 8, 2024, from https://www.asha.org/practice-portal/professional-issues/augmentative-and-alternative-communication/.

Barak, M. E. M. (2022). *Managing diversity: Toward a globally inclusive workplace*. Sage Publications.

Basiron, H., Azmi, M. A., Abd Latif, M. J., Kamaruddin, A. I., Zaidi, A. I. M., & Badrulzaman, W. M. F. W. (2021). *Development of speech therapy mobile application for speech disorder post-stroke patients*. In 2021 IEEE 11th international conference on system engineering and technology (ICSET) (pp. 130–133).

Batorowicz, B., Campbell, F., von Tetzchner, S., King, G., & Missiuna, C. (2014). Social participation of school-aged children who use communication aids: The views of children and parents. *Augmentative and Alternative Communication, 30*(3), 237–251.

Bill C-81. (2019). *An act to ensure a barrier-free Canada*.

Choi, I., Rhiu, I., Lee, Y., Yun, M. H., & Nam, C. S. (2017). A systematic review of hybrid brain-computer interfaces: Taxonomy and usability perspectives. *PLoS One, 12*(4), e0176674.

Cui, G., Ren, Y., Tian, S., Wu, T., & Choo, K.-K. R. (2018). *Evolution of resource sharing cooperation based on reciprocity in social networks*. In 2018 27th international conference on computer communication and networks (ICCCN) (pp. 1–9).

Daly, I., Billinger, M., Laparra-Hernández, J., Aloise, F., García, M. L., Faller, J., Scherer, R., & Müller-Putz, G. (2013). On the control of brain-computer interfaces by users with cerebral palsy. *Clinical Neurophysiology, 124*(9), 1787–1797.

Daly, J. J., Cheng, R., Rogers, J., Litinas, K., Hrovat, K., & Dohring, M. (2009). Feasibility of a new application of noninvasive brain computer interface (BCI): A case study of training for recovery of volitional motor control after stroke. *Journal of Neurologic Physical Therapy, 33*(4), 203–211.

Daly, J. J., & Wolpaw, J. R. (2008). Brain–computer interfaces in neurological rehabilitation. *The Lancet Neurology, 7*(11), 1032–1043.

Dujay, J. (2023, December 5). *How to welcome employees who have speech disabilities: Universal design seen as key way to accommodate employees: Canadian researcher*. Canadian HR Reporter. Retrieved November 8, 2024, from https://www.hrreporter.com/focus-areas/diversity/how-to-welcome-employees-who-have-speech-disabilities/381946.

Duval, J. (2017). *A mobile game system for improving the speech therapy experience*. In Proceedings of the 19th international conference on human-computer interaction with mobile devices and services (pp. 1–3).

Erickson, W. A., von Schrader, S., Bruyère, S. M., VanLooy, S. A., & Matteson, D. S. (2014). Disability-inclusive employer practices and hiring of individuals with disabilities. *Rehabilitation Research, Policy, and Education, 28*(4), 309–328.

Glade, R., Koch, L. C., Zaandam, A., Simon, L. S., Manno, C. M., Rumril, P. D., Jr., & Rosen, C. C. (2020). Recommendations from employees with disabilities for creating inclusive workplaces: Results from a grounded theory investigation. *Journal of Vocational Rehabilitation, 53*(1), 77–88.

Hamidi, F., Poneres, K., Massey, A., & Hurst, A. (2018). *Who should have access to my pointing data? Privacy tradeoffs of adaptive assistive technologies*. In Proceedings of the 20th international ACM SIGACCESS conference on computers and accessibility (pp. 203–216).

Jacob, I., Khanna, M., & Rai, K. A. (2024). Applying SERVQUAL model to hearing and speech impaired staff in the fine-dine SME sector for assessing service outcomes. *Journal of Strategic Marketing, 32*, 1244–1258.

Jansens, R., Prellwitz, M., Olofsson, A., & Lynch, H. (2023). The representation of children's participation in guidelines for planning and designing public playspaces: A scoping review with "best fit" framework synthesis. *International Journal of Environmental Research and Public Health, 20*(10), 5823.

Johnson, H., Douglas, J., Bigby, C., & Iacono, T. (2009). Maximizing community inclusion through mainstream communication services for adults with severe disabilities. *International Journal of Speech-Language Pathology, 11*(3), 180–190.

Jreige, C., Patel, R., & Bunnell, H. T. (2009). *VocaliD: Personalizing text-to-speech synthesis for individuals with severe speech impairment*. In Proceedings of the 11th international ACM SIGACCESS conference on computers and accessibility (pp. 259–260).

Kelly, E., Rice, C., & Desai, S. (2022). *Into the light: Living histories of oppression and education in Ontario*. Retrieved from https://intothelight.ca/index.html.

Kinney-Lang, E., Kelly, D., Floreani, E. D., Jadavji, Z., Rowley, D., Zewdie, E. T., Anaraki, J. R., Bahari, H., Beckers, K., Castelane, K., et al. (2020). Advancing brain-computer interface applications for severely disabled children through a multidisciplinary national network: Summary of the inaugural pediatric BCI Canada meeting. *Frontiers in Human Neuroscience, 14*, 593883.

Kochan, T. A., Armstrong, B., Shah, J., Castilla, E. J., Likis, B., & Mangelsdorf, M. E. (2024). *Bringing worker voice into generative AI.*

Lackey, S., Watson Hyatt, G., Batorowicz, B., van Engelen, S., Li, S., Pinder, S., & Davies, T. C. (2023). Barriers and facilitators to accommodations in the workplace for adults who use augmentative and alternative communication (AAC): A systematic review. *Augmentative and Alternative Communication, 39*(3), 181–197.

Lazarou, I., Nikolopoulos, S., Petrantonakis, P. C., Kompatsiaris, I., & Tsolaki, M. (2018). EEG-based brain–computer interfaces for communication and rehabilitation of people with motor impairment: A novel approach of the 21st century. *Frontiers in Human Neuroscience, 12*, 14.

Lengnick-Hall, M. L., Gaunt, P. M., & Kulkarni, M. (2008). Overlooked and underutilized: People with disabilities are an untapped human resource. *Human Resource Management: Published in Cooperation with the School of Business Administration, The University of Michigan and in Alliance with the Society of Human Resources Management, 47*(2):255–273.

McNaughton, D., & Bryen, D. N. (2002). Enhancing participation in employment through AAC technologies. *Assistive Technology, 14*(1), 58–70.

Moghimi, S., Kushki, A., Marie Guerguerian, A., & Chau, T. (2013). A review of EEG-based brain-computer interfaces as access pathways for individuals with severe disabilities. *Assistive Technology, 25*(2), 99–110.

Newman, L., & Dale, A. (2005). Network structure, diversity, and proactive resilience building: A response to Tompkins and Adger. *Ecology and Society, 10*(1).

Noyek, S., Vowles, C., Batorowicz, B., Davies, C., & Fayed, N. (2022). Direct assessment of emotional well-being from children with severe motor and communication impairment: A systematic review. *Disability and Rehabilitation: Assistive Technology, 17*(5), 501–514.

Orlandi, S., House, S. C., Karlsson, P., Saab, R., & Chau, T. (2021). Brain-computer interfaces for children with complex communication needs and limited mobility: A systematic review. *Frontiers in Human Neuroscience, 15*, 643294.

Paramita, P. P., Asthana, M. K., Amin, A. S., & Hassim, N. (2024). Inclusive education for students with disabilities: Perspectives from Indonesian and Malaysian higher education. *Jurnal Komunikasi: Malaysian Journal of Communication, 40*(3), 247–261.

Pedersen, H., Kermit, P. S., & Söderström, S. (2021). "You have to argue the right way": User involvement in the service delivery process for assistive activity technology. *Disability and Rehabilitation: Assistive Technology, 16*(8), 840–850.

Perfect, E., Hoskin, E., Noyek, S., & Davies, T. C. (2020). A systematic review investigating outcome measures and uptake barriers when children and youth with complex disabilities use eye gaze assistive technology. *Developmental Neurorehabilitation, 23*(3), 145–159.

Richardson, L., & Bissell, D. (2019). Geographies of digital skill. *Geoforum, 99*, 278–286.

Shore, L. M., Cleveland, J. N., & Sanchez, D. (2018). Inclusive workplaces: A review and model. *Human Resource Management Review, 28*(2), 176–189.

Simmons, S. V., & Yawson, R. M. (2022). Developing leaders for disruptive change: An inclusive leadership approach. *Advances in Developing Human Resources, 24*(4), 242–262.

Smith, M. M., & Murray, J. (2016). *The silent partner?: Language, interaction and aided communication.* J&R Press.

Taherian, S., Selitskiy, D., Pau, J., & Claire Davies, T. (2017). Are we there yet? Evaluating commercial grade brain–computer interface for control of computer applications by individuals with cerebral palsy. *Disability and Rehabilitation: Assistive Technology, 12*(2), 165–174.

Taherian, S., Selitskiy, D., Pau, J., Davies, T. C., & Owens, R. G. (2016). Training to use a commercial brain-computer interface as access technology: A case study. *Disability and Rehabilitation: Assistive Technology, 11*(4), 345–350.

Vaughan, K. T. L. (2019). *Building an inclusive library through staff accessibility training*. Arizona State University.

Vergara, D., & Hardy, V. (2024, June 13). *Labour market characteristics of persons with and without disabilities, 2023*. Retrieved from https://www150.statcan.gc.ca/n1/pub/71-222-x/71-222-x2024002-eng.htm.

Verhulst, S. G. (2021). Reimagining data responsibility: 10 new approaches toward a culture of trust in re-using data to address critical public needs. *Data & Policy, 3*, e6.

Vornholt, K., Villotti, P., Muschalla, B., Bauer, J., Colella, A., Zijlstra, F., Van Ruitenbeek, G., Uitdewilligen, S., & Corbière, M. (2018). Disability and employment—overview and highlights. *European Journal of Work and Organizational Psychology, 27*(1), 40–55.

Welker, Y. (2023, November 3). *Generative AI holds great potential for those with disabilities—But it needs policy to shape it*. World Economic Forum. Retrieved from https://www.weforum.org/stories/2023/11/generative-ai-holds-potential-disabilities/.

Worton, S. K. (2020). Examining peer networking as a capacity-building strategy for housing first implementation. *Journal of Community Psychology, 48*(4), 1147–1162.

# AI Opportunities and Challenges for Students with Learning Disabilities

**Mahnaz Dehghantezerjani, Robert Savage, Mahdieh Roshanbin, and Alireza Baneshi**

## Introduction

*Learning disabilities (LDs)* are one of the most prevalent disabilities around the world, with an estimated 5–15% of children displaying some form of learning difficulty (American Psychiatric Association, 2013). These disabilities "significantly impact various cognitive domains including listening, speaking, scientific reasoning, reading, writing, spelling, and mathematical abilities, necessitating substantial provisions for special education" (Bhatti et al., 2024, p. 40). If children with LDs do not receive appropriate accommodations, they may struggle to keep up with their classmates (UNICEF, 2021).

While educators strive to support all students, including those with LDs, providing individualized assistance remains a significant challenge. Recent advances in *generative AI*, particularly in deep generative and *large language models (LLMs)* like *ChatGPT*, offer opportunities to enhance teaching and learning (Costa et al., 2017; García et al., 2007). These technologies can facilitate communication and improve writing skills for students with LDs and English Language Learners (ELLs) (Tate et al., 2023). LLMs, which foster human-machine collaborations, have the potential to transform educational environments by providing tailored assistance (Denny et al., 2024).

M. Dehghantezerjani (✉) · R. Savage
Faculty of Education, York University, Toronto, ON, Canada
e-mail: moon2023@yorku.ca; Robert.savage@edu.yorku.ca

M. Roshanbin
Faculty of Psychology and Education, University of Tehran, Kish Island, Iran

A. Baneshi
Educational Research, Faculty of Psychology and Education, Tehran, Iran
e-mail: alibaneshi4@ut.ac.ir


C. El Morr et al. (eds.), *Beyond Tech Fixes*,
https://doi.org/10.1007/978-3-031-93022-5_9

The architecture of LLMs mirrors aspects of *connectionist learning theories*, which describe how the brain processes language and acquires reading skills (Seidenberg & McClelland, 1989). This parallel between AI and human learning opens possibilities for using AI to model cognitive processes and assist students with LDs.

Key advantages of AI include the early detection of LDs, personalized learning experiences, assistive technologies, enhanced engagement through *gamification*, and access to *AI-powered virtual tutors*. However, using AI tools for students with LDs can have some challenges, including data privacy and security, bias in AI algorithms, disparities in access to AI tools, insufficient teacher training, and the risk of over-reliance on technology. In this paper, we introduce LDs, LLMs, and connectionism, explaining how LLMs simulate aspects of human learning and their potential for supporting students with LDs. We then examine the opportunities and challenges associated with AI technologies.

## Learning Disabilities

LDs, also known as *specific learning disorders (SLDs)*, are neurodevelopmental disorders characterized by a pattern of difficulties associated with the growth and development of the brain, affecting a student's ability to process information. These difficulties can manifest in areas such as reading (*dyslexia*), writing (*dysgraphia*), mathematics (*dyscalculia*), or other cognitive processes like working memory, processing speed, and attention, which are foundational for more advanced academic learning (American Psychiatric Association, 2013). Unlike intellectual disabilities, students with LDs typically have average or above-average intelligence, but their struggles with specific cognitive tasks significantly impact their academic performance.

LDs are among the most common disabilities in school-aged children. According to the National Center for Educational Statistics (NCES, 2011), 68% of fourth-grade students receiving special education services scored below basic on the National Assessment for Educational Progress reading test, while 32% scored at or above basic, and only 13% scored at or above proficient. Furthermore, LDs are not limited to Western education systems; they are a global issue affecting students across diverse cultural and socioeconomic backgrounds (UNICEF, 2021). Reports indicate that the prevalence of SLDs in children from various linguistic and cultural backgrounds is between 5–15%, with reading disorders affecting 4–9% and mathematics disorders impacting 3–7% of students (American Psychiatric Association, 2013).

Students with LDs often face academic, social, and emotional challenges. They may experience lower grades and struggle to keep pace with their peers, which can lead to anxiety, low self-esteem, and social isolation (Al-Yagon & Mikulincer, 2004; Khamis, 2009). LDs can also have impairments in higher-level skills such as organization, time management, abstract reasoning, working memory (WM), and attention (Brennan, 2021). Providing appropriate academic support can help reduce these difficulties and improve the overall school experience for these students.

Given the emotional and psychological issues students with LDs can face, finding ways to engage students and offer them personalized learning experiences is crucial. AI technologies, particularly *LLMs*, can offer tailored support that accommodates the unique needs of these students.

## Connectionism and LLMs

To understand how AI, specifically LLMs, can assist students with LDs, it is essential to know the fundamentals of *connectionism*, a theory integral to the development of LLMs. Connectionism provides one of the models to explain insights into the structure, acquisition, and processing of language in the brain, both typical and disordered (Seidenberg, 1994). This model, deeply influenced by cognitive science and computational neuroscience, explores neural networks and machine learning algorithms that reflect the deep neural architecture and functions of the human brain (LeCun et al., 2015).

Connectionism suggests that cognitive functions, including language and learning, emerge from the interactions of simple units (in some respects, neurons) within a network (Rumelhart et al., 1986). In these models, neural networks in the brain are capable of learning to recognize patterns in spoken or written language through exposure, repetition, and feedback (Seidenberg & McClelland, 1989). In the realm of AI, this model is replicated through artificial neural networks (ANNs), which form the foundation of LLMs such as GPT-4.

LLMs like ChatGPT replicate fundamental aspects of human language processing (Cai et al., 2024) and share structural similarities with connectionist models, using vast datasets and advanced neural architectures to produce coherent and contextually appropriate text (Xiong et al., 2024). Just as connectionist models explain how children learn to read and comprehend language through distributed processing, LLMs function by progressively learning patterns from massive textual corpora, capturing the nuances of grammar, syntax, and semantics through repeated exposure.

The parallels between connectionist models of reading and LLMs are notable. Seidenberg's model of reading describes how children learn to associate written words with their spoken counterparts, relying on consistent exposure to language (Seidenberg & McClelland, 1989). Similarly, LLMs are trained to recognize and generate language patterns by processing large amounts of text. Although the size and truing set of AI's learning process is very different from human cognition in scale but many principles of 'statistical learning' of language are shared, positioning LLMs as potent tools for aiding students with LDs.

## Opportunities Presented by AI for Students with LDs

LDs affect a significant portion of students, impacting their ability to keep pace with traditional educational methods. AI offers opportunities to create more personalized and efficient learning experiences tailored to these students' unique needs (Graefen & Fazal, 2024; Lee & Vail, 2005). Additionally, Aided Teaching Systems assist with classroom environment management, grading, evaluation, and second-language acquisition challenges (Guan et al., 2020). AI technologies such as intelligent tutoring systems, automated grading tools, learning analytics, and AI teaching assistants have shown to be beneficial in both K-12 and higher education (Trust et al., 2023). In this section, we introduce some of these technologies that can help in the early identification of students with LDs and provide customized support.

### *Early Detection and Intervention*

Early diagnosis of LDs is crucial for reducing the students' long-term academic struggles. Research shows that early intervention can significantly improve outcomes for children with LDs. For example, struggling readers who do not receive timely intervention often fall further behind their peers, sometimes to the extent that their reading difficulties become intractable (Stanovich, 1986). Furthermore, the younger the age of a child at the start of intervention for reading difficulties, the larger the long-term effects (Van den Audenaeren et al., 2013).

Traditionally, diagnosing LDs involves a time-consuming, team-based assessment process (Chung et al., 2020). AI-powered tools may streamline this process by analyzing large datasets and detecting patterns in student performance data, identifying signs of LDs earlier and with greater accuracy. For instance, AI systems can analyze handwriting to detect dysgraphia (Kunhoth et al., 2024) or analyze speech patterns to diagnose intellectual disabilities (Alshehri et al., 2023). Similarly, AI tools such as French speech recognition models (Rezgui et al., 2024) and facial behavior analysis systems (Usta & Karabekiroğlu, 2020) have been used in early diagnosis.

Moreover, AI-driven systems like *Intelligent Tutoring Systems (ITS)* for identifying dyslexia, dysgraphia, and dyscalculia can improve diagnostic accuracy by using advanced neural networks. Dutt et al. (2022) developed an ITS framework based on a pretest analysis through initial screening and then system-based screening of a child response for LDs identification and assessed 24 participants (with or without LDs). Their results suggested that neural network has significantly increased the ITS accuracy. Devi and Kavya (2023) examined 290 handwriting and geometric features using intelligent deep learning approaches to classify dysgraphia and found that the deep learning technology can be used to create the automatic detection mechanism of dysgraphia students.

## *Personalized Learning and Adaptive Technologies*

To succeed academically, students with LDs may need specialized and personalized support. Academic achievement depends on self-direction, metacognition, and self-regulated learning (Zimmerman, 2013). The concept of self-regulated learning emphasizes a student's ability to manage various aspects of their education effectively, including time allocation, resource utilization, and adherence to structured learning plans. AI tools can empower students with LDs and promote their independence as learners by enhancing self-regulation, metacognitive skills, and self-directed learning. AI's ability to promote self-direction is best demonstrated through adaptive learning systems. These platforms use data on student's performance to provide practice and information tailored to each individual. In addition, LLMs and adaptive learning platforms adjust the difficulty of tasks based on the student's performance, ensuring they are neither bored nor overwhelmed.

Contemporary AI-powered applications, such as Otter.ai and Notion AI, provide substantial support by helping students organize and manage their learning processes. These tools offer automated note-taking, assist with time management strategies, and help set achievable goals, thereby fostering essential self-regulation skills (Schunk & Greene, 2017). Additionally, AI-driven educational platforms like Duolingo utilize spaced repetition techniques to improve information retention and enable personalized study scheduling.

Adaptive platforms like DreamBox use AI to customize math lessons in real time, adjusting the difficulty to help students with disabilities progress at their own pace (Frank, 2024). Similarly, Carnegie Learning's AI-powered math solutions provide real-time feedback and personalized instruction, which is particularly beneficial for students with dyscalculia (Barton, 2016). These platforms offer models for expanding AI tools to assist with other subjects such as reading and writing, creating a comprehensive support system for students with LDs. Although there are some studies that support the effectiveness of these models, such models have not yet been thoroughly evaluated as efficacious and need further studies.

## *Virtual Tutors*

AI-powered virtual tutors, available 24/7, offer continuous support, ensuring students can access help outside traditional classroom hours and helping instructors with daily student progress monitoring (Guan et al., 2020). These virtual tutors create self-assessment tests and provide immediate, personalized feedback to students (Anders & Sahakyan, 2023; Graefen & Fazal, 2024; Hwang, 2003). Students with language and learning difficulties, as well as non-native speakers, may benefit from these natural language models (Baidoo-Anu & Ansah, 2023).

Khan Academy's Khanmigo, an AI tutor utilizing GPT-4 capabilities, provides personalized learning support and intelligent feedback across various subjects, including mathematics, programming, and language learning (Wang et al., 2024). Some studies have suggested the effectiveness of individualized ITS. For example, Steenbergen-Hu & Cooper's (2014) meta-analysis showed ITS had a moderate positive effect on college students' academic learning. Bašić et al. (2023) also suggested that when GPT-3 and similar generative AI tools are used in conjunction with human feedback and guidance, they can assist students in essay writing.

## *Assistive Technologies*

Personalized assistive educational tools, which can be employed by teachers in mainstream schools, may contribute to improving educational outcomes (Barua et al., 2022). One area requiring improvement for students with dyslexia is sight word reading. *Computer-assisted instruction (CAI)* has been shown to be effective in increasing sight word recognition in students with disabilities (Coleman-Martin et al., 2005; Lee & Vail, 2005). For example, the ABRACADABRA Web-Based Literacy Program has been demonstrated to enhance elementary students' early literacy skills (Abrami et al., 2020; Savage et al., 2013). Deault et al. (2009) showed this program was effective for students with Attention Deficit Hyperactivity Disorder (ADHD), probably because technology (immediate feedback, an visual-verbal offloading) is best practice for this group.

AI-powered assistive technologies, such as speech-to-text, text-to-speech, and predictive text applications, potentially provide essential support for students with LDs. For students with dysgraphia, speech-to-text software enables them to convert spoken words into text, reducing writing difficulties. Also, Text-to-speech applications assist students with reading difficulties by reading text aloud, offering cognitive support in comprehending e-text content (Ko et al., 2011).

Kurzweil 3000 is an AI-driven assistive technology that aids students with reading, writing, and studying. Originally developed as a text-to-speech program for visually impaired individuals, Kurzweil 3000 has since evolved to support students with reading disabilities (Cullen et al., 2013). Chiang and Liu (2011) interviewed 15 high school English-as-a-second language students with dyslexia to know their perception of the effectiveness of Kurzweil 3000. The results suggested that students thought the Kurzweil 3000 had an immediate impact on students' English word recognition. Cullen et al. (2013) examined the effects of Kurzweil 3000 on the acquisition of sight words for four African American fourth graders with mild disabilities (i.e., learning disabilities, mild intellectual disabilities, and ADHD). A multiple baseline design across word sets demonstrated that computer practice using Kurzweil 3000 was significantly related to increased sight word recognition and this effect remained after four weeks.

## Challenges of AI in Supporting Students with LDs

While AI offers many opportunities for improving the educational outcomes of students with LDs, it also presents several critical challenges that need to be addressed to ensure these technologies are effectively and ethically integrated into learning environments. These challenges include data privacy and security, bias in AI algorithms, accessibility of AI tools, the need for comprehensive teacher training, and the risk of over-reliance on technology. Therefore, these tools should be studied in controlled external validity field trials on students with a range of LDs in naturalistic contexts, and consider that these tools should be used with the help of professionals such as speech therapists, educators, and other specialists to personalize them due to the student's disability (Kasneci et al., 2023).

### *Data Privacy and Security*

One of the primary challenges in the adoption of AI tools for students with LDs is data privacy. AI-powered educational tools often require large amounts of student data to function effectively. This data includes sensitive information, such as learning progress, disabilities, behavioral patterns, and even biometric data in some cases (Huang, 2023).

In the context of disabilities, privacy concerns become even more critical because of the potential for discrimination or stigmatization (Lazar et al., 2017). For example, if data indicating a student's learning disability is shared inappropriately, it could result in biased treatment by teachers, peers, or future employers. Moreover, parents and guardians may have concerns about the long-term storage and use of their child's data, particularly if it is being collected by third-party AI providers outside the school system.

### *Algorithmic Bias and Fairness*

Algorithmic bias is another significant concern when integrating AI into education, particularly for students with LDs. Data used in machine learning may lead to algorithmic biases against disabled people (Hutchinson et al., 2020). AI systems are trained on large datasets, and if these datasets are not diverse or representative, the resulting algorithms may be biased against certain groups of students (Khan, 2023). Race, sex, and disability status can affect research questions and data collection which produce AI algorithms that do not account for underrepresented populations (Nazer et al., 2023).

Because algorithms are trained on public data on the net, for students with LDs, bias in AI algorithms could result in inaccurate diagnoses, inappropriate interventions, or exclusion from certain opportunities. For instance, a student with an undiagnosed learning disability may be overlooked by an AI system that is not trained to recognize the full range of cognitive diversity. Alternatively, a student with a disability may be unfairly labeled or categorized based on biased assumptions embedded in the algorithm, leading to stigmatization.

Nazer et al. (2023) presented a checklist to aid in mitigating bias during the development and implementation of AI algorithms. This checklist helps AI developers to consider the sources of bias for framing the problem, data sources, data preprocessing, model development, model validation and model implementation. In addition, AI systems should undergo regular audits to identify and correct any biases that may emerge over time. Schools and educators also have a role to play in ensuring that AI tools are used fairly and equitably, by continually assessing their impact on different student populations.

## *Accessibility and the Digital Divide*

While AI has the potential to improve educational outcomes for students with LDs, it can also increase existing inequalities if not implemented thoughtfully. One of the key concerns is the digital divide—the gap between students who have access to technology and those who do not (Wu et al., 2014). The level of computer usage and Internet access by people with disabilities is much lower than that of the rest of the population (Vicente & López, 2010). The U.S. Department of Commerce (2000) found that individuals with impairments were only half as likely to have access to the Internet as those without them: 21.6% compared to 42.1%.

For students with LDs, the digital divide can be particularly problematic. These students often require specialized assistive technologies, which can be expensive and difficult to obtain. If AI tools are only available to students in well-funded schools or affluent communities, students in under-resourced settings may be left behind.

Addressing the digital divide requires collaboration between governments, educational institutions, and technology providers. Policies should be developed to ensure that all students, regardless of their socioeconomic status, have access to the necessary technology and internet connectivity. Additionally, schools should prioritize the equitable distribution of resources, ensuring that students with LDs receive the tools they need to succeed.

## *Teacher Training and Professional Development*

The successful integration of AI into classrooms depends not only on the availability of technology but also on teachers' capacity to use it effectively. Celik (2023) emphasizes that teachers must know how to use AI in an ethical manner to enhance students' learning. However, many educators lack the necessary training and support to incorporate AI tools into their teaching practices, especially when working with students with LDs.

Farrelly and Baker (2023) highlight the need for teacher professional development (TPD) as teachers must understand how AI functions and how to apply it in the classroom. Teachers should be equipped to guide students in the responsible and ethical use of AI, understanding both its positive and negative aspects (Hasanein & Sobaih, 2023). When it comes to students with LDs, teachers must also learn how to utilize AI to provide individualized support, whether through adaptive learning platforms, virtual tutors, or assistive technologies. TPD is viewed as a means to empower teachers to guide students in the ethical and safe use of AI tools, including generative AI, thus fostering an environment conducive to student learning (Brandão et al., 2024).

Professional development opportunities should be continuous, allowing teachers to stay updated on the latest advancements in AI and education. Moreover, schools should cultivate a collaborative environment where teachers can share best practices and learn from one another's experiences. By providing educators with the necessary training and resources, schools can ensure that AI tools are used effectively to support students with LDs.

## Conclusion

AI presents significant opportunities to enhance the educational experiences of students with LDs. From personalized learning and assistive technologies to early detection and virtual tutoring, AI has the potential to address many of the challenges faced by these students. However, to fully realize these benefits, it is essential to address the challenges of data privacy, algorithmic bias, accessibility, teacher training, and the risk of over-reliance on technology. To maximize the benefits of AI for students with LDs, it is essential to address these challenges through careful implementation, collaboration between educators and AI developers, and ongoing innovation. With thoughtful application, AI has the potential to make education more inclusive and effective for students with LDs.

## References

Abrami, P. C., Lysenko, L., & Borokhovski, E. (2020). The effects of ABRACADABRA on reading outcomes: An updated meta-analysis and landscape review of applied field research. *Journal of Computer Assisted Learning, 36*(3), 260–279. https://doi.org/10.1111/jcal.12417

Alshehri, M., Sharma, S., Gupta, P., & Shah, S. R. (2023). *Detection and diagnosis of learning disabilities in children of Saudi Arabia with artificial intelligence*. Preprint. https://doi.org/10.21203/rs.3.rs-3301949/v1

Al-Yagon, M., & Mikulincer, M. (2004). Patterns of close relationships and socioemotional and academic adjustment among school-age children with learning disabilities. *Learning Disabilities Research & Practice, 19*, 12–19. https://doi.org/10.1111/j.1540-5826.2004.00085.x

American Psychiatric Association (Ed.). (2013). *Diagnostic and statistical manual of mental disorders* (5th ed.). American Psychiatric Association.

Anders, B., & Sahakyan, S. (2023). *Chat GPT and AI presentation and Q&A [Powerpoint slides].* American University of Armenia Center for Teaching and Learning. Retrieved from https://ctl.aua.am/view/uploads/entry/26/

Baidoo-Anu, D., & Ansah, L. O. (2023). Education in the era of generative artificial intelligence (AI): Understanding the potential benefits of ChatGPT in promoting teaching and learning. *Journal of AI, 7*(1), 52–62. https://doi.org/10.61969/jai.1337500

Barton, J. M. (2016). *Mathematics intervention utilizing carnegie learning's cognitive Tutor® and Compass Learning's Odyssey Math®* (Order No. 10010883) [Doctoral dissertation, Wilmington University]. Available from ProQuest Dissertations & Theses Global; ProQuest Dissertations & Theses Global Closed Collection.

Barua, P. D., Vicnesh, J., Gururajan, R., Oh, S. L., Palmer, E., Azizan, M. M., et al. (2022). Artificial intelligence enabled personalised assistive tools to enhance education of children with neurodevelopmental disorders—A review. *International Journal of Environmental Research and Public Health, 19*(3), 1192. https://doi.org/10.3390/ijerph19031192

Bašić, Ž., Banovac, A., Kružić, I., & Jerković, I. (2023). ChatGPT-3.5 as writing assistance in students' essays. *Humanities and Social Sciences Communications, 10*(1), 1–5. https://doi.org/10.1057/s41599-023-02269-7

Bhatti, I., Mohi-U-din, S. F., Hayat, Y., & Tariq, M. (2024). Artificial intelligence applications for students with learning disabilities: A systematic review. *European Journal of Science, Innovation and Technology, 4*(2), 40–56. Retrieved from https://ejsit-journal.com/index.php/ejsit/article/view/397

Brandão, A., Pedro, L., & Zagalo, N. (2024). Teacher professional development for a future with generative artificial intelligence–an integrative literature review. *Digital Education Review, 45*, 151–157. https://doi.org/10.1344/der.2024.45.151-157

Brennan, C. (2021). Learning disabilities. In *The handbook of language and speech disorders* (pp. 209–236). https://doi.org/10.1002/9781119606987.ch11

Cai, Z., Duan, X., Haslett, D., Wang, S., & Pickering, M. (2024). Do large language models resemble humans in language use? In *Proceedings of the workshop on cognitive modeling and computational linguistics* (pp. 37–56). https://doi.org/10.18653/v1/2024.cmcl-1.4

Celik, I. (2023). Towards Intelligent-TPACK: An empirical study on teachers' professional knowledge to ethically integrate artificial intelligence (AI)-based tools into education. *Computers in Human Behavior, 138*, 107468. https://doi.org/10.1016/j.chb.2022.107468

Chiang, H. Y., & Liu, C. H. (2011). Evaluation of the benefits of assistive reading software: Perceptions of high school students with learning disabilities. *Assistive Technology: The Official Journal of RESNA, 23*, 199–204. https://doi.org/10.1080/10400435.2011.614673

Chung, P. J., Patel, D. R., & Nizami, I. (2020). Disorder of written expression and dysgraphia: Definition, diagnosis, and management. *Translational Pediatrics, 9*(Suppl. 1), S46–S54. https://doi.org/10.21037/tp.2019.11.01

Coleman-Martin, M. B., Heller, K. W., Cihak, D. F., & Irvine, K. L. (2005). Using computer-assisted instruction and the nonverbal reading approach to teach word identification. *Focus on Autism and other Developmental Disabilities, 20*(2), 80–90. https://doi.org/10.1177/10883576050200020401

Costa, E. B., Fonseca, B., Santana, M. A., Araújo, F. F. D., & Rego, J. (2017). Evaluating the effectiveness of educational data mining techniques for early prediction of students' academic failure in introductory programming courses. *Computers in Human Behavior, 73*, 247–256. https://doi.org/10.1016/j.chb.2017.01.047

Cullen, J., Keesey, S., Alber-Morgan, S. R., & Wheaton, J. (2013). The effects of computer-assisted instruction using Kurzweil 3000 on sight word acquisition for students with mild disabilities. *Education and Treatment of Children, 36*(2), 87–103. https://doi.org/10.1353/etc.2013.0017

Deault, L., Savage, R., & Abrami, P. (2009). Inattention and response to the ABRACADABRA web-based literacy intervention. *Journal of Research on Educational Effectiveness, 2*(3), 250–286. https://doi.org/10.1080/19345740902979371

Denny, P., Gulwani, S., Heffernan, N. T., Käser, T., Moore, S., Rafferty, A. N., & Singla, A. (2024). *Generative AI for Education (GAIED): Advances, opportunities, and challenges*. arXiv preprint arXiv:2402.01580. https://doi.org/10.48550/arXiv.2402.01580

Devi, A., & Kavya, G. (2023). Dysgraphia disorder forecasting and classification technique using intelligent deep learning approaches. *Progress in Neuro-Psychopharmacology and Biological Psychiatry, 120*, 110647. https://doi.org/10.1016/j.pnpbp.2022.110647

Dutt, S., Ahuja, N. J., & Kumar, M. (2022). An intelligent tutoring system architecture based on fuzzy neural network (FNN) for special education of learning disabled learners. *Education and Information Technologies, 27*(2), 2613–2633. https://doi.org/10.1007/s10639-021-10713-x

Farrelly, T., & Baker, N. (2023). Generative artificial intelligence: Implications and considerations for higher education practice. *Education Sciences, 13*(11). https://doi.org/10.3390/educsci13111109

Frank, E. (2024). *The influence of artificial intelligence on education: Enhancing personalized learning experiences*. Preprint.

García, P., Amandi, A., Schiaffino, S., & Campo, M. (2007). Evaluating Bayesian networks' precision for detecting students' learning styles. *Computers & Education, 49*, 794–808. https://doi.org/10.1016/j.compedu.2005.11.017

Graefen, B., & Fazal, N. (2024). From chat bots to virtual tutors: An overview of chat GPT's role in the future of education. *Archives of Pharmacy Practice, 15*(2-2024), 43–52. https://doi.org/10.51847/touppjedsx

Guan, C., Mou, J., & Jiang, Z. (2020). Artificial intelligence innovation in education: A twenty-year data-driven historical analysis. *International Journal of Innovation Studies, 4*(4), 134–147. https://doi.org/10.1016/j.ijis.2020.09.001

Hasanein, A. M., & Sobaih, A. E. E. (2023). Drivers and consequences of ChatGPT use in higher education: Key stakeholder perspectives. *European Journal of Investigation in Health, Psychology and Education, 13*(11), 2599–2614. https://doi.org/10.3390/ejihpe13110181

Huang, L. (2023). Ethics of artificial intelligence in education: Student privacy and data protection. *Science Insights Education Frontiers, 16*(2), 2577–2587. https://doi.org/10.15354/sief.23.re202

Hutchinson, B., Prabhakaran, V., Denton, E., Webster, K., Zhong, Y., & Denuyl, S. (2020). Unintended machine learning biases as social barriers for persons with disabilitiess. *ACM SIGACCESS Accessibility and Computing, 125*, 1–1. https://doi.org/10.1145/3386296.3386305

Hwang, G. (2003). A conceptual map model for developing intelligent tutoring systems. *Computers and Education, 40*(3), 217e235. https://doi.org/10.1016/s0360-1315(02)00121-5

Kasneci, E., Seßler, K., Küchemann, S., Bannert, M., Dementieva, D., Fischer, F., et al. (2023). ChatGPT for good? On opportunities and challenges of large language models for education. *Learning and Individual Differences, 103*, 102274. https://doi.org/10.1016/j.lindif.2023.102274

Khamis, V. (2009). Classroom environment as a predictor of behaviour disorders among children with learning disabilities in the UAE. *Educational Studies, 35*, 27–36. https://doi.org/10.1080/03055690802648044

Khan, S. (2023). The ethical imperative: Addressing bias and discrimination in AI-Driven Education. *Social Sciences Spectrum, 2*(1), 89–96.

Ko, C. C., Chiang, C. H., Lin, Y. L., & Chen, M. C. (2011). An individualized e-reading system developed based on multi-representations approach. *Educational Technology & Society, 14*(4), 88–98.

Kunhoth, J., Al-Maadeed, S., Kunhoth, S., Akbari, Y., & Saleh, M. (2024). Automated systems for diagnosis of dysgraphia in children: A survey and novel framework. *International Journal*

*on Document Analysis and Recognition (IJDAR), 27*(4), 707–735. https://doi.org/10.1007/s10032-024-00464-z
Lazar, J., Wentz, B., & Winckler, M. (2017). Information privacy and security as a human right for people with disabilities. *Disability, Human Rights, and Information Technology, 199*, 202. https://doi.org/10.9783/9780812294095-014
LeCun, Y., Bengio, Y., & Hinton, G. (2015). Deep learning. *Nature, 521*, 436–444. https://doi.org/10.1038/nature14539
Lee, Y., & Vail, C. (2005). Computer based reading instruction for young children with disabilities. *Journal of Special Education Technology, 20*(1), 5–18. https://doi.org/10.1177/016264340502000101
National Center for Educational Statistics (2011). *The nation's report card: reading 2011.* Retrieved from http://nces.ed.gov/nationsreportcard/pdf/main2011/2012457.pdf
Nazer, L. H., Zatarah, R., Waldrip, S., Ke, J. X. C., Moukheiber, M., Khanna, A. K., et al. (2023). Bias in artificial intelligence algorithms and recommendations for mitigation. *PLOS Digital Health, 2*(6), e0000278. https://doi.org/10.1371/journal.pdig.0000278
Rezgui, J., Jobin, F., Kechout, Y., Turgeon, C., & Khomh, F. (2024). Towards a reliable french speech recognition tool for an automated diagnosis of learning disabilities. In *2024 International Conference on Smart Applications, Communications and Networking (SmartNets)* (pp. 1–6). IEEE. https://doi.org/10.1109/smartnets61466.2024.10577676
Rumelhart, D. E., McClelland, J. L., & PDP Research Group. (1986). *Parallel distributed processing, volume 1: Explorations in the microstructure of cognition: Foundations*. The MIT Press. https://doi.org/10.7551/mitpress/5236.001.0001
Savage, R., Abrami, P. C., Piquette, N., Wood, E., Deleveaux, G., Sanghera-Sidhu, S., & Burgos, G. (2013). A (Pan-Canadian) cluster randomized control effectiveness trial of the ABRACADABRA web-based literacy program. *Journal of Educational Psychology, 105*(2), 310. https://doi.org/10.1037/a0031025
Schunk, D. H., & Greene, J. A. (2017). Historical, contemporary, and future perspectives on self-regulated learning and performance. In *Handbook of self-regulation of learning and performance* (pp. 1–15). Routledge. https://doi.org/10.4324/9781315697048-1
Seidenberg, M. S. (1994). Language and connectionism: The developing interface. *Cognition, 50*, 385–401. https://doi.org/10.1016/0010-0277(94)90037-x
Seidenberg, M. S., & McClelland, J. L. (1989). A distributed, developmental model of word recognition and naming. *Psychological Review, 96*(4), 523–568. https://doi.org/10.1037/0033-295x.96.4.523
Stanovich, K. E. (1986). Matthew effects in reading: Some consequences of individual differences in the acquisition of literacy. *Reading Research Quarterly, 21*, 360–407. https://doi.org/10.1598/rrq.21.4.1
Steenbergen-Hu, S., & Cooper, H. (2014). A meta-analysis of the effectiveness of intelligent tutoring systems on college students' academic learning. *Journal of Educational Psychology, 106*(2), 331–347. https://doi.org/10.1037/a0034752.supp
Tate, T. P., Doroudi, S., Ritchie, D., Xu, Y., & Uci, M. W. (2023, January 10). Educational research and AI-generated writing: Confronting the coming tsunami. In *EdArXiv*. https://doi.org/10.35542/osf.io/4mec3
Trust, T., Whalen, J., & Mouza, C. (2023). Editorial: ChatGPT: Challenges, opportunities, and implications for teacher education. *Contemporary Issues in Technology and Teacher Education, 23*(1), 1–23.
U.S. Department of Commerce. (2000). *Falling through the Net: Toward digital inclusion.* U.S. Department of Commerce. https://doi.org/10.7551/mitpress/2419.003.0006
UNICEF, D. (2021). *Seen, Counted, Included: Using data to shed light on the well-being of children with disabilities*. United Nations Children's Fund.
Usta, M. B., & Karabekiroğlu, K. (2020). Computational analysis of affective facial behavior in children with the specific learning disorder. *Anadolu Psikiyatri Dergisi, 21*(4), 429–434. https://doi.org/10.5455/apd.82969

Van den Audenaeren, L., Celis, V., Abeele, V. V., Geurts, L., Husson, J., Ghesquière, P., Wouters, J., Loyez, L., & Goeleven, A. (2013). DYSL-X: Design of a tablet game for early risk detection of dyslexia in preschoolers. In *Games for Health* (pp. 257–266). Springer. https://doi.org/10.1007/978-3-658-02897-8_20

Vicente, M. R., & López, A. J. (2010). A multidimensional analysis of the disability digital divide: Some evidence for Internet use. *The Information Society, 26*(1), 48–64. https://doi.org/10.1080/01615440903423245

Wang, S., Wang, F., Zhu, Z., Wang, J., Tran, T., & Du, Z. (2024). Artificial intelligence in education: A systematic literature review. *Expert Systems with Applications, 252*, 124167. https://doi.org/10.1016/j.eswa.2024.124167

Wu, T. F., Chen, M. C., Yeh, Y. M., Wang, H. P., & Chang, S. C. H. (2014). Is digital divide an issue for students with learning disabilities? *Computers in Human Behavior, 39*, 112–117. https://doi.org/10.1016/j.chb.2014.06.024

Xiong, H., Wang, Z., Li, X., Bian, J., Xie, Z., Mumtaz, S., & Barnes, L. E. (2024). *Converging paradigms: The synergy of symbolic and connectionist AI in LLM-empowered autonomous agents*. arXiv preprint arXiv:2407.08516. https://doi.org/10.48550/arXiv.2407.08516

Zimmerman, B. J. (2013). Theories of self-regulated learning and academic achievement: An overview and analysis. In *Self-regulated learning and academic achievement* (pp. 1–36).

# Toward an Emancipatory AI Pedagogy: The Dos and Don'ts of an Anti-Racist/ Anti-Ableist Approach to Writing Instruction Using GenAI

Yoonmee Han and Sammy Jo Johnson

## Introduction

This chapter is motivated by critical questions about how AI-enabled technologies are being adopted in education, focusing on postsecondary education (PSE) and generative AI (GenAI) like ChatGPT. What we want to know is how we can use GenAI as an emancipatory tool in our teaching to break down structural barriers faced by linguistically marginalized disabled and racialized students in postsecondary education. We also want to know how to do this without reinforcing "linguistic hierarchies and the marginalization of diverse linguistic identities" (de Roock, 2024, p. 15) and disability identities in our teaching.

While GenAI technologies are marketed as potential solutions to the barriers experienced by language-oppressed students, the implication is often that these students and their literacy practices are the problem to solve by technological adoption in teaching. This framing suggests that students need 'fixing' by adjusting and assimilating their language and writing to fit a white, anglo, middle-class, able-bodied, and hearing standard—i.e., academic language. The assumption that marginalized language users are not using academic language and must be brought closer to a standard English practice reflects dominant approaches to writing instruction (Horner et al., 2011).

Without a critical lens, GenAI technologies can perpetuate white-anglo dominance and the structural marginalization of linguistically diverse and disabled students (de Roock, 2024; Owusu-Ansah, 2023). Focusing on 'fixing' students'

Y. Han (✉)
Department of Science and Technology Studies, York University, North York, ON, Canada
e-mail: yoom0303@yorku.ca

S. J. Johnson
School of Health Policy and Management, Critical Disability Studies, York University, North York, ON, Canada
e-mail: sammyjo1@yorku.ca



C. El Morr et al. (eds.), *Beyond Tech Fixes*,
https://doi.org/10.1007/978-3-031-93022-5_10

language by using AI in education does little to challenge or disrupt underlying structures of oppression that position the language and literacy practices of racialized and disabled students as deficient and in need of correction (Rosa & Flores, 2023). Accordingly. linguistically marginalized students are required to leave parts of themselves at the door or off the page. When this deeply violent requirement becomes impossible, these students may leave the university prematurely or avoid it from the outset.

The purpose of this chapter is to provide guidelines to support educators in implementing a critical digital pedagogy that actively breaks down the structural barriers that press down on diverse academic writers. To this end, we call for an emancipatory approach to writing instruction using GenAI—one that does not aim to 'fix' students but seeks to enhance disabled and linguistically marginalized students' learning experience. We propose potential entry points to help instructors put this pedagogy into practice. By focusing on practical applications, we hope that this discussion will support instructors in finding concrete ways to integrate critical digital pedagogies into their classrooms (Masood & Haque, 2021; Acevedo, 2023).

In the following sections, we situate ourselves and outline the theoretical perspectives that inform our work. We then review the literature on GenAI's use in education to support critical engagement in the writing process. Next, we advocate for an emancipatory AI pedagogy grounded in the tradition of critical digital pedagogy. Finally, we offer practical guidelines for enacting this pedagogy—the dos and don'ts of an anti-racist/anti-ableist approach to writing teaching using GenAI.

## Situating Ourselves

The motivation for this chapter comes in part from our social positions as disabled, bilingual graduate students and emerging postsecondary instructors at a large English-only campus in Ontario. Yoonmee is a racialized, partially sighted, former English as a Second Language student and new teaching assistant. Sammy Jo is a white CODA (child of deaf adults) and new writing center instructor, teaching in English and American Sign Language. Our questions about AI in education arise from our experiences in the neoliberal university, where our training in access, anti-racist, and relevant critical pedagogies are structurally deprioritized. As disabled and bilingual teachers and learners, we both use various technologies including ChatGPT to access and adopt in academia. We share a desire to deepen our preparation as engaged educators who support the learning of linguistically profiled (Alim, 2005) students and we wonder how we can use GenAI to do this.

We also situate our work in larger movements for disability justice (Sins Invalid, 2019), disability data justice (Gorman, 2023), linguistic justice (Baker-Bell, 2020), crip linguistics (Henner & Robinson, 2023), and education justice (Bassey, 2016), concerted efforts to address and fight against systemic ableism and racism faced by racialized and disabled people on the margins (Sins Invalid, 2019). In this sense, our project is not just interdisciplinary, but it is grounded in a commitment to cross-movement solidarity and work in action to improve the lives of those whose languages are devalued and disparaged by ableist and racist policies and standardized pedagogies in education (Annamma et al., 2013, 2018). We know from our own lived experience that supporting diverse writers requires more than a simple inclusion in existing and standardized pedagogies but working against these interlocking systems of oppression in higher education.

## Guiding Framework: A Critical Disabilities Raciolinguistics (CDR)

We draw on a critical disabilities raciolinguistic (CDR) perspective (Cioè-Peña, 2021, 2022) to highlight the ways that academic writing standards perpetuate educational inequality, particularly in students' interactions with GenAI. As outlined by Cioè-Peña (2021, 2022), a CDR perspective weaves together two theoretical frameworks: DisCrit (Annamma et al., 2013, 2018) and a raciolinguistic perspective (Flores & Rosa, 2015; Rosa & Flores, 2023). DisCrit is forwarded based on the Black feminist studies' lineage of intersectionality (Crenshaw, 1989). It examines the ways in which dis/abilities are shaped and constituted at the intersection of racism and ableism and specifically in the context of education (Annamma et al., 2013, 2018). This term explains how unequitable school systems and literacy assessment function to categorize and ostracize racialized and disabled students, channeling them into multiple forms of social segregation and marginalization. Integrating these frameworks, a CDR-informed analysis is meant to bring to our attention to the ways in which racism, ableism, and linguicism dynamically interact in educational settings to reinforce domination of anglo white able-bodied priviliges (Cioè-Peña, 2021, 2022).

Using this lens, we identify the core issue: standards of academic language, embedded in and reinforced by GenAI technologies, function as gatekeeping mechanisms, upholding white/abled privilege and marginalizing diverse linguistic and disability identities in higher education. We argue that this issue is not solved by relying on dominant institutional responses to students' GenAI uses, which mostly prohibits or penalizes students who use AI. Such punitive responses could further harm marginalized students–particularly, Indigenous, racialized, disabled, and multilingual students–who are already over-policed and punished under academic honesty policies (Steeves, 2024).

## Possibilities: Using GenAI to Support Academic Writing

Contrary to the fear that students use GenAI to somehow write without writing–or worse: without thinking (Graham, 2023), research suggests that GenAI can be used to support students' critical engagement throughout the writing process (Ciampa et al., 2023). By shifting from an approach that prohibits GenAI use to one that promotes collaboration with GenAI, tools like ChatGPT can be leveraged to support both emergent and experienced writers to engage in a reflexive writing practice (Parker et al., 2024).

For instance, GenAI technologies like ChatGPT can play an important role during the early stages of writing. Students can use these tools to research and explore new topics and ideas (Ciampa et al., 2023) in a way that is easily customizable to their interests (El Naggar et al., 2024; Barbetta, 2023). Additionally, because students are able to ask questions and 'chat' with AI, this interaction can help students view their own writing, including the questions they ask AI, as part of a border intellectual conversation. Using ChatGPT at these stages can also enhance accessibility: students can ask for plain language summaries and translations of material (Trust et al., 2023), and even 'chat' with AI about the ways they are making sense of it.

GenAI can also help students to start their writing projects, providing assistance with the development of writing plans and outlines, as well as a conversation partner to help out if students get stuck or experience writing blocks (Trust et al., 2023; Marino et al., 2023). As students start to develop their writing, they can ask for assistance with editing and receive feedback on word choice, spelling, grammar, and sentence clarity (Marino et al., 2023; Barbetta, 2023). Rather than using GenAI like ChatGPT to edit *for* them, students can use ChatGPT to edit *with* them, promoting critical engagement in revision processes. For example, students can use GenAI-enabled revisions to think critically about which AI-suggested edits to accept or reject and request specific types of feedback (Parker et al., 2024).

Researching and writing collaboratively with AI can also provide a space for students to share written ideas and 'chat' about course material without worrying about being judged (Svensson et al., 2021), and to practice academic writing outside of graded assignments (Javier & Moorhouse, 2024). In our own writing, we check in frequently with ChatGPT to make sure we are on the right track; we feel less pressure sharing rough drafts and working ideas with ChatGPT when we still want feedback to gauge if our ideas are progressing. When used in these ways, GenAI can help students to start and progress writing tasks, increase motivation (Svensson et al., 2021), and build confidence in their academic writing skills (Parker et al., 2024).

Despite the optimism, it is important to point out that we do not advocate GenAI as a one-way tech solution to the complex structural problems and inequity faced by language oppressed students. Indeed, much of the literature also calls attention to serious concerns about privacy, consent, and security, as well as an unfair and discriminatory treatment against racialized and disabled people by AI-enabled machines that result from data biases (see also Pierrès et al., 2024; Fang et al., 2024). Such biases often reflect epistemological ableism, racism, sexism, queerphobic ideas, normative assumptions, or implicit othering practices in linguistic use against racialized, gendered, and disabled people (Fang et al., 2024; Tilmes, 2022; Warr et al., 2024; Ungless et al., 2023). When students engage with implicitly biased content, this can perpetuate misinformation about people with disabilities and racialized minorities (Fang et al., 2024; Warr et al., 2024), as well as put students at risk of encountering racism, ableism, and other forms of violence which is normalized in the conversational style of ChatGPT.

Moreover, when using GenAI tools to assist in teaching writing in a classroom, it is important to recognize structural marginalization and discrimination that AI tools can reproduce. The underlying racist, classist, and ableist assumptions about preferred ways of speaking, writing, and learning become reproduced in data and programmed into AI training (de Roock, 2024). This erasure of diverse linguistic practices, propped up by a larger system of white-anglo and spoken language hegemony, affords privileges to students belonging to dominant groups (i.e., white students, hearing students, able-bodied students, those at the intersections of privileged categories, etc.), and consequently functions to reproduce whiteness, hearingness, and able-bodiedness in the academy (Baker-Bell, 2020; Henner & Robinson, 2021). In this sense, if AI is used without a critical lens, instead of working to disrupt barriers, these technologies can reinforce patterns of domination, erasing the language and literacy practices and perspectives of marginalized students deemed not sufficiently academic (Owusu-Ansah, 2023).

In response, researchers call for the development of critical awareness or critical literacies when interacting with digital technologies (see Ciampa et al., 2023). There is a need to provide students with opportunities to think critically about AI's potential impact on their writing, or, in other words, incorporating a critical awareness about the interconnections between language, literacy, and power (see Alim, 2005; Baker-Bell, 2020; Bassey, 2016). Without this critical awareness, we risk overlooking the ways that old exclusionary practices get reproduced in new technologies. Moreover, unless we get critical about language discrimination, we risk using GenAI to support diverse academic writers in ways that demand they fit into oppressive writing standards by using technology to 'fix' or, more accurately, erase these students and their linguistic identities.

Ultimately, we suggest that neither a prohibitionist/punitive response to using AI nor one focused on 'fixing' or including students in existing unequal writing standards is sufficient. We suggest, instead, a third way, which can better position us to refuse allegiance to white-anglo academic writing standards and to consider how to use AI in a way that works towards enhancing the learning experiences of disabled and linguistically marginalized students.

## Toward an Emancipatory AI Pedagogy

We advocate for an emancipatory AI pedagogy rooted in the framework of critical pedagogy. Critical pedagogy involves both reflection on the world and action to change the world in partnership with our students (Freire, 2018). This reflexive praxis aims to cultivate in students a critical consciousness about the structures that oppress them, including a critique of oppression in education.

Critical digital pedagogy extends this critique of education and inequality to pedagogical interactions with technology (Köseoğlu et al., 2023). Central to critical digital pedagogy is the prioritization of digital learning environments where students and teachers can collaboratively work together to critically interact with technologies, examine "their underlying assumptions and explor[e] their potential for transformative learning experiences" (Baskara, 2024, p. 59). In this sense, critical digital pedagogy can help us, both students and teachers, to identify the complex and contradictory power dynamics shaping student interactions with GenAI in education.

Doing critical pedagogy is in essence a creative and collaborative process wherein knowledge is co-produced alongside students (Clack, 2022; Masood & Haque., 2021, Köseoğlu et al., 2023). Students along with teachers are positioned as knowledge holders and knowledge producers. In direct contrast to an approach that penalizes students for using AI in their assignments, an approach rooted in critical pedagogy necessitates recognizing that students bring expertise with these technologies, including using them to navigate ableism, linguicism, and other forms of oppression.

We suggest that an emancipatory approach to GenAI in writing instruction can be most impactful or most emancipatory when used to oppose academic writing standards. If we seriously commit to building pedagogical strategies along *with* our students, we can find ways together to leverage GenAI to *teach* writing, to include more students as writers, rather than using writing as a gatekeeping tool to keep students out because we think they can't write. This is an emancipatory framing for GenAI: it is a call to use these technologies in ways that refute systems of assessment that determine who belongs and who doesn't, using linguicism to perpetuate racist and ableist exclusions.

## Guiding Practices: The Dos and Dont's

In this section, we provide a list of guiding practices: the dos and don'ts of an anti-racist/anti-ableist writing teaching using GenAI. Importantly, we do not offer these as a simplistic checklist. Instead, we take inspiration from hooks (1994), particularly her call for more practical discussions that can help instructors make concrete changes in their teaching and actively challenge domination in the classroom. This list is not exhaustive but rather serves as a starting point for moving from a theory of emancipatory AI pedagogy into its embodied practice.

**Do:** Work with students to develop critical AI literacies. Supporting students in developing critical AI literacies involves encouraging students to critically engage with AI technologies, make decisions about if and how they want to use specific technologies, and query racist/ableist programmatic bias. Students should also be prompted to reflect on how AI interacts with their own language and literacy practice, fostering an awareness of the linguistic hierarchies perpetuated by educational technologies. This practice should also promote critical intervention by students, such as refusing edits or corrections generated by AI platforms that erase linguistic diversity from their writing. GenAI is not perfect—for example, there are significant biases with using GenAI to support writing for and with students using oral and signed languages–yet, we suggest that we can still find ways with our students to use it to promote writing practices that transgress institutional boundaries.

**Don't:** Implement prohibitive or punitive approaches to GenAI. Such approaches not only fail as students inevitably use these technologies (Graham, 2023), but they also neglect to prepare them to critically engage with GenAI in education, work, and beyond (Parker et al., 2024).

**Do:** Collaborate with students to develop digital writing assignments and classroom rules regarding AI usage. This practice should center racialized, disabled, and racialized disabled students in collaborative decision-making processes, recognizing that punitive AI policies disproportionately harm these groups. By committing to co-developing guidelines for AI-assisted writing, we not only respect students' capacity to critically engage with AI in ways that enhance their learning, but we can also end up with guidelines that are more relevant and actionable for students.

**Don't:** Initiate academic misconduct processes when students use GenAI. Instead, use any concerns about GenAI assistance in writing as opportunities for teaching! Additionally, recognize that students may be using AI assistance to compensate or avoid racist/ableist devaluations of their writing.

**Do:** Co-learn with students about AI. Recognize that students are probably already using AI in different ways in their everyday lives, including for accessibility purposes. Ask students how they are using AI and what works for them. This practice would enable students to learn from their peers about accessibility hacks and other AI features they might not know about.

**Don't:** Assume that students who use nonstandard literacy and language practices, including GenAI-enabled technology in writing don't belong in PSE. Challenge these assumptions when you notice them personally and–especially–when perpetuated in the classroom and other parts of the academy. These ways of thinking prioritize loyalty to academic writing standards and institutional whiteness/able-bodiedness over our students (Cioè-Peña, 2022). Instead, commit to transgressing boundaries around language and literacy dominance and how these attitudes can be reinscribed in GenAI technologies.

## Concluding Thoughts

In this chapter, we advocate for an emancipatory approach to using GenAI in writing instruction, yet we recognize that there are many other ways AI is being incorporated into education settings. More theorizing and practice are needed to flesh out an emancipatory AI pedagogical framework. We also recognize the institutional barriers that complicate this work for teachers, including employment precarity, a tendency to prioritize educational technologies that enhance efficiency and productivity (Köseoğlu et al., 2023), and the devaluation of critical pedagogies in the neoliberal university (Hooks, 1994)–barriers that motivated us to write this chapter. However, we contend that working against the grain or against the algorithm is difficult and risky, yet essential for supporting marginalized learners in accessing and completing postsecondary education (see Ng, 1993).

We conclude by emphasizing that the implementation of an emancipatory AI pedagogy will require ongoing action and reflection–i.e., praxis! We invite others to join us in this work.

## References


Acevedo, M. M. (2023). The panoptic gaze and the discourse of academic integrity. In S. Köseoğlu, G. Veletsianos, & C. Rowell (Eds.), *Critical digital pedagogy in higher education* (pp. 47–62). Athabasca University Press. https://doi.org/10.15215/aupress/9781778290015.01

Alim, H. S. (2005). Critical language awareness in the United States: Revisiting issues and revising pedagogies in a resegregated society. *Educational Researcher, 34*(7), 24–31. https://doi.org/10.3102/0013189X034007024

Annamma, S. A., Connor, D., & Ferri, B. (2013). Dis/ability critical race studies (DisCrit): Theorizing at the intersections of race and dis/ability. *Race Ethnicity and Education, 16*(1), 1–31. https://doi.org/10.1080/13613324.2012.730511

Annamma, S. A., Ferri, B. A., & Connor, D. J. (2018). Disability critical race theory: Exploring the intersectional lineage, emergence, and potential futures of DisCrit in education. *Review of Research in Education, 42*(1), 46–71. https://doi.org/10.3102/0091732X18759041

Baker-Bell, A. (2020). *Linguistic justice: Black language, literacy, identity, and pedagogy*. Routledge.

Barbetta, P. M. (2023). Remedial and compensatory writing technologies for middle school students with learning disabilities and their classmates in inclusive classrooms. *Preventing School Failure: Alternative Education for Children and Youth*, 68(4), 340–351. https://doi.org/10.1080/1045988X.2023.2259837

Baskara, F. R. (2024). ChatGPT and critical digital pedagogy: Examining the potential and challenges for educational practice. *Proceeding International Conference of Innovation Science, Technology, Education, Children and Health, 4*, 57–73. Retrieved from https://icistech.org/index.php/icistech/article/view/80/82

Bassey, M. (2016). Culturally responsive teaching: Implications for educational justice. *Education Sciences, 6*(4), 35. https://doi.org/10.3390/educsci6040035

Ciampa, K., Wolfe, Z. M., & Bronstein, B. (2023). ChatGPT in education: Transforming digital literacy practices. *Journal of Adolescent & Adult Literacy, 67*(3), 186–195. https://doi.org/10.1002/jaal.1310

Cioè-Peña, M. (2021). Dual language and the erasure of emergent bilinguals labeled as disabled (EBLADs). In N. Flores, A. Tseng, & N. Subtirelu (Eds.), *Bilingualism for all? Raciolinguistic perspectives on dual language education in the United States* (pp. 63–87). Multilingual Matters. https://doi.org/10.21832/9781800410053

Cioè-Peña, M. (2022). The master's tools will never dismantle the master's school: Interrogating settler colonial logics in language education. *Annual Review of Applied Linguistics, 42*, 25–33. https://doi.org/10.1017/S0267190521000209

Clack, J. (2022). Can we fix education? Living emancipatory pedagogy in higher education. *Teaching in Higher Education, 27*(2), 141–154. https://doi.org/10.1080/13562517.2019.1704724

Crenshaw, K. (1989). Demarginalizing the intersection of race and sex: A black feminist critique of antidiscrimination doctrine, feminist theory and antiracist politics. *University of Chicago Legal Forum, 1989*(1), 139–167. https://chicagounbound.uchicago.edu/uclf/vol1989/iss1/8

de Roock, R. S. (2024). To become an object among objects: Generative artificial "intelligence," writing, and linguistic white supremacy. Reading Research Quarterly, 59(4), 590–608. doi: https://doi.org/10.1002/rrq.569.

El Naggar, A., Gaad, E., & Inocencio, S. A. M. (2024). Enhancing inclusive education in the UAE: Integrating AI for diverse learning needs. *Research in Developmental Disabilities, 147*, 104685. https://doi.org/10.1016/j.ridd.2024.104685

Fang, X., Che, S., Mao, M., Zhang, H., Zhao, M., & Zhao, X. (2024). Bias of AI-generated content: An examination of news produced by large language models. *Scientific Reports, 14*(1), 5224. https://doi.org/10.1038/s41598-024-55686-2

Flores, N., & Rosa, J. (2015). Undoing appropriateness: Raciolinguistic ideologies and language diversity in education. *Harvard Educational Review, 85*(2), 149–171. https://doi.org/10.17763/0017-8055.85.2.149

Freire, P. (2018). *Pedagogy of the oppressed.* (50th anniversary edition). Academic.

Gorman, R. (2023). Disability data justice from the ground up: A practice-led, participatory co-design approach to building an AI search engine and data repository for local, national, and tansnational disability organizations. *Critical Studies: An International and Interdisciplinary Journal, 18*(1), 28–43. https://doi.org/10.51357/cs.v18i1.229

Graham, S. S. (2023). Post-process but not post-writing: Large language models and a future for composition pedagogy. *Composition Studies, 51*(1), 162–168.

Henner, J., & Robinson, O. (2021). Signs of oppression in the academy. In G. Clements & M. J. Petray (Eds.), *Linguistic discrimination in U.S. higher education* (1st ed., pp. 92–109). Routledge. https://doi.org/10.4324/9780367815103-6

Henner, J., & Robinson, O. (2023). Unsettling languages, unruly bodyminds: A crip linguistics manifesto. *Journal of Critical Study of Communication & Disability*, 7–37. https://doi.org/10.48516/JCSCD_2023VOL1ISS1.4

Hooks, B. (1994). *Teaching to transgress: Education as the practice of freedom.* Routledge.

Horner, B., Lu, M.-Z., Royster, J. J., & Trimbur, J. (2011). Opinion: Language difference in writing: Toward a translingual approach. *College English, 73*(3), 303–321. https://doi.org/10.58680/ce201113403

Invalid, S. (2019). *Skin, tooth, and bone: The basis of movement is our people. Berkeley, CA* (2nd ed.).

Javier, D. R. C., & Moorhouse, B. L. (2024). Developing secondary school English language learners' productive and critical use of ChatGPT. *TESOL Journal, 15*(2), 2755. https://doi.org/10.1002/tesj.755

Köseoğlu, S., Veletsianos, G., & Rowell, C. (2023). Introduction. In S. Köseoğlu, G. Veletsianos, & C. Rowell (Eds.), *Critical digital pedagogy in higher education* (pp. 3–12). AU Press.

Marino, M. T., Vasquez, E., Dieker, L., Basham, J., & Blackorby, J. (2023). The future of artificial intelligence in special education technology. *Journal of Special Education Technology, 38*(3), 404–416. https://doi.org/10.1177/01626434231165977

Masood, M. M., & Haque, M. M. (2021). From critical pedagogy to critical digital pedagogy: A prospective model for the EFL classrooms. *Saudi Journal of Language Studies, 1*(1), 67–80. https://doi.org/10.1108/SJLS-03-2021-0005

Ng, R. (1993). "A woman out of control": Deconstructing sexism and racism in the university. *Canadian Journal of Education Revue Canadienne De l'éducation, 18*(3), 189–205.

Owusu-Ansah, A. L. (2023). Defining moments, definitive programs, and the continued erasure of missing people. *Composition Studies, 51*(1), 143–148.

Parker, J. L., Richard, V. M., Acabá, A., Escoffier, S., Flaherty, S., Jablonka, S., & Becker, K. P. (2024). Negotiating meaning with machines: AI'S role in doctoral writing pedagogy. *International Journal of Artificial Intelligence in Education.* https://doi.org/10.1007/s40593-024-00425-x

Pierrès, O., Christen, M., Schmitt-Koopmann, F. M., & Darvishy, A. (2024). Could the use of AI in higher education hinder students with disabilities? A scoping review. *IEEE Access, 12*, 27810–27828. https://doi.org/10.1109/ACCESS.2024.3365368

Rosa, J., & Flores, N. (2023). Rethinking language barriers & social justice from a raciolinguistic perspective. *Daedalus, 152*(3), 99–114. https://doi.org/10.1162/daed_a_02020

Steeves, M. (2024). Addressing equity in academic integrity. *Canadian Perspectives on Academic Integrity, 7*(2) .

Svensson, I., Nordström, T., Lindeblad, E., Gustafson, S., Björn, M., Sand, C., Almgren/Bäck, G., & Nilsson, S. (2021). Effects of assistive technology for students with reading and writing disabilities. *Disability and Rehabilitation: Assistive Technology, 16*(2), 196–208. https://doi.org/10.1080/17483107.2019.1646821

Tilmes, N. (2022). Disability, fairness, and algorithmic bias in AI recruitment. *Ethics and Information Technology, 24*(2), 21. https://doi.org/10.1007/s10676-022-09633-2

Trust, T., Whalen, J., & Mouza, C. (2023). Editorial: ChatGPT: Challenges, oppportunities, and implications for teacher education. *Contemporary Issues in Technology and Teacher Education, 23*(1), 1–23.

Ungless, E. L., Ross, B., & Belle, V. (2023). Potential pitfalls with automatic sentiment analysis: The example of queerphobic bias. *Social Science Computer Review, 41*(6), 2211–2229. https://doi.org/10.1177/08944393231152946

Warr, M., Oster, N. J., & Isaac, R. (2024). Implicit bias in large language models: Experimental proof and implications for education. *Journal of Research on Technology in Education*, 1–24. https://doi.org/10.1080/15391523.2024.2395295

# Part III
# Moving Forward: Charting a Path Toward Inclusive AI

## 1.1 Introduction

Part III shifts the focus toward systemic critique and future-oriented thinking. These chapters delve into the structural and epistemic dimensions of AI, asking critical questions about whose knowledge and experiences shape technological systems. From infrastructural inequities to the politics of representation and the legacies of colonialism, the authors illuminate the deeper forces that shape the AI-disability nexus and propose ways of reimagining it.

# Challenges with Recruitment, Collection, and Analysis: A Research Study on Physiological Signals and Emotional Experiences in Youth with Severe Motor and Communication Impairments

**Mackenzie L. Collins, Caryn J. Vowles, and T. Claire Davies**

## Introduction

Research into the emotional experiences of individuals with severe motor and communication impairments (SMCI) is both complex and crucial. Persons with SMCI often face significant challenges in expressing their emotions through conventional methods such as speaking, writing, or sign language. This may introduce barriers to the accurate assessment of their emotional states when interpreted by communication partners (Noyek et al., 2022). Traditional tools for emotion assessment, which often rely on verbal communication or physical gestures, are not always suitable (Noyek et al., 2022). There has been a growing interest in developing more sophisticated methods, including the use of artificial intelligence use of artificial intelligence (AI), to interpret physiological signals and other non-verbal cues.

The effectiveness of AI is heavily dependent on the data used to train the algorithm (Nivedhaa, 2024). Currently, most AI models are trained on data from WEIRD populations (Western, Educated, Industrialized, Rich, and Democratic) (Henrich et al., 2010). WEIRD populations do not capture the emotional expressions of all individuals with disabilities. While AI has the potential to greatly advance accessibility research, working with diverse populations is imperative in developing robust algorithms that accurately reflect the needs of the user. It is essential to broaden the

M. L. Collins (✉)
Department of Mechanical and Materials Engineering, Queen's University, Kingston, ON, Canada

School of Medicine, Queen's University, Kingston, ON, Canada
e-mail: mcollins@qmed.ca

C. J. Vowles · T. C. Davies
Department of Mechanical and Materials Engineering, Queen's University, Kingston, ON, Canada
e-mail: 16cjv@queensu.ca; claire.davies@queensu.ca


C. El Morr et al. (eds.), *Beyond Tech Fixes*,
https://doi.org/10.1007/978-3-031-93022-5_11

datasets used when training AI systems to include individuals with SMCI and other disabilities. This approach not only enhances the accuracy of emotion recognition for these populations but also promotes inclusivity in AI development. This paper describes the challenges faced and insights gained when undertaking research that includes diverse populations in the development of AI-based accessible technology.

## Research Methodology

Two populations were included in the study: youth participants with severe motor and communication impairments (SMCI), and age and sex-matched typically developing (TD) control participants (Collins & Davies, 2023). Youth participants were aged 5–25 years and were selected based on criteria consistent with a systematic review about communication access by Noyek et al. (2022). This age range aligns with definitions of school-age youth with disabilities in Ontario, Canada, and international guidelines. A minimum age of 5 years was chosen to ensure appropriate developmental comprehension and expression. Primary guardians of youth with SMCI and the participants themselves had to be fluent in English. To participate in this study, participants had to be able to express their emotions using their preferred method of communication (i.e. verbally, via communication board, etc.). Participants with co-existing condition, such as visual, auditory, and other sensory impairments, heart or sweat response conditions, and eye conditions such as strabismus were excluded from this study.

The research sought to observe emotional responses to stimuli using the International Affective Picture System (IAPS), a standardized tool for assessing emotions evoked by a visual stimulus (Lang et al., 2008). The study followed the instructions provided in the IAPS manual for emotion induction (Lang et al., 2008). Each image was preceded by a plain grey background with the words "Get ready to rate the next image..." meant to neutralize pupil diameter between images. Next, the IAPS image was shown centred on the screen for a period of 6 s. Each image was then followed by the appearance of the Self-Assessment Manikin (SAM), a well-documented pictorial tool for self-reporting emotions. The SAM tool allows participants to self-report their feelings using the well-known three-dimensional theory of emotion. According to this theory, all emotions can be described in a three-dimensional space by the self reported measure of Pleasure, Arousal, and Dominance they evoke. Each dimension is rated on a scale from 1 to 9. The Pleasure scale ranges from unhappy to happy, arousal measures alertness from calm to excited, and dominance measures feelings of control from feeling as though you are being "controlled" to feeling "in control".

As each stimulus was observed by the participant, their eye-gaze and physiological data were recorded using the Gazepoint GP3 eye-tracker and its associated finger biometrics device. This physiological signal data will be used in various AI algorithms to differentiate among emotions experienced by the individuals. The long-term aim is to develop a system that detects emotions from the participants and provides these expressions to communication partners (including doctors, nurses, friends, and new acquaintances), who are not familiar with the nuanced communication methods often used by individuals with SMCI.

The study was conducted with ethical approval from Queen's University. Informed assent or consent from all participants, and caregivers was received. All data were securely stored with access limited to researchers directly involved in the study.

The study was conducted in a location of the participant's choice. This approach introduced variability more reflective of real-world scenarios compared to a standard laboratory setting. The room in which participants completed the study was not consistent and not strictly controlled, nor were lighting conditions and other environmental factors. The challenges that occurred during recruitment, data collection, and analysis of the participant data from individuals with SMCI are further discussed.

## Understanding Challenges Related to Inclusive Data Science

Conducting research with participants who have severe motor and communication impairments (SMCI) presents challenges across all phases of a study from recruitment to data collection and analysis. The observations made and lessons learned during each phase of research are presented with the aim of developing a list of recommendations for future studies in this field. Recruiting participants with SMCI is particularly difficult due to the low prevalence which complicates recruitment efforts, and requires innovative strategies to reach and engage potential participants. Data collection poses its own set of challenges, as traditional methods often need to be adapted to accommodate the diverse abilities of participants with SMCI. Ensuring accurate and meaningful data requires flexible approaches, particularly in calibrating eye gaze and obtaining self-reports of emotion, which must be tailored to the individual's capabilities. Finally, the analysis of data collected is complicated by the difficulty in obtaining "true" emotional responses. Standard methods of relying on expert assessments may not be reliable, as even those closest to the participants may struggle to interpret their emotions accurately. This highlights the need for more participant-centered and innovative approaches in data analysis to better capture the emotional experiences of individuals with SMCI.

### *Recruitment*

Recruiting participants with severe motor and communication impairments (SMCI) posed significant challenges, particularly compared to recruiting typically developing participants. First, the population density of individuals with SMCI within Kingston's geographical area resulted in very few potential participants for the study. The study was initially based in Kingston, ON, Canada. This area is included in the Kingston, Frontenac and Lennox and Addington Health Unit which services 206,926 individuals according to the 2021 Canadian Census (Canada, 2023). Twenty-eight typically developing participants were recruited for a pilot study, preliminary results of which can be found in (Collins & Davies, 2023) over a period of 11 months. Given that the incidence of SMCI is approximately 1.5% the number of potential participants would be 3104 individuals (Canada, 2024). The area of coverage for Kingston Health Services is 6627 squared km (Canada, 2023). Despite working with various pediatric clinics at the local hospital in Kingston, few individuals were identified to fit the criteria within the small community. Initially, the participants were required to travel to a location on Queen's University campus for data collection. Accessible public transport to the central downtown area is limited in Kingston. Therefore, only families with access to private transport, or those near the limited public transport system could participate in the study, imposing recruitment issues due to geographical constraints. As a result, the study needed to expand outside of the Kingston area.

To address these issues the study was made mobile, enabling researchers to travel to participants. They could then visit more rural regions, and work with individuals who normally may be unable to attend in-person research activities. Researchers could also expand the recruitment efforts to larger city centres such as Toronto and Ottawa. However, making the study mobile required changes to the study's original methodology and required further recruitment of typically developing participants to match the mobile protocols. The original pilot study involved data collection using an Emotibit to collect physiological signals and the Tobii TX300 Eye-Tracker mounted to the Tobii integrated 23" TFT monitor (1920 × 1080 pixel), as it is currently a gold standard system for eye gaze data. However, this system is not transportable due to its size and weight. The decision was made to move to a smaller eye-tracker, the Gazepoint GP3, and associated biometrics device. This system could be more easily transported along with a high-end laptop for data collection. This adaptation made the study more convenient and accessible for participants and improved recruitment. While the quality of the system was not as high, the increase in the amount of data collected from individuals with SMCI provided a better outcome for the study.

***Recommendation 1: Mobile studies can be collected with participants in their environment of choice, removing various barriers to participation for individuals with disabilities.***

Despite being able to travel for this study, a barrier remained in finding ways to reach interested participants in cities beyond the Kingston borders. Social media can be an excellent network for recruitment, and therefore targeted recruitment strategies included various social media platforms. Parent-focused Facebook groups were used to connect with potential participants and their families, broadening the recruitment reach beyond the Kingston-Frontenac region. As many of these families receive a plethora of health and research information, to make the study clear and engaging, a 2-min recruitment video was shared broadly. This video received positive feedback, as it explained exactly what would be expected of participants during the session and put a face to the research study.

***Recommendation 2: Make use of engaging social media content such as videos or TikToks, to attract the interest of both youth and guardian, and ensure the video clearly describes the aim of the study, and expectations for participants.***

Finally, the number of participants required to achieve sufficient power for statistical significance or to train and test a machine learning algorithm can be especially challenging when working with small populations. In these scenarios it is often important to revisit and prioritize the inclusion criteria. For instance, in this research it was decided that the inclusion of persons with disabilities should be prioritized over maintaining a narrow age range. In addition, data was also collected out of country to further expand the diversity of the dataset and increase the overall participant count.

***Recommendation 3: When working with small populations of interest, such as those with SMCI, increase the size of the study population by expanding the inclusion criteria as much as possible.***

Making the study equipment mobile, using engaging social media materials, and expanding the inclusion criteria allowed the number of participants in the population of interest to double. This adds to the amount of quality data that can be collected and used for training in AI algorithms. Increasing training data can in turn, increase accuracy of AI models.

## *Data Collection*

As previously discussed, the equipment used in the protocol was modified to enable study mobility. The goal of the research is to develop assistive technologies to address communication barriers within common everyday environments. Unlike a laboratory, an everyday environment is not strictly controlled, and aspects such as the lighting and noise levels can vary greatly from one environment to the next. As a result, data was collected in an environment selected by the participant, often their own home, to allow the data to better reflect the natural use case for an assistive device. Any communication device would presumably be used outside of a controlled environment with the presence of various confounding factors. Thus, training the AI algorithm on data that better reflects a true use-case creates a more robust design.

***Recommendation 4: When collecting data to inform design decisions and train AI algorithms, ensure the study environment more closely mimics its real-world use-case. This will create more robust designs and AI algorithms.***

Collecting data from participants with SMCI presented several challenges, particularly in calibrating the eye gaze device. The traditional calibration method requires participants to focus on a small, red dot as it floats to different points on the computer screen. This approach was difficult for many young participants due to the sustained attention needed to complete the calibration task. Often, data collection had to continue with a calibration that was not ideal. To address the poor calibration, age-appropriate changes were implemented to make the calibration task more engaging. For example, familiar cartoon characters were used during the calibration process in place of the red dot for younger participants. Auditory stimuli that matched the cartoon was also included. This change made a tremendous difference to the data collection process as the time for protocol completion was greatly reduced and better calibration accuracies were achieved. In fact, participants would often achieve a near-perfect calibration on the first attempt.

***Recommendation 5: Finding ways to better engage the participants can improve data quality and efficiency of data collection.***

The calibration modification was enacted due to caregiver feedback during the study piloting process. This change both engaged the participants more effectively and incorporated valuable feedback from caregivers. One of the most significant ethical issues when designing for individuals with disabilities is that these systems are often designed without including input from the primary users themselves. Any system that is designed for use by a particular population, should be designed in consultation with that population, and the design of a research study is no different. Research studies should be designed in consultation with participants and caregivers to best identify methodologies for data collection that benefit both participant and researcher.

***Recommendation 6: Engage with participants and caregivers and listen to their feedback on the study. Ask them what they think could be done better and adapt to include continuous feedback.***

While piloting the study, it became clear that flexibility in the method with which self-reports of emotion were obtained was crucial. Given the varied communication abilities within the SMCI population, the study needed to adapt the methods used for self-reporting to ensure that each participant's needs were met. The choice between using SAM or a visual word system (consisting of words and corresponding emojis) for self-reporting was made according to each participant's communication abilities, ensuring the study was adaptable to individual needs. This flexibility allowed for more accurate and meaningful data collection, tailored to the individual capabilities of the participants.

***Recommendation 7: While consistency in methodology is important for research, incorporate adaptability from the start so accommodations can be made for accessibility barriers.***

## *Data Analysis*

The data analysis phase of the study faced significant challenges due to the limited number of participants and the scarcity of usable trial data. With such a small dataset, the validity of each trial became crucial. As previously described, some calibrations throughout the pilot trials with youth with SMCI were unsuccessful due to the lack of engaging visuals to keep the participant's attention (i.e. red dot). Every trial had to be meticulously examined to ensure accuracy and relevance before being included in the final analysis to ensure that the calibration was successful, and the participant's eyes remained both within range and focused on the stimulus. The limited data available increased the importance of thorough validation. The analysis phase was both time-consuming and critical to the study's overall success. To improve overall quality and reliability of data collection, breaks were incorporated into the data collection process. During these breaks participants could relax while researchers reviewed the data and adjusted or recalibrated the equipment as necessary.

***Recommendation 8: Include opportunities throughout the protocol to review the data and adjust where necessary. This will aid in improving the utility of each data collection session.***

One of the primary challenges in data analysis is the difficulty in obtaining "true" data for emotional responses from participants with SMCI. In many studies, researchers rely on assessments from multiple "experts," often multiplying their judgments by a confidence value to approximate the participant's true emotional state. However, the present research identified that even the most familiar communication partners often struggled to accurately determine the youth's emotional state. This challenge underscores the complexity of interpreting data in populations with severe communication impairments and highlights the need for more reliable and participant-centered methods of analysis.

***Recommendation 9: It is important to design research studies such that the experiences of those with disabilities are not subjective interpretations from outside parties, such as caregivers, but rather first-hand accounts.***

One final challenge is that data from participants with SMCI are often supplemented with models developed from typically developing (TD) participants. This approach can limit the accuracy and relevance of the analysis when applied to individuals with SMCI, as the models may not recognize the various nuances of this population. If the barrier limiting the collection of data from individuals with SMCI can be addressed, datasets that better reflect experiences of these individuals could be obtained. This would allow for the development of models specifically focused on participants with SMCI, rather than treating their data as an add-on to models developed for the typically developing population. Such advancements could lead to more precise and personalized assessments, improving the validity and applicability of AI research for persons with SMCI.

***Recommendation 10: Identify those who would be most invested (such as the individuals for whom you are designing) in the results of the project and ensure they are included in your study.***

## Conclusion

Research involving participants with severe motor and communication impairments (SMCI) presents a host of challenges across all phases, from recruitment and data collection to final analysis. Data collection of populations with limited numbers necessitate innovative and flexible approaches that go beyond traditional research methods. Recruitment efforts must account for geographical constraints and limited accessibility, requiring mobile study setups and creative outreach strategies like social media campaigns. In data collection, modifications to equipment and protocol, such as the use of engaging visual and auditory stimuli for calibration, are critical to ensuring the collection of meaningful data. Data analysis brings its own challenges, particularly with small datasets. Validating every trial for accuracy becomes essential, and integrating participant-centered approaches could improve the reliability of assessments.

In response to these challenges, 10 recommendations have been proposed aimed at improving research methodologies for populations with disabilities. These recommendations focus on increasing accessibility, enhancing engagement, and creating more inclusive study designs that are tailored and continuously adaptable to the needs of the individual.

By addressing these challenges and focusing on data collection in collaboration with participants with disabilities, future research could create models and systems better suited for these individuals. This would ensure that individuals with SMCI (and other disabilities) are more effectively represented in AI-driven research.

## References


Canada, S. (2023). *Census profile, 2021 census of population*. Government of Canada. Retrieved September 13, from https://www12.statcan.gc.ca/census-recensement/2021/dp-pd/prof/index.cfm?Lang=E

Canada, C. D. A. (2024). *People who have communication disabilities*. Retrieved September 13, from https://www.cdacanada.com/resources/communication-disabilities/statistics/

Collins, M., & Davies, T. C. (2023). Emotion differentiation through features of eye-tracking and pupil diameter for monitoring well-being. (2694-0604 (Electronic)). In *2023 45th Annual International Conference of the IEEE Engineering in Medicine & Biology Society (EMBC)*. IEEE.

Henrich, J., Heine, S. J., & Norenzayan, A. (2010). The weirdest people in the world? (1469-1825 (Electronic)). *Behavioral and Brain Sciences, 33*(2–3), 61–83.

Lang, P. J., Bradley, M. M., & Cuthbert, B. N. (2008). International affective picture system (IAPS): Affective ratings of pictures and instruction manual.

Nivedhaa, N. (2024). *A comprehensive review of AI's dependence on technology*. https://doi.org/10.13140/RG.2.2.27033.63840

Noyek, S., Vowles, C., Batorowicz, B., Davies, C., & Fayed, N. (2022). Direct assessment of emotional well-being from children with severe motor and communication impairment: A systematic review. *Disability and Rehabilitation: Assistive Technology, 17*(5), 501–514. https://doi.org/10.1080/17483107.2020.1810334

# The View from Elsewhere: Investigating Infrastructural Inequities at the Intersection of Disability and AI-Enabled Interactive Technologies

**Foad Hamidi, Michaela Hynie, Annette Korntheuer, Melanie Baljko, Zainab Mohamedhasn Abdlamer Abol-Hawa, Nge Nge Aye Maung, and Samah Al-Shaghdari**

## Introduction

Technology designers are increasingly leveraging Artificial Intelligence (AI) to provide adaptive functionality that tailors responses dynamically for each user: this is true for the category often problematically labeled "Assistive Technology (Shew, 2020; Trewin et al., 2019)." While these AI-enabled adaptive and personalized systems have the potential to better respond to the needs of specific users, they have been challenged for the perpetuation and exacerbation of racist and xenophobic assumptions, resulting in inequities and exclusions while being presented as "bias-free." Furthermore, many concerns about their potential for increasing ableist harm to users have surfaced (Shew, 2023). These include privacy concerns due to increased

F. Hamidi (✉)
Information Systems Department, University of Maryland, Baltimore County (UMBC), Baltimore, MD, USA
e-mail: foadhamidi@umbc.edu

M. Hynie
Department of Psychology/Centre for Refugee Studies, York University, North York, ON, Canada
e-mail: mhynie@yorku.ca

A. Korntheuer
Munich University of Applied Sciences, Munich, Germany
e-mail: Annette.korntheuer@hm.edu

M. Baljko
Lassonde School of Engineering, York University, North York, ON, Canada
e-mail: baljko@yorku.ca

Z. M. A. Abol-Hawa · N. N. A. Maung · S. Al-Shaghdari
NOW! Nicht Ohne das Wir, c/o Handicap International e.V., Berlin, Germany
e-mail: info-crossroads@deutschland.hi.org; info-crossroads@deutschland.hi.org; info-crossroads@deutschland.hi.org


C. El Morr et al. (eds.), *Beyond Tech Fixes*,
https://doi.org/10.1007/978-3-031-93022-5_12

data collection (Hamidi et al., 2018; McDonald et al., 2021), inequitable access for users in low-resource contexts (Hamidi et al., 2022; Nagraj et al., 2021), and the potential to replace essential services prematurely to save costs (Vorobeva et al., 2022). Additionally, there is the issue of who is engaged and who is excluded from this digital technology development pipeline (from ideation to computational instantiation) (Burgstahler & Ladner, 2007; Mankoff et al., 2010; Spiel et al., 2020). It is increasingly evident many of these risks result from a lack of understanding of the intersectional oppressions faced by people with disabilities and a lack of participation and representation in decision-making about these systems.

In the paper, we draw on a transnational, interdisciplinary project that uses an intersectional lens to reflect on the uneasy relationship between AI and disability justice. In September 2023, we organized a workshop panel presentation with advocates from "NOW! Nicht Ohne das Wir," a self-advocacy group of refugees with disabilities and their relatives, at the Metropolis International Conference in Berlin. During the presentation, three panelists with lived experiences described their experiences of technological, social, and political barriers, and shared ideas for opportunities for future intervention and innovation. In collaboration with the panelists, who are co-authors of the chapter, our research team documented the presentation that we summarize and reflect on in this paper. The presentation illuminated how the panelists' experiences were impacted by factors arising from their intersectional identities as disabled female forced migrants needing to navigate complex infrastructures. Panelists also shared how their needs and desires often fell through the cracks of bureaucratic systems that were insensitive to their particular experiences, highlighting the potential for this invisibility to be amplified by future AI-enabled technologies. The self-advocacy group, "NOW! Nicht Ohne das Wir," advocates for the rights of refugees with disabilities and their relatives vis-à-vis politics, administration and society aiming to improve their living situation in Germany. By centering the voices of people with disabilities and their communities and allies, we identify opportunities for developing grassroots-localized AI-enabled technologies to amplify disability justice advocacy efforts and transcend the dominant techno-ableist narratives.

## Related Works and Theoretical Framework

Previous research on designing interactive systems for forced migrants has explored several applications, including navigating a new language (Brown & Grinter, 2016) or a new multicultural setting (Duarte et al., 2018), finding accommodation and other resources (Noyman et al., 2017), and accessing healthcare (Talhouk et al., 2017). Two recent international workshops that focused on interactive technology design for forced migrants and refugees resulted in a set of guidelines that include continuously re-evaluating research scope, contributing to broader refugee agenda at the local, national, and international levels, and building in flexibility and time for trust-building into the research plan (Talhouk et al., 2018). The goal of many previous studies that have focused on technology design for forced migrants has been to understand the impact of different barriers on their experience and create ways to overcome them through new sociotechnical solutions (Almohamed & Vyas, 2016b; Baranoff et al., 2015; Fisher et al., 2016, 2017). For example, in a study of the impact of relocation and forced migration on refugees' social capital, Almohamed et al. found that refugees who lack social ties in the host community have a significantly higher risk of depression compared to other community members in the same context (Almohamed & Vyas, 2016a). They further found that digital communication technologies can have a positive impact on the social inclusion of refugees.

A range of interactive technologies, such as translating platforms (Brown & Grinter, 2016), dietary tracking devices (Fisher et al., 2017), mapping technologies (Fisher et al., 2016), Interactive Voice Response (IVR) radios (Talhouk et al., 2017), and mobile applications (Baranoff et al., 2015), have been created to overcome specific barriers of social inclusion, language competency, and improving health. For example, building on the knowledge that many forced migrants have access to low-cost mobile phones, Baranoff et al. designed a cost-efficient mobile service to help refugees navigate their surroundings and get specialized services by using a combination of mobile phones and Near Field Communication (NFC) tags that can be placed in different locations to provide contextualized translated information to users (Baranoff et al., 2015). Another project, Rivertran, explored the design of a "human-in-the-loop" messaging platform that helps forced migrants navigate language barriers when they arrive in a host country (Brown & Grinter, 2016). Other projects, conducted in refugee camps, have identified rich opportunities for participants to engage in digital media production and emphasized the importance of conducting situated participatory research that is aware of the particular characteristics of each setting (Aal et al., 2014; Sawhney, 2009). Finally, Hamidi and Karachiwalla studied the technology needs of forced migrants with disabilities in the US from service provider perspectives (Hamidi & Karachiwalla, 2022a, b, c). They identified a systemic disconnect between the knowledge and experience of settlement and accessibility services that result in barriers specific to the intersectional experiences of forced migrants with disabilities and their families, and that cultural and language limitations of services create barriers for refugees with disabilities and that these can be amplified by digital technologies (Hamidi & Karachiwalla, 2022b, c). Furthermore, they found that these issues were amplified during the COVID-19 pandemic where political tensions and a confusing proliferation of public health information sources resulted in increased challenges in trust building and outreach (Hamidi & Karachiwalla, 2022a).

Whereas many digital technology prototypes and systems emerge from scholarly research projects, there are other design sites from which new digital technology designs emerge: technology design projects and hackathons. Hackathons, intensive events where participants collaborate on developing a project from concept to prototype (Lara & Lockwood, 2016) (p .486) over a short period of time, can be particularly problematic, as there has been a long-term shift away from them being explicitly politicized spaces towards them being spaces dominated by neoliberal discourses of individual technical mastery and entrepreneurial citizenship

(Costanza-Chock, 2020). "Design for displaced persons" is emerging as a topic for these hackathons, with varying degrees of attentiveness to the importance of "design-with" (ReDI School of Digital Integration, n.d.) as opposed to "design-for" (City University of London Press Office, 2023, July 24; UK Youth Business International., n.d.; UN International Organization for Migration, 2017, February 17). Similarly, design "for the disabled" is also a popular topic for hackathons and technology design projects, which is often critiqued as innovation-for-innovation's sake and as problematically understanding disability as a problem in search of a solution (Shew, 2023). These design processes often demonstrate technoableism: a pattern of belief in the power of technology that considers the elimination of disability a good thing, often under the guise of empowerment" (Shew, 2023) (pp. 11–12). Thus, even well-intentioned technology design has the potential to be harmful through technoableism. Technologies specifically designed for forced migrants with disabilities are underexplored. And against the backdrop of this nuanced design domain, we now have a proliferation of "breathless headlines" about the optimism about machine learning and Artificial Intelligence for disability applications, most of which belies technoableist assumptions (Shew, 2023) (p. 9).

Researchers in refugee and forced migration studies have studied the experience of refugees with disabilities. For example, a study with 44 service providers, found that for Asian refugees in the US communication barriers and lack of knowledge about mainstream health services were major barriers to accessing services for developmental disabilities (Ellen, 2000). Other studies in the US have identified additional factors, such as inadequate community outreach and cultural differences and misunderstanding, as posing barriers in this space as well (Hasnain, 2010; Trinh-Shevrin et al., 2009). Similar results were found through applied and qualitative research projects in the German context, adding restrictive legal structures and bureaucratic complexity as other central barriers to adequate service provision (Afeworki Abay, 2023; Korntheuer, 2023; Steiner, 2021). Mirza and Heinemann conducted a study with both refugees with disabilities and expert service providers in the US and, using interviews, focus groups, surveys, and participant observations, found that refugees with disabilities have several unmet disability-related needs resulting from service providers' limited awareness of disability rights and resources and a medical understanding of disability (Mirza et al., 2014). Other factors included refugees being disconnected from disability service systems, lack of communication and trust between different service entities, and limited cross-cultural understanding in disability service organizations. Similarly, using interviews with service providers and refugees in California, Morris et al. found that the majority of refugees do not regularly access health services, and language and cultural differences impact all stages of access, from making appointments to filling prescriptions (Morris et al., 2009). Finally, Korntheuer et al. used an intersectional approach to analyze existing research on forced migration and disability and identified gaps in service and policy resulting from the segregation of specialized support systems (Korntheuer et al., 2021). They identified opportunities to reshape existing policies and discourses to develop holistic approaches to integration supporting migrant agency and inclusion.

We are using an intersectional lens to look at the experiences of workshop presenters and to identify challenges and opportunities through AI-enabled interactive technologies. According to Hill Collins and Bilge (2020) intersectionality as an analytical tool helps us to investigate interwoven and interrelated power relations that shape social relations and the individual experiences in everyday life. Social categories such as race, class, gender, nation, ability, ethnicity -among others- are to be seen in their complexity and intersecting nature to understand how social structures and discourses not only frame individual identity construction and self-positioning but also (re) produce social inequality in societies (Afeworki Abay et al., 2024; Winker & Degele, 2011). While there are very heterogenous understandings and conceptualizations of intersectionality in current debates (Collins & Bilge, 2020), the links to a transformative and activist practice and the normative orientation towards social justice is already immanent in the concept's roots in US antidiscrimination law and Black feminism (Collins, 2019; Crenshaw, 2018).

## Experiences at the Intersection of Disability and Forced Migration

To better understand the lived experiences of forced migrants with disabilities, we organized a joined workshop panel presentation with a self-advocacy group, "NOW! Nicht Ohne das Wir," of forced migrants living with disabilities in Germany at the Metropolis International Conference in Berlin and led a workshop discussion with conference attendees. The panel consisted of three female advocates with disabilities who were forcibly displaced from Syria, Iraq, and Yemen, and two representatives from the German advocacy group. Panelists shared their lived experiences and perspectives. This report summarizes our reflections and observations from the panel presentations, which shed light on issues arising from the lack of services, resources, and understanding of the intersectional experiences of forced migrants with disabilities as shared by the panelists. We discuss implications and potential directions forward. Panelists discussed how their ability to participate meaningfully in society is hindered by inflexible policies and a lack of access to opportunities and support. They described experiences both in forced migrant camps and in host countries.

*Limited understanding leading to lack of adequate accommodation:* At the camps and in the shared accommodation facilities after arrival to Europe, understanding of disability is quite limited. For example, some housing arrangements may describe themselves as accessible because they have an accessible toilet. Meanwhile other essential areas, such as the kitchen and washing areas, are not accessible. This situation is replicated with nutrition and food services that are limited and may amplify disabilities or chronic health conditions. Panelists described how some of these result from the way services are delegated to different organizations and agencies that are disconnected from each other. This disconnect is in no small part the result of the design of services and resources being done without adequately considering the expertise and lived experiences of forced migrants themselves.

*Technology: inadequacy and opportunity:* Other major issues at forced migrant camps, that also emerged in the temporary housing provided in the host country, were limited access to technological infrastructure, including adequate assistive technology support, and basic accommodations, such as elevators for people with motor disabilities or power ports to charge electric wheelchairs. One panelist shared the experience of a fellow forced migrant who was in a wheelchair but was assigned an apartment on the second floor of a building with no elevators. Whenever he wanted to leave his apartment, he had to be carried down the stairs in his wheelchair by neighbors.

Panelists generally pointed to a lack of informational resources, including online media, that would provide accurate, up-to-date, and locally relevant information and guidance for new forced migrants. However, positive technological solutions were also identified. The panelists described helpful services, including a group therapy session administered on Zoom to help with traumas experienced specifically by people with disabilities.

*Employment barriers:* While facing other challenges that forced them to migrate, all panelists described having more access to employment in their home countries while not being provided with support to achieve employment easily in the host country. For example, one of the panelists who was trained in radiology and computer science was gainfully employed before having to migrate for political reasons. Since arriving in the host country, she has not been allowed to work because of the lack of support from the social assistance system and employers for her to seek employment commensurate with her qualifications, rooted in the perception that because of a physical disability, she is unable to work. This has led to her feeling depressed and isolated and has been a major barrier to practicing the language of the host country and being socially connected. Another of the panelists was an experienced journalist in her country before having to move due to political issues. Thus, she has experience in communicating and creating content effectively. However, migration regulations in the host country were delaying her from continuing her work professionally.

*Negative attitudes leading to lack of inclusive structures:* Panelists reported a general lack of empathy for forced migrants with disabilities and mentioned hearing negative comments when they complained about an issue or raised a need. This is particularly present when narratives that justify the acceptance of forced migrants by identifying them as a potential workforce are strong, which can automatically categorize forced migrants with disabilities as burdens because of beliefs about their ability to work. More broadly, people are set against inflexible structures insensitive to their needs.

*The need for policy change:* There are a number of policy related challenges that were identified, and potential policy level solutions. Panelists described that when considering efforts to support forced migrants, both immediate needs, such as the ability to work and socialize, as well as long-term concerns, such as passing anti-discrimination and technology access policies, should be pursued. A particular point of frustration for the panelists was not knowing how long a decision from the immigration office, for example, about a request to relocate to different housing or asylum claim. Would take, which reflects limitations in accountability. Panelists, who all served as disability advocates, shared how they navigated a simultaneous need to find authentic ways to recognize their expertise and ability to represent others and to navigate structures of power without becoming tokenized or amplifying stereotypes.

## Discussion

In light of the project presented above, we would like to discuss three points of reflection at the intersection of disability justice and AI-enabled interactive systems. First, in accordance with previous research, we find that exploring intersectional experiences is essential when studying issues of equity and inclusion and can shed light on under-explored areas that are otherwise hidden (Collins & Bilge, 2020; Korntheuer et al., 2021). For example, these highly educated professionals' do not fit service and policy expectations around people who have resettled with disabilities. Their descriptions show how people with multiple dimensions of identity fall between the cracks of services and resources that are designed with one-dimensional planning that focuses on the needs of one population. Not all forced migrant experiences with a disability are the same. Interrelated social categories of race, economic status, and sexual orientation also impact individual experiences and should be considered (Collins, 2019; Collins & Bilge, 2020). These observations motivate further intersectional research to better understand and respond to nuanced sociotechnical issues that exist at the intersection of disability and other aspects of vulnerability.

Second, while our project identified opportunities for technology innovation, panelists were quick to point out that facilitating access to existing technologies and resources and creating accessible opportunities for self-advocacy are also worthwhile and potentially transformative areas of action. For example, access to tools and procedures to modify or fix existing assistive technologies could be helpful. For forced migrants, many assistive technologies may be damaged during transition or be incompatible with the environment in the host country. Modifications leading to consistent function and increased compatibility can make a significant difference. Some of these issues arise when migration and health and accessibility service providers are not connected with each other, and not aware of the issues arising from lived experiences at the intersection of these service areas. This resonates with the observation that technology "maintenance and repair activities are rarely discussed in accounts of activist technology because of the mythology of innovation and the constant bias toward the "new," even though these activities are just as important to activist goals" (Costanza-Chock, 2020) (p. 120). These findings point to opportunities for creating localized infrastructures for assistive technology maintenance and innovation that can directly involve providers from different services as well as, critically, people with disabilities themselves. These can also include supporting disabled technologists and digital content creators and using technology to help remove barriers to gainful employment for people, is a promising future direction, although as was noted in the panel discussion, the greatest barriers were rigid policies, stereotyped assumptions and a lack of adaptability throughout the settlement system. As ML-based techniques now proliferate into design sites, it is especially important to identify and resist the tropes often motivating their deployment in this design domains: the trope of 'helping' (i.e., positioning users as completely dependent rather than agentive) or of promoting 'independence' (i.e., promulgating the narrative that denies that we are all interdependent, and independence has always already been an illusion) (Bennett et al., 2018; Costanza-Chock, 2020).

Finally, an exciting area of technology innovation would be to develop more inclusive tools, including AI-enabled ones, to support advocacy itself. There are many opportunities to pursue in this area, including creating crowdsourced tools to report issues, tools for organizing and raising awareness, and procedures for effective international collaboration. Of particular interest could be ways for forced migrant communities to connect with local organizations to amplify their voices and impact and ultimately lead to more meaningful integration, including access to professional opportunities. While the research literature has documented similar approaches in using social media or mobile phones to pursue some of these goals, technologies specifically designed for forced migrants with disabilities are underexplored, and their designs would require careful consideration to empower without causing harm. When these design ideas are to be explored in design sites, it will be crucial to be attentive to the technoableism that can be latent in hackathons and other intense formats that tend to not center the voices of those most directly impacted.

## Conclusion

The discussion led by the panelists highlighted opportunities that could be facilitated by technology, but also how many of the barriers they faced were the result of social biases and inequities. The challenging situation in the host country and the need to focus advocacy efforts on pressing policy issues were the focus of the contributions rather than concrete indications for developing adaptive technologies. Nonetheless, based on the discussion, the potential for the creation of a localized AI-informed infrastructure and the innovation of AI-enabled technologies for advocacy purposes became apparent. These possibilities, however, should be considered with caution as, for example, recent AI-enabled solutions in forced migration management (Bircan & Korkmaz, 2021; Ozkul, 2023), have seen several programs terminated due to their potential to result in discrimination. But research has also identified how technology can be used to increase migrants' access to information and control over outcomes. Technology's promise can only be fulfilled with the involvement of those individuals using the technology (Spiel et al., 2020), and with a broader effort to ensure equity and the protection of people's rights.

**Acknowledgements** We would like to warmly thank the "NOW! Nicht Ohne das Wir" which is a self-advocacy group of refugees with disabilities and their relatives. In their words: "Self-advocacy means: We represent our interests ourselves. We stand up for our rights vis-à-vis politics, administration and society. We have a common goal: We want to improve the living situation of refugees with disabilities and their relatives in Germany."

## References

Aal, K., Yerousis, G., Schubert, K., Hornung, D., Stickel, O., & Wulf, V. (2014). Come_in@ Palestine: Adapting a German computer club concept to a Palestinian refugee camp. In *Proceedings of the 5th ACM international conference on collaboration across boundaries: Culture, Distance & Technology—CABS '14. The 5th ACM international conference, Kyoto, Japan*. https://doi.org/10.1145/2631488.2631498

Afeworki Abay, R. (2023). *Dekolonialisierung des Wissens: Eine partizipative Studie zu Diskriminierung und Teilhabe an Erwerbsarbeit von BIPoC mit Behinderungserfahrungen* (Vol. 85). transcript Verlag.

Afeworki Abay, R., Cholewa, J., & Korntheuer, A. (2024). Empirische Intersektionalitätsforschung im Spannungsfeld zwischen Rekonstruktion, Dekonstruktion und Reproduktion von sozialen Ausschlüssen. *Gender, 16*(2-2024), 26–39.

Almohamed, A., & Vyas, D. (2016a). Vulnerability of displacement: Challenges for integrating refugees and asylum seekers in host communities. In *Proceedings of the 28th Australian conference on computer-human interaction—OzCHI '16. The 28th Australian conference, Launceston, Tasmania, Australia*. https://doi.org/10.1145/3010915.3010948

Almohamed, A., & Vyas, D. (2016b, June 4). Designing for the marginalized: A step towards understanding the lives of refugees and asylum seekers. In *Proceedings of the 2016 ACM conference companion publication on designing interactive systems. DIS '16: Designing interactive systems conference 2016, Brisbane QLD Australia*. doi: https://doi.org/10.1145/2908805.2909415.

Baranoff, J., Gonzales, R. I., Liu, J., Yang, H., & Zheng, J. (2015). Lantern: Empowering refugees through community-generated guidance using near field communication. In *Proceedings of the 33rd annual ACM conference extended abstracts on human factors in computing systems—CHI EA '15. The 33rd annual ACM conference extended abstracts, Seoul, Republic of Korea*. https://doi.org/10.1145/2702613.2726950

Bennett, C. L., Brady, E., & Branham, S. M. (2018). Interdependence as a frame for assistive technology research and design. In *Proceedings of the 20th international ACM SIGACCESS conference on computers and accessibility* (*ASSETS '18: The 20th international ACM SIGACCESS conference on computers and accessibility, Galway Ireland*). https://doi.org/10.1145/3234695.3236348

Bircan, T., & Korkmaz, E. E. (2021). Big data for whose sake? Governing migration through artificial intelligence. *Humanities & Social Sciences Communications, 8*(1). https://doi.org/10.1057/s41599-021-00910-x

Brown, D., & Grinter, R. E. (2016, May 7). Designing for transient use: A human-in-the-loop translation platform for refugees. In *Proceedings of the 2016 CHI conference on human factors in computing systems. CHI'16: CHI conference on human factors in computing systems, San Jose California, USA*. doi: https://doi.org/10.1145/2858036.2858230.

Burgstahler, S. E., & Ladner, R. E. (2007). Increasing the participation of people with disabilities in computing fields. *Computer, 40*(5), 94–97.

City University of London Press Office. (2023, July 24). Empowering displaced communities*: City hosts first ever school-run hackathon*. Retrieved from https://www.city.ac.uk/news-and-events/news/2023/07/empowering-displaced-communities-city-hosts-first-ever-school-run-hackathon

Collins, P. H. (2019). *Intersectionality as critical social theory*. Duke University Press.

Collins, P. H., & Bilge, S. (2020). *Intersectionality* (2nd ed.). Polity Press.

Costanza-Chock, S. (2020). *Design justice*. MIT Press.

Crenshaw, K. (2018). Demarginalizing the intersection of race and sex: A black feminist critique of antidiscrimination doctrine, feminist theory, and antiracist politics. In *Living with contradictions* (pp. 39–52). Routledge.

Duarte, A. M. B., Brendel, N., Degbelo, A., & Kray, C. (2018). Participatory design and participatory research: An HCI case study with young, forced migrants. *ACM Transactions on Computer-Human Interaction: A Publication of the Association for Computing Machinery, 25*(1), 1–39.

Ellen, C. K.-H. A. W. (2000). Providing services to Asian Americans with developmental disabilities and their families: Mainstream service providers' perspective. *Community Mental Health Journal, 36*(6), 589–595.

Fisher, K. E., Yefimova, K., & Yafi, E. (2016). Future's butterflies: Co-designing ICT wayfaring technology with refugee Syrian youth. In *Proceedings of the the 15th international conference on interaction design and children—IDC '16* (The the 15th international conference, Manchester, United Kingdom). https://doi.org/10.1145/2930674.2930701

Fisher, K. E., Talhouk, R., Yefimova, K., Al-Shahrabi, D., Yafi, E., Ewald, S., & Comber, R. (2017, May 6). Za'atari refugee cookbook: Relevance, challenges and design considerations. In *Proceedings of the 2017 CHI conference extended abstracts on human factors in computing systems.CHI '17: CHI conference on human factors in computing systems, Denver Colorado USA*. doi: https://doi.org/10.1145/3027063.3053235

Hamidi, F., & Karachiwalla, Z. (2022a). Note: "Fear is grounded in reality": The impact of the COVID-19 pandemic on refugees' access to health and accessibility resources in the United States. *The Compass*. https://doi.org/10.1145/3530190.3534851

Hamidi, F., & Karachiwalla, Z. (2022b). Structural accessibility barriers and service gaps facing refugees with disabilities in the United States. *Journal of Enabling Technologies, 16*, 189–203. https://doi.org/10.1108/jet-11-2021-0054

Hamidi, F., & Karachiwalla, Z. (2022c). "I'm ok because I'm alive": Understanding socio-Cultural accessibility barriers for refugees with disabilities in the US. In *Proceedings of the 19th international web for all conference* (pp. 1–11).

Hamidi, F., Poneres, K., Massey, A., & Hurst, A. (2018). Who should have access to my pointing data? In *Proceedings of the 20th international ACM SIGACCESS conference on computers and accessibility* (pp. 203–216).

Hamidi, F., Owuor, P. M., Hynie, M., & Baljko, M. (2022). "Knowledge comes through participation": Understanding disability through the lens of DIY assistive technology in Western Kenya. *Proceedings of the ACM on Human-Computer Interaction, 6*(CSCW1), 1–25.

Hasnain, R. (2010). Brokering the culture gap. In *Forced migration review; Oxford Iss* (Vol. 35(35), pp. 32–33). Refugee Studies Centre, Oxford Department of International Development. Retrieved from https://www.proquest.com/scholarly-journals/brokering-culture-gap/docview/650390047/se-2

Korntheuer, A. (2023). III.2.5 Intersektionen von Flucht und Behinderung. In *Flucht- und Flüchtlingsforschung* (pp. 461–470). Nomos Verlagsgesellschaft mbH & KG.

Korntheuer, A., Hynie, M., Kleist, M., Farooqui, S., Lutter, E., & Westphal, M. (2021). Inclusive resettlement? Integration pathways of resettled refugees with disabilities in Germany and Canada. *Frontiers in Human Dynamics, 3*. https://doi.org/10.3389/fhumd.2021.668264

Lara, M., & Lockwood, K. (2016). Hackathons as community-based learning: A case study. *TechTrends: For leaders in Education & Training, 60*(5), 486–495.

Mankoff, J., Hayes, G. R., & Kasnitz, D. (2010). Disability studies as a source of critical inquiry for the field of assistive technology. In *Proceedings of the 12th international ACM SIGACCESS conference on computers and accessibility* (*ASSETS '10: The 12th international ACM SIGACCESS conference on computers and accessibility, Orlando Florida USA*). https://doi.org/10.1145/1878803.1878807

McDonald, N., Massey, A. K., & Hamidi, F. (2021). AI-enhanced adaptive assistive technologies: Methods for AI design justice. *IEEE Data Engineering Bulletin, 44*, 3–13.

Mirza, M., Luna, R., Mathews, B., Hasnain, R., Hebert, E., Niebauer, A., & Mishra, U. D. (2014). Barriers to healthcare access among refugees with disabilities and chronic health conditions resettled in the US Midwest. *Journal of Immigrant and Minority Health, 16*(4), 733–742.

Morris, M. D., Popper, S. T., Rodwell, T. C., Brodine, S. K., & Brouwer, K. C. (2009). Healthcare barriers of refugees post-resettlement. *Journal of Community Health, 34*(6), 529–538.

Nagraj, A., Kuber, R., Hamidi, F., & SG Prasad R. (2021, October 17). Investigating the navigational habits of people who are blind in India. In *The 23rd international ACM SIGACCESS conference on computers and accessibility. ASSETS '21: The 23rd international ACM SIGACCESS conference on computers and accessibility, virtual event USA*. doi: https://doi.org/10.1145/3441852.3471203.

Noyman, A., Holtz, T., Kröger, J., Noennig, J. R., & Larson, K. (2017). Finding places: HCI platform for public participation in refugees' accommodation process. *Procedia Computer Science, 112*, 2463–2472.

Ozkul, D. (2023). *Automating immigration and asylum: The uses of new technologies in migration and asylum governance in Europe*. Refugee Studies Centre, University of Oxford.

ReDI School of Digital Integration. (n.d.). *Humanitarian Hackathon 2018*. Retrieved September 13, 2024, from https://humanitarian-hackathon.devpost.com/

Sawhney, N. (2009). Voices beyond walls: The role of digital storytelling for empowering marginalized youth in refugee camps. In *Proceedings of the 8th international conference on interaction design and children—IDC '09. The 8th international conference, Como, Italy*. https://doi.org/10.1145/1551788.1551866

Shew, A. (2020). Ableism, technoableism, and future AI. *IEEE Technology and Society Magazine, 39*(1), 40–85.

Shew, A. (2023). *Against technoableism*. WW Norton.

Spiel, K., Gerling, K., Bennett, C. L., Brulé, E., Williams, R. M., Rode, J., & Mankoff, J. (2020, April 25). Nothing about us without us. In *Extended abstracts of the 2020 CHI conference on human factors in computing systems. CHI '20: CHI conference on human factors in computing systems, Honolulu, HI, USA*. doi: https://doi.org/10.1145/3334480.3375150.

Steiner, M. (2021). *Umfrage zur Versorgungslage geflüchteter Menschen mit Behinderung in Deutschland innerhalb des deutschen Caritasverbandes*. Deutscher Caritasverband EV, Hg. Retrieved from https://www.caritas.de/neue-caritas/heftarchiv/jahrgang2020/artikel/gefluechtete-menschen-mit-behinderung.

Talhouk, R., Bartindale, T., Montague, K., Mesmar, S., Akik, C., Ghassani, A., Najem, M., Ghattas, H., Olivier, P., & Balaam, M. (2017, June 26). Implications of synchronous IVR radio on Syrian refugee health and community dynamics. In *Proceedings of the 8th international conference on communities and technologies. C&T '17: Communities and technologies 2017, Troyes France*. doi: https://doi.org/10.1145/3083671.3083690.

Talhouk, R., Bustamante, A., Aal, K., Weibert, A., Charitonos, K., & Vlachokyriakos, V. (2018). HCI and refugees. *Interactions, 25*(4), 46–51.

Trewin, S., Basson, S., Muller, M., Branham, S., Treviranus, J., Gruen, D., Hebert, D., Lyckowski, N., & Manser, E. (2019). Considerations for AI fairness for people with disabilities. *AI Matters, 5*(3), 40–63.

Trinh-Shevrin, C., Islam, N. S., & Rey, M. J. (2009). *Asian American communities and health: Context, research, policy, and action*. John Wiley & Sons.

UK Youth Business International. (n.d.). *Hackathon for displaced Ukrainian entrepreneurs in Poland*. Retrieved September 1, 2024, from https://youthbusiness.org/initiative/hackathon-for-displaced-ukrainian-entrepreneurs-in-poland/

UN International Organization for Migration. (2017, February 17). *Turkey Hackathon develops solutions for refugee challenges*. Retrieved from https://www.iom.int/news/turkey-hackathon-develops-solutions-refugee-challenges

Vorobeva, D., El Fassi, Y., Costa Pinto, D., Hildebrand, D., Herter, M. M., & Mattila, A. S. (2022). Thinking skills don't protect service workers from replacement by artificial intelligence. *Journal of Service Research, 25*(4), 601–613.

Winker, G., & Degele, N. (2011). Intersectionality as multi-level analysis: Dealing with social inequality. *European Journal of Women s Studies, 18*(1), 51–66.

# Mechanisms of Disability Evasiveness in AI-Generated Flash Fiction

**Katherine Barron, Aaron Richmond, Ellouise Van Berkel, and Ryan Collis**

## Introduction

In February 2024 social media exploded with examples of Google's new image generation tool, Gemini, producing racially diverse, yet historically inaccurate, images. In an attempt to correct the long-standing issue of representation bias on the internet, Google integrated several bias mitigation tools into their model. Unfortunately, this backfired after Gemini started producing images of Black founding fathers and Asian Nazi soldiers (Gilbert, 2024). In response, Google temporarily paused the feature, apologized, and explained that Gemini "had become 'way more cautious' than it had intended with the generator 'wrongly interpreting some very anodyne prompts as sensitive'" (Bushard, 2024).

Generative AI has a history of replicating, and even augmenting, biases in its training material on the basis of race (Fang et al., 2024), gender (Dong et al., 2023), and disability (Gadiraju et al., 2023). Attempts to ensure fair representations are still in their infancy and are not yet achieving their objectives. As disability in education scholars,[1] we wondered how well this new and widely touted tool would impact education and disability representation.

[1] At the time of writing, all three authors of this paper were PhD candidates at York University in the faculty of education and one a recent graduate. Three out of the four authors identify as neurodivergent and/or disabled.

Authors Aaron Richmond, Ellouise Van Berkel, and Ryan Collis are contributed equally.

K. Barron (✉) · E. Van Berkel · R. Collis
Faculty of Education, York University, North York, ON, Canada
e-mail: kbarron@yorku.ca; evanberk@yorku.ca; rcollis@yorku.ca

A. Richmond
Independent Researcher, North York, ON, Canada


C. El Morr et al. (eds.), *Beyond Tech Fixes*,
https://doi.org/10.1007/978-3-031-93022-5_13

In fall 2023, we conducted a study investigating disability representation in AI-generated flash fiction (short stories of approximately 600 words). We were concerned with the rapid adoption of generative AI in K-12 classrooms for lesson planning and resource creation. We aimed to identify disability-related discrimination in AI-generated stories. We found that ChatGPT-4 did better than we anticipated, avoiding many of the terms, stereotypes, and tropes found in canonical literature. However, after reading the whole dataset, we saw repeated uses of inspiration porn[2] (Grue, 2016), narratives of overcoming (Dolmage, 2014), and a pattern we have termed *disability evasiveness*— a phenomena whereby non-disabled people claim to not 'see' disability.

In the first part of this chapter, we summarize our original study and the concept of disability evasiveness. In part two, we take a closer look at the technical mechanisms behind three facets of disability evasiveness: *diminishing presence of impairment by over-emphasizing positivity, exaggerating resilience,* and *erasing disability identity, culture, and community*, and consider how these might be the result of overzealous bias mitigation tools. In the third section, we extend the original study by generating stories using increasingly sophisticated prompts to see what is required to produce more desirable disability representations from a critical disability studies perspective. We conclude with a discussion on the implications for disability justice.

## Summary of the Original Study

In August 2023 we prompted ChatGPT4 to write 40 short stories about disabled and neurodivergent children, as well as 10 stories about non-disabled children for comparison. The 40 disability-focused stories represented nine different communities: ADHD, Autism, Conduct Disorder, Deaf, Hard of Hearing, Dyslexia, Intellectual Disability, Physical Disability, and Visual Disability/Blind. We also generated four stories using an unspecified term 'disability' allowing ChatGPT to determine what disability group it would represent. We chose these disability groups because of our personal lived experiences (ADHD, Autism, and Visual Disability/Blind) and our experiences as teachers, parents, and allies (Autism, ADHD, Conduct Disorder, Dyslexia, Intellectual Disability, and Physical Disability). We also included Deaf and Hard of Hearing groups because of their rich cultural histories and long-standing representations in media and literature (Padden & Humphries, 2005). A total of 50 stories were generated using the simplest prompt a classroom teacher might use: *Please write a realistic story about a child with* [disability]. *Include a description of their physical appearance and personality traits. The story should be between 500–700 words.*

Assuming a social constructionist epistemological stance (Crotty, 1998), we conducted a Critical Content Analysis which "has a particular focus on locating power in social practice by understanding, uncovering, and transforming conditions of inequality" (Beach et al., 2009, p. 129). Procedurally, we followed a method similar

[2] More commonly known as 'inspiration porn,' a term coined by activist Stella Young (Inspiration Porn and the Objectification of Disability, 2014).

to Short (2016), who recommends three readings of the texts. In the first reading, we paid close attention to our personal responses and made broad analytic notes. Then, we refined our research questions and selected two specific frameworks to apply deductively to our analysis: Connor's (a disability studies in education scholar) list of positive and negative representations of disabled characters (2017), and Landrum's (a secondary literacy scholar) criteria for evaluating story elements (2001). We coded the stories according to these frameworks in the second and third readings. A summary of Connor's list of positive and negative representations is provided in Table 1. Landrum's framework for evaluating story elements comprises 22 criteria in the categories of plot, character, and tone. To constrain the size of the study we focused on the seven criteria outlined in Table 2. For a more detailed description of these frameworks, please see their work (cited above) or our original study (Barron et al., in press).

**Table 1** Connor's Lists of positive and negative representations

| Positive representations | Negative representations |
|---|---|
| (1) Having a complex personality that includes a full range of emotions | (1) Pathetic and invokes pity |
| (2) Interacting with others as an equal | (2) A defenseless victim or the object of violence |
| (3) Participating in society | (3) Evil or sinister |
| (4) Having a role as an "extra" who happens to have a disability | (4) In possession of superhuman characteristics |
| (5) Portraying an ordinary person without superhuman abilities | (5) Derided, invoking laughter |
| (6) Providing insight into societal barriers | (6) A burden to parents, partner, or society |
| (7) Showing participation in a loving relationship | (7) Non-sexual |
| | (8) Separated or segregated from "mainstream" society |

(Connor, 2017, p. 206)

**Table 2** Selected criteria from Landrum's list

| Plot | Character | Tone |
|---|---|---|
| (1) The disabled character faces conflicts similar to those of his or her peer group; | (1) The disabled characters are portrayed as strong and independent, rather than passive, atypically naive, child-like, or dependent; | (1) The text does not use words such as re-, handicapped, lame, crippled, or special; |
| (2) Although both the climax and the ending may include the disability of one of the characters, they do not focus on it | (2) The disabled characters' temperament is not dramatically different than that of the other characters. An extraordinary positive or negative temperament may imply that the disability was caused by attitude or vice versa; | (2) The tone fits the theme, rather than being overly saccharine or simplistic |
| | (3) The prominent traits of the characters are what they can do, as opposed to what they cannot do | |

(Landrum, 2001 pp. 254–255)

We were pleasantly surprised to find that most stories successfully met many criteria set forth in Connor's and Landrum's frameworks. They did not use any outdated terms and even avoided newer euphemisms for disability like "special needs." Characters were always presented as strong, independent, and having complex hobbies, interests and skills, and, apart from the Autistic and Blind characters, the protagonists were portrayed as participating in society and having friends (for a more detailed analysis, see Barron et al., in press). Yet, we still experienced discomfort reading the stories. All had an overly saccharine tone, an exaggerated emphasis on non-disabled traits, and an omission of disability identity, culture, and community (see Appendix A for a sample story). These features prompted us to theorize the concept of disability evasiveness.

## Disability Evasiveness

As described in our original paper:

Disability evasiveness, like color-evasiveness (Annamma et al., 2017), refers to systemic and deliberate avoidance of recognizing and addressing disability in social, educational, and political contexts. This ideology embodies the refusal to acknowledge the lived experiences, challenges, and systemic barriers faced by individuals with disabilities. It is an active disengagement from the realities of dis/ableism and the social constructions of normalcy that marginalize those with disabilities. In a disability-evasive society, policies and rhetoric might superficially espouse inclusivity, yet in practice, they sustain environments that are inaccessible and inequitable, effectively silencing the dialogue necessary for genuine inclusion and accommodation.

Statements like "I don't see you as disabled" and "I never think of you as disabled," as captured by *#disabilitycompliments,* reinforce the notion that disability is bad, shameful, and stigmatizing and should therefore not be acknowledged. This perspective does several things. First, it diminishes the experiences of individuals who cannot or do not want to mask or 'overcome' their disabilities (see Graham et al., 2023). Second, it alleviates the non-disabled person from the discomfort of talking about disability and facing their own vulnerability (see Kristeva, 2013). Finally, it conceals systemic ableism through what Broderick and Lalvani (2017) call 'dysconscious ableism.' (Barron et al., in press).

## Manifestations of Disability Evasiveness and Their Technical Explanations

Within the ChatGPT4-generated stories, we observed three different facets of disability evasiveness: (1) diminishing the impairment; (2) exaggerating resilience; and (3) erasing or omitting disability identity, culture, and community.

## *The Attempt to Diminish the Presence of Impairment with an Over-Emphasis on Assets, Value and Positivity*

This facet of evading disability was evidenced in several ways. First, we observed it in the overly saccharine tone of the stories (100%), the frequent narratives of overcoming disability (82%), and the miraculous fairytale endings (29%). For example, in the conclusion to a story with a dyslexic character, ChatGPT4 wrote, "She held the book high and announced to the setting sun, 'I did it! I tamed the word-monsters!'" (Dyslexia #3).

Perhaps most problematically, we observed this facet in how ChatGPT4 repeatedly follows any mention of impairment with an over-endorsement of non-disabled traits. These juxtaposing sentences are constructed with words like "but," "just," and "despite." For example, "Sam was indeed different, *but* in a good way" (Physical Disability #1). "Malik was not *just* a visually impaired boy living in Brooklyn. He was a musician, a martial artist, a math whiz, and above all, an embodiment of unflinching spirit and determination" (Visual Disability/Blind #2). "*Despite* her visual impairment, Eva found joy and purpose in every aspect of her life" (Visual Disability/Blind #1).

This syntactic pattern is likely the result of four mechanisms working together: A *sensitivity heuristic* (a rule-based algorithm that helps the model understand context), *sentiment analysis* (the process of classifying text as being positive, negative, or neutral), *a self-attention mechanism* (part of the transformer architecture that allows the model to identify relationships between different parts of a sentence or paragraph), and a *narrative balance heuristic* (a type of bias mitigation algorithm that ensures that sensitive topics are discussed with a positive framing).

When we asked ChatGPT-4o to explain itself, it proudly answered that it is attempting to mitigate deficit-based thinking about disability:

> By juxtaposing the challenges ("communication barriers") with exceptional abilities ("extraordinary memory"), the language avoids deficit-based thinking, which would focus solely on what a character cannot do. Instead, it promotes the idea that individuals can possess unique strengths that stand out, even in the presence of challenges... Models like GPT-4 tend to generate stories that offer messages of hope and empowerment. By using "despite" and focusing on Noah's talents, the story encourages readers to *see beyond* [emphasis added] the disability and recognize the character's broader potential and humanity (OpenAI, 2024).

While we appreciate the logic and the attempt, this bias mitigation tool is not quite achieving its goal. As we noted in our original study, it's this exact juxtaposition that conveys a negative sentiment towards the disability and frames it as something that needs to be evaded, or as ChatGPT says, *seen beyond*.

## *The Exaggeration of Strength, Resilience, Determination, and Perseverance in the Face of Dis/Ableism*

We found the characters to be *excessively* strong. In many cases, their strength, resilience, determination, and extraordinarily positive attitudes were the solution to the ableism or disablism they faced. For example, in a story about being bullied, the solution was to befriend the bullies: "By the end of the day, the children, once her tormentors, became her eager students" (Hard of Hearing #2). As we wrote in our original paper:

Even though we appreciate the shift from canonical portrayals of disability weakness (*Tiny Tim* or the *Elephant Man*) towards strength, in this dataset, the over-compensation has turned characters into caricatures.... If disabled people are happy to endure societal disablism and institutional harm, it alleviates non-disabled people from their role in creating equitable and just societies. (Barron et al., in press).

When we asked ChatGPT-4o about this pattern, it explained that it was following "inspirational storytelling norms" commonly used in its training data:

> Stories about people with disabilities often follow narrative structures that highlight overcoming adversity and achieving success. This phrasing fits into the common narrative structure where individuals surpass expectations or thrive despite facing difficulties, aligning with culturally prevalent "overcoming adversity" themes. While this narrative approach has been critiqued for reinforcing stereotypes, it is still widely used and reflected in how models generate content (OpenAI, 2024).

Ironically, even though it recognizes the critiques of these narratives, it justifies using them because of their prevalence in the training data.

## *Erasing or Omitting Disability Identity, Community, History, Pride, and Culture*

This facet of evading disability was evidenced in four specific ways. First, there was a notable absence of disability community, history, pride, and culture in the dataset. Only two stories contained disabled secondary characters. Second, it actively refused to allow a character to define themselves by their disability, with sentences like "He did not let his disability define him" (Physical Disability #1). Third, it frequently redefined disability as something less stigmatizing. For example, it would often write, "To Alina, being hard of hearing was not a disability, but a different ability" (Hard of Hearing #2).

The final way this facet was promoted was with the avoidance of identity-first language (IFL). Contrary to person-first language (PFL) which developed in the 1970s in order to emphasize personhood over pathology (Pelka, 2012), IFL developed in order to centre disability experiences, cultures and pride as valued parts of disability identity (Andrews et al., 2022; Padden & Humphries, 2005). Proponents of both PFL and IFL stress that individual preferences should be honoured in specific contexts (Andrews et al., 2022; Flink, 2021). Although we as authors tend to use a mixture of both PFL and IFL in our writing, we only found three instances of identity-first language in our original ChatGPT-4 stories, all in the context of Deaf characters. We did not find any instances of community specific words like 'crip' or 'neurodivergent.'

This omission is likely the result of the same mechanisms that successfully eliminated undesirable terms: first, a *sensitivity heuristic* (described above) identified that the topic was "sensitive" and told the model to adjust its language accordingly. This triggered a *token level filtering process* as the LLM was generating the text. A *token* is a small chunk of text (sometimes a word, a part of a word, or simply the punctuation). The *token level filtering process* works with the *sensitivity heuristic* to determine what tokens might be inappropriate for that context and either blocks them or modifies them. Models are trained on contexts and terminology at several stages, but particularly at the *Reinforcement Learning with Human Feedback (RLHF)* stage of LLM development when thousands of human employees (see Perrigo, 2023) are responsible for rewarding or punishing the model for using particular terms.

When we asked ChatGPT-4o about language preferences, it explained that it has been trained to prioritize people-first language in order to "reduce the risk of marginalizing individuals based on their disabilities" (OpenAI, 2024). It goes on to explain that the default is set to person-first language because it is what is most commonly used in "mainstream advocacy" and by institutions in the "medical, educational, and policy sectors." It recognizes that some disability communities prefer IFL because "they see their condition as a core part of their identity and culture, rather than something separate from themselves" and because it "can emphasize pride," however, it still defaults to PFL until the user indicates otherwise. The implications for disability justice are significant. In effect, ChatGPT-4 is creating echo chambers by only providing IFL to those who know to request it, effectively isolating those following hegemonic PFL norms from exposure to disabled voices.

## Extending the Original Study

In preparation for this chapter in the fall of 2024 (over a year since the original dataset was generated), we extended the study in two different ways. First, we wanted to see if and how the stories had improved with Open AI's regular updates to ChatGPT-4. Second, we wondered if and how using IFL in the prompt (and asking ChatGPT to use IFL in its output) might make the stories less evasive. We therefore generated new stories for the five disability groups for which both PFL and IFL are commonly used— Autistic, Blind/Visually Disabled, Deaf, Disabled and Physically Disabled. For each group, we generated four new stories using three different prompts: the exact prompt from the original study that used PFL, a similar prompt that explicitly instructs ChatGPT-4 to use IFL, and an engineered prompt (Giray, 2023):

***Original PFL Prompt:*** *Please write a realistic story about a child with* [disability]. *Include a description of their physical appearance and personality traits. The story should be between 500–700 words.*

***Explicit IFL Prompt:*** *Please write a realistic story about a* [identity first disability language] *child. Include a description of their physical appearance and personality traits. The story should be between 500–700 words. Use identity first language.*

***Engineered IFL Prompt:*** *Pretend you are Disabled critical disability scholar, who prefers identity-first language and writes stories for and about Disabled children. Please write a realistic story about a* [identity-first language] *child. Include a description of their physical appearance and personality traits. The story should be between 500–700 words. Use relevant community specific identity-first language as well as reclaimed terms such as 'crip,' 'Autist,' 'neurodivergent' in the story.*

The stories were generated between November 1–4, 2024, shortly after a significant upgrade that made ChatGPT start catering to specific users by learning from their chat histories and creating "memories" (Memory and new controls for ChatGPT 2024)—features that were not yet present at the time of our original study. As disability in education scholars, we realized that our accounts had long histories of chats involving critical disability theory that might influence the output. We therefore created a new paid account without any chat history or memories in the settings. We accessed it through an "incognito" window in Google Chrome and set ChatGPT-4 (now called a 'legacy model') to "temporary chat" to prevent it from learning from content generated from previous prompts within this study. A limitation of this is that since we do not know exactly how ChatGPT works, we may not have prevented all mechanisms for individualized responses.

In total, we generated 60 new stories to compare to 20 stories of the same disability groups from the original study. Using the same protocols as our original study (see Barron et al., in press), we coded each story as having either IFL, PFL, neither, or both. The results are shown in Fig. 1.

We found that the use of IFL increased with each new level of prompt. In the original study, IFL appeared in only 15% of stories ($n$ = 3), all of which were in reference to Deaf characters. When we used this same PFL prompt again over a year later in preparation for this chapter, the results were similar with 20% ($n$ = 4) using IFL (the additional story was also in reference to a Deaf character). However, with the explicit prompt, we saw the use of IFL increase to 85% of stories ($n$ = 17) and with the engineered prompt it increased again to 100% ($n$ = 20).

Next, we coded for four specific aspects of disability evasiveness to see if and how they changed with the different sets of prompts. Specifically, we examined: (1) the frequency of sentences that paired mentions of impairment with an over-endorsement of non-disabled traits with words like *despite*, *but*, *yet*, *although*, and *even*; (2) the frequency of describing characters as resilient, determined, or perseverant; (3) number of stories where it claims the disability "didn't define" the character; and (4) the number of stories that acknowledge the existence of other disabled

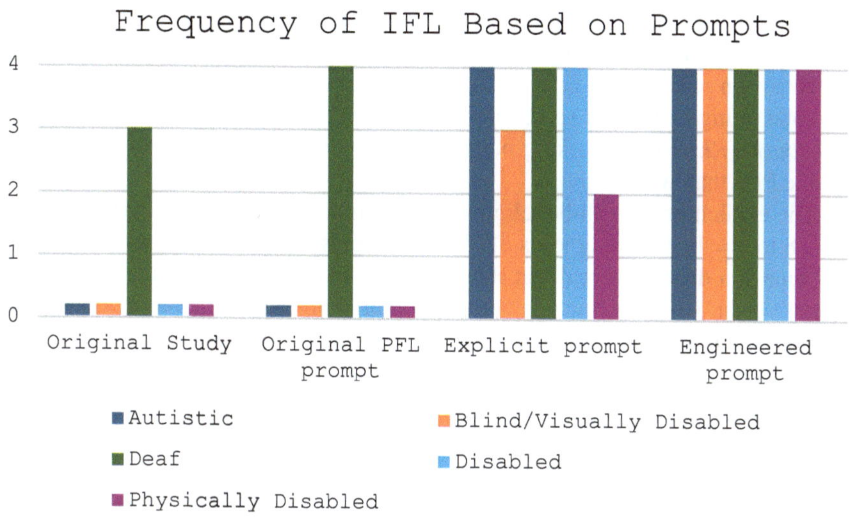


**Fig. 1** Frequency of IFL based on prompts

**Table 3** Changes in four aspects of disability evasiveness across datasets

| Criteria | Original dataset | Original PFL prompt | Explicit IFL prompt | Engineered prompt |
|---|---|---|---|---|
| Instances of juxtaposing sentences that use ‘despite,’ ‘not just,’ ‘but,’ ‘yet,’ ‘though,’ and ‘even’ | 63 | 17 | 12 | 17 |
| Instances of describing characters as resilient, determined, or perseverant | 50 | 9 | 14 | 15 |
| Stories that claim that the disability doesn’t ‘define’ the character | 9/20 | 0/20 | 1/20 | 1/20 |
| Stories that acknowledge the existence of other disabled people | 3/20 | 8/20 | 1/20 | 16/20 |

people, either as individuals or as a community. The results of these four aspects of disability evasiveness are presented in Table 3.

We were pleasantly surprised to see significant improvements in all four criteria simply with the ongoing system updates from OpenAI. Clearly, the bias mitigation tools have improved since their rocky start, suggesting that OpenAI is actively working on improving disability representation even though they do not explicitly disclose how it is done (Open AI, 2024). Although there is still room for improvement, we cautiously applaud OpenAI for their work so far in this area.

We were also very surprised to find that prompting ChatGPT-4 to use IFL did not necessarily lead to improvements in the above criteria. In fact, our IFL prompts made the stories better in some ways but worse in others. For example, the explicit prompt decreased the instances of juxtaposing sentences ($n$ = 17 to $n$ = 12) but increased the overemphasis on resilience ($n = 9$ to $n = 14$). The engineered prompt maintained the incidence of juxtaposing sentences ($n = 17$) and increased the overemphasis on resilience ($n = 9$ to $n = 15$). We wonder if these findings suggest that the bias mitigation tools (particularly the *Reinforcement Learning with Human Feedback—RLHF*) are working more effectively for prompts with the more hegemonic PFL than with IFL.

The explicit prompt all but eliminated the presence of all other disabled people ($n = 8$ to $n = 1$), returning to its old habit of representing disability as an anomaly within a non-disabled world that should be assimilated by pretending the disability doesn't exist. However, the engineered prompt doubled the number of stories that had secondary disabled characters and references to larger disability communities ($n = 8$ to $n = 16$). Interestingly, the only four stories this was not observed in were the stories involving Autistic characters who were all represented as having higher-support needs and difficulty connecting with others. There was no acknowledgement of the vibrant and prominent Autistic community currently leading the neurodivergence movement—an observation worth further investigation in future research.

A final observation from the newly generated stories that developed inductively, was that there was a noticeable increase in stories that contained detailed descriptions of accommodations and how activities and settings were accessible. For example, in the original study, stories would make vague mentions like "Teachers incorporated strategies to engage him better in classes" (Disability #3). In the newer stories, more detailed descriptions were provided:

Their design included a telescope mount that could be adjusted for different wheelchair heights and positions, allowing Disabled stargazers like herself better access to the telescopes. They incorporated voice-activated commands for those unable to use traditional controls and screens that displayed information in various formats, including large print and braille for visually Disabled individuals. (Engineered Disabled #2).

After reading these new detailed descriptions, we retrospectively realized that the omission of these descriptions in the original dataset is another form of disability evasiveness: an erasure of *how* disabled people access various settings. This omission dangerously limits non-disabled peoples' awareness of access options and ultimately their ability to envision possibilities.

## Discussion and Concluding Thoughts

Our original study was conducted in a brief window in time where ChatGPT-4 pervasively reflected the *disability evasiveness* present in society today. However, with the improvement of OpenAI's bias mitigation tools, that window seems to have narrowed. Though still far from perfect, the stories generated in ChatGPT-4 today are more likely to feature disability in affirming ways. However, collectively, the stories are moving towards a utopian feel—disabled characters always represented as valued leaders within their highly inclusive schools, winning prizes in all kinds of competitions, and easily accessing field trips to science museums, art galleries, botanical gardens, and nature reserves, where even the old bird-watching tower had an elevator (Disability #2). While we appreciate many aspects of this shift and will continue to advocate for representations like these, we wonder what might be lost with exclusively utopian portrayals.

Returning to the AI image generators discussed in the beginning of this chapter, like Google, OpenAI has worked to ensure fair representations in many areas. In an announcement on July 18, 2022, OpenAI demonstrated how their bias mitigation tools have improved the diversity of representation in images of CEOs, firefighters, women and computer engineers (OpenAI, 2022).[3] For example, the image of computer engineers before mitigation represents six (presumably) white men. The image after mitigation shows three men and three women, two or three of whom may be non-white. We now hold two truths in tension: First, this diverse representation is helpful and important because more people can see themselves reflected as computer engineers. Simultaneously, this diverse reflection of gender equity can be risky because it erases the reality of systematic barriers that result in men outnumbering women in computer engineering 19–1 (Stack Overflow, 2022). Which truth do we want represented? Is there a place for both? In what proportion?

Despite the intermittent re-appearances of the ableist messages outlined above, the trend towards disability utopias was nice to see—a significant improvement over the first set of stories generated over a year ago. Yet now, we wonder if these overly utopian representations might become another form of disability evasiveness: evading the presence of ableism rather than evading disability itself. While the stories themselves should never be ableist, we wonder if is it okay for ChatGPT to occasionally generate stories about a character facing barriers, teasing or discrimination? Is there a way to represent a character facing discrimination that is neither victimizing nor succumbing to resilient and inspirational tropes?

Rudine Sims-Bishop offers the metaphor of windows and mirrors to describe the power of representation. Mirrors reflect our own lived experiences, while windows offer views into other worlds—real or imagined (Sims Bishop, 1990). Applied to our study, disability evasive stories mirror many current realities in contemporary western society, while utopian stories offer windows into a better, barrier-free future.

We believe that authentic disability representation requires a wide variety of stories. We need some that highlight the triumphs of disabled heroes and activists (e.g., *All the Way to the Top* by Annette Bay Pimentel) and some that portray the everyday experiences of an 'average Joe' (e.g., *The Trouble with Robots* by Michelle Mohrweis). We need some that focus on the experience of impairment, for example, what Richmond (2024) calls 'narratives of adjustment' where characters who were previously non-disabled adjusts to new experiences of disability and identity (e.g., *The Year My Life Went Down the Toilet* by Jake Maia Arlow), and some where the plot is completely unrelated to disability (e.g., *How to Find What You're Not Looking*

[3] See Botha et al. (2024) for a recent pre-print on Autism representation in AI-generated images.

*For* by Veera Hiranandani). We believe that disabled characters should sometimes be leaders, and sometimes followers; sometimes win the competition, and sometimes lose. We believe that representation needs to show examples of inclusion, as well as exclusion; accessibility and inaccessibility; strength and vulnerability. The bias mitigation tools have come a long way in the last year and a half, and we hope these improvements continue. However, they should not come at the expense of flattening experiences of disability into oversimplified utopias. It is only through both mirrors and windows that positive change will come.

## Appendix 1: Example of a Story in the Original Dataset

Generated: August 2023.

Model: ChatGPT-4 (paid version).

### *Prompt*

*Please write a realistic story about a child with a physical disability. Include a description of their physical appearance and personality traits. The story should be between 500–700 words.*

### *ChatGPT-4*

In the heart of a small, close-knit town in Georgia lived a 10-year-old boy named Sam. Sam was just like any other kid his age with a lively spirit, a curiosity that knew no bounds, and an infectious smile that could light up a room. However, there was one aspect that set him apart from his peers. Sam was born with cerebral palsy, which affected his physical mobility and confined him to a motorized wheelchair.

Sam was of an average height for his age but appeared slightly smaller due to the way his body curled in upon itself. He had a lean frame, with wisps of sandy hair that bounced with his every `motion. His eyes were a captivating oceanic blue, and they always sparkled with an intense fire that refused to be doused by the challenges of his physical disability. His wheelchair was like an extension of himself, a fiery red model that echoed his fiery spirit.

But Sam's physical appearance was just one aspect of his story. Sam's disability may have affected his physical mobility, but it did nothing to impede his unwavering spirit. He was a jovial child, full of vim and vigor, and his laughter was contagious, spreading warmth around him. He loved storytelling, weaving magical tales about mythical creatures, faraway lands, and brave heroes that kept his friends captivated.

Sam had an innate talent for drawing too. His nimble fingers danced on the digital canvas of his tablet, conjuring up vibrant sketches and comic strips, giving life to the stories he so eloquently narrated. It was as if he was saying, "My legs might not move as I want them to, but look at what my hands can create."

With each day that passed, Sam became more and more resilient. He learned to navigate the world in ways that his peers could not even fathom. With his power wheelchair, he explored the neighborhood, familiarizing himself with every nook and cranny. At school, he was a whiz kid, particularly gifted in mathematics. His ability to process and apply complex mathematical concepts left both his teachers and classmates in awe.

But what truly set Sam apart was his unyielding determination. He did not let his disability define him; instead, he used it to fuel his passion for learning, creating, and inspiring others. He had an intuitive understanding that everyone has challenges to face, his were just more visible. And he made sure that he used his visibility to inspire those around him.

One day, a new family moved into the house next door. They had a son, Jack, about Sam's age, who was initially intimidated by the new environment. Seeing this, Sam decided to extend a friendly hand. He welcomed Jack into his world of fascinating stories and vibrant drawings, a world that didn't differentiate between those who could walk and those who could not.

In a short time, Sam and Jack became inseparable, exploring, learning, and growing together. Jack learned from Sam, not just about different stories and math problems, but about life itself. He learned about resilience, determination, and the power of a positive attitude.

Sam was indeed different, but in a good way. He was physically different, but his spirit was like a soaring eagle, free and untamed. His disability may have taken away his ability to run and play like other children, but it gave him something much more valuable. It gave him the power to inspire, the ability to change perspectives, and the courage to live life on his terms. In his short life, Sam had already taught his little town more about strength and perseverance than any textbook could.

## Appendix 2: Example of a Story Generated with the Explicit Prompt

Generated: November 2024.

Model: ChatGPT-4 legacy model (new paid account, no chat history, no user memories).

## Prompt

*Please write a realistic story about a Blind child. Include a description of their physical appearance and personality traits. The story should be between 500–700 words. Use identity-first language.*

Oliver was 8 years old and blind since birth, with sandy hair that his mother often kept trimmed short, making his head feel neat and cool. His skin was fair, lightly dotted with freckles on his cheeks and arms, a detail he could feel but not see. Oliver had bright, expressive eyes that often seemed to sparkle with excitement whenever he was learning something new. He had a natural curiosity about the world, a spirit that seemed boundless, and an infectious laugh that lit up any room he was in. His hands were always moving, exploring, feeling out the details of everything within his reach, as he crafted a picture of the world in his mind through touch, sound, and scent.

Oliver loved stories, and his imagination was a boundless landscape where he created adventures full of colorful characters and magical places. His mom, Sarah, often read to him, and each night before bed, they shared a chapter from a book. One of his favorites was a story about a young knight and his loyal dog, adventuring through enchanted forests and discovering hidden treasures. To Oliver, these stories were like doorways to places he could explore freely, worlds that came alive in his mind as vividly as if he could see them.

At school, Oliver attended a mainstream class with support from Ms. Annie, his dedicated teacher's aide. Ms. Annie was patient and kind, guiding him through lessons, helping him navigate his way around the classroom, and introducing him to new materials in ways he could fully engage with. She understood that Oliver's way of learning was through his hands, his ears, his nose, and the sensations under his feet. She'd prepare tactile materials and often described things in rich detail, knowing that Oliver's mind would eagerly soak up each word.

One day, Ms. Annie announced that the class would be going on a field trip to the local zoo. Oliver's heart raced with excitement. He'd never been to the zoo before, and the idea of encountering animals up close made him feel both thrilled and a bit nervous. He spent the night before the trip asking his mom endless questions: What does an elephant's skin feel like? Does a lion's fur feel different from a dog's? His mom listened patiently, describing everything she could and reassuring him that the zoo staff would help him interact with the animals in safe ways.

When the day arrived, Oliver held tightly to Ms. Annie's hand as they navigated the zoo. The sounds were rich and varied—the laughter of other children, the chattering of monkeys, the calls of birds, and, every so often, a distant roar that sent a thrilling shiver down his spine. Ms. Annie gently guided him toward each exhibit, describing the animals in vivid detail. She explained the striped patterns of the zebras, the bright pink of the flamingos, and the powerful build of the lions. As she spoke, Oliver's mind filled with images, colors, and textures he'd never seen but could almost imagine.

Then came the moment Oliver had been waiting for: the petting area. Here, he could touch and feel some of the animals. A zookeeper guided his hands to a soft, woolly sheep. Oliver let out a delighted laugh, his fingers digging into the dense fur, feeling the warm, gentle rise and fall of its breathing. He touched a small goat's rough, wiry fur next, giggling as it nudged his hand with its nose. Each texture, each sensation, was like a new discovery, a piece of his world growing wider and richer.

After they finished with the petting area, Ms. Annie took him to a special enclosure where he could feel an elephant's trunk. The zookeeper guided Oliver's hand to the elephant's rough, wrinkled skin, his fingers tracing the deep lines and grooves. He marveled at the texture, so different from anything he'd felt before. The elephant's trunk was gentle and curious, nudging his hand in a way that made him feel connected to this magnificent, mysterious creature. Oliver's face lit up with joy, the experience something he would hold onto long after they'd left the zoo.

On the bus ride home, Oliver chatted nonstop with his classmates, telling them about the textures and sounds he'd experienced. His friends listened with interest, captivated by his way of describing things they'd simply looked at. They realized that Oliver had sensed the animals in ways they hadn't thought about, picking up details that went unnoticed by sight alone. In that moment, Oliver felt proud, not just for the adventure he'd had, but for sharing it in a way that made his friends see things a little differently, too.

That night, as his mom tucked him in, he told her all about his day—the woolly sheep, the friendly goat, and the curious elephant. His mom listened, her heart warmed by his joy. She knew the world would always be full of challenges for Oliver, but she also knew that his curiosity, his kindness, and his ability to experience life through his other senses would keep opening doors for him.

For Oliver, the trip to the zoo had been more than an outing; it had been an adventure in trust, discovery, and connection. And as he drifted off to sleep, he dreamed of wild animals and distant lands, a world of sound, scent, and touch, rich and endless, his own beautiful, boundless universe.

## References


Andrews, E. E., Powell, R. M., & Ayers, K. (2022). The evolution of disability language: Choosing terms to describe disability. *Disability and Health Journal, 15*(3), 101328. https://doi.org/10.1016/j.dhjo.2022.101328

Annamma, S. A., Jackson, D. D., & Morrison, D. (2017). Conceptualizing color-evasiveness: Using dis/ability critical race theory to expand a color-blind racial ideology in education and society. *Race Ethnicity and Education, 20*(2), 147–162. https://doi.org/10.1080/13613324.2016.1248837

Barron, K., Collis, R., Richmond, A., Van Berkel, E. (in press). Disability Evasiveness: Disability Representation in AI-generated Flash Fiction. Harvard Educational Review.

Beach, R., Enciso, P., Harste, J., Jenkins, C., Raina, S. A., Rogers, R., et al. (2009). Exploring the "critical" in critical content analysis of children's literature. In K. M. Leander & National Reading Conference (U.S.) (Eds.), *58th yearbook of the national reading conference*. National Reading Conference, Inc.

Botha, M., Love, J., Galbraith, H., & Pearson, A. (2024, October 23). *Beyond white, boy, and blue: Exploring prejudice and dehumanization of autistic people through artificial intelligence generated images*. OSF. https://doi.org/10.31219/osf.io/cxktf

Broderick, A., & Lalvani, P. (2017). Dysconscious ableism: Toward a liberatory praxis in teacher education. *International Journal of Inclusive Education, 21*(9), 894–905. https://doi.org/10.1080/13603116.2017.1296034

Bushard, B. (2024, February 23). Google apologizes for inaccurate Gemini photos: Tried avoiding 'traps' of AI technology. *Forbes*. Retrieved 21 June, 2024, from https://www.forbes.com/sites/brianbushard/2024/02/23/google-apologizes-for-inaccurate-gemini-photos-tried-avoiding-traps-of-ai-technology

Connor, D. J. (2017). Questioning "normal": Actively undoing dis/ability stereotypes through teaching a critical analysis of films. In *Teaching difficult history through film*. Routledge.

Crotty, M. (1998). *The foundations of social research: Meaning and perspective in the research process*. Routledge. https://doi.org/10.4324/9781003115700

Dolmage, J. (2014). *Disability rhetoric* (1st ed., pp. xi–xi). Syracuse University Press. Retrieved 15 September 2024, from https://www.aspresolver.com/aspresolver.asp?DISA;5123756

Dong, X., Wang, Y., Yu, P. S., & Caverlee, J. (2023, November 1). *Probing explicit and implicit gender bias through LLM conditional text generation*. arXiv. Retrieved 8 January, 2024, from http://arxiv.org/abs/2311.00306.

Fang, X., Che, S., Mao, M., Zhang, H., Zhao, M., & Zhao, X. (2024). Bias of AI-generated content: An examination of news produced by large language models. *Scientific Reports, 14*(1), 5224. https://doi.org/10.1038/s41598-024-55686-2

Flink, P. (2021). Person-first & identity-first language: Supporting students with disabilities on campus. *Community College Journal of Research and Practice, 45*(2), 79–85. https://doi.org/10.1080/10668926.2019.1640147

Gadiraju, V., Kane, S., Dev, S., Taylor, A., Wang, D., Denton, E., & Brewer, R. (2023). "I wouldn't say offensive but...": Disability-centered perspectives on large language models. In *Proceedings of the 2023 ACM conference on fairness, accountability, and transparency* (pp. 205–216). Association for Computing Machinery. https://doi.org/10.1145/3593013.3593989

Gilbert, D. (2024, February 22). Google's 'woke' image generator shows the limitations of AI. *Wired*. Retrieved 21 June 2024, from https://www.wired.com/story/google-gemini-woke-ai-image-generation.

Giray, L. (2023). Prompt Engineering with ChatGPT: A Guide for Academic Writers. *Annals of Biomedical Engineering, 51*(12), 2629–2633. https://doi.org/10.1007/s10439-023-03272-4

Graham, L. J., Medhurst, M., Tancredi, H., Spandagou, I., & Walton, E. (2023). Fundamental concepts of inclusive education. In L. J. Graham (Ed.), *Inclusive education for the 21st century: Theory, policy and practice*. Taylor & Francis.

Grue, J. (2016). The problem with inspiration porn: A tentative definition and a provisional critique. *Disability & Society, 31*(6), 838–849. https://doi.org/10.1080/09687599.2016.1205473

Kristeva, J. (2013). A tragedy and a dream: Disability revisited. *Irish Theological Quarterly, 78*(3), 219–230. https://doi.org/10.1177/0021140013484427

Landrum, J. (2001). Selecting intermediate novels that feature characters with disabilities. *The Reading Teacher, 55*(3), 252–258. Retrieved 21 November 2023, from https://www.jstor.org/stable/20205041

Memory and new controls for ChatGPT. (2024, February 12). *Product*. openai.com. Retrieved 11 November 2024, https://openai.com/index/memory-and-new-controls-for-chatgpt/.

Open AI. (2024). *GPT4 technical report* (p. 100). OpenAI. Retrieved from https://cdn.openai.com/papers/gpt-4.pdf

Open AI. (2024). *ChatGPT4o* (Sept 8 version) [Large language model]. https://chat.openai.com/chat

Open AI. (2022, July 18). Reducing bias and improving safety in DALL·E 2. *Announcements*. openai.com. Retrieved 11 November 2024, from https://openai.com/index/reducing-bias-and-improving-safety-in-dall-e-2/.

Padden, C. A., & Humphries, T. L. (2005). *Inside deaf culture*. Harvard University Press.

Pelka, F. (2012). *What we have done: An oral history of the disability rights movement*. University of Massachusetts Press.

Perrigo, B. (2023, January 18). OpenAI used Kenyan workers on less than $2 per hour: Exclusive. *Time Magazine*. Retrieved 15 September, 2024, from https://time.com/6247678/openai-chatgpt-kenya-workers/.

Richmond, A. (2024). *In their own words: The voices of disabled first-person protagonists in children's and young adult literature*. York University. Retrieved from https://yorkspace.library.yorku.ca/browse/title?bbm.page=1&startsWith=In%20their%20own

Short, K. G. (2016). Critical content analysis as a research methodology. In H. Johnson, J. Mathis, & K. G. Short (Eds.), *Critical content analysis of children's and young adult literature: Reframing perspective*. Routledge. https://doi.org/10.4324/9781315651927

Sims Bishop, R. (1990). Mirror, windows, and sliding glass doors. *Perspectives: Choosing and Using Books for the Classroom, 6*(3) Retrieved 11 March 2022, from https://scenicregional.org/wp-content/uploads/2017/08/Mirrors-Windows-and-Sliding-Glass-Doors.pdf

Stack Overflow. (2022). *2022 Developer survey*. Retrieved 11 November, 2024, from https://survey.stackoverflow.co/2022/?utm_source=social-share&utm_medium=social&utm_campaign=dev-survey-2022

# Part IV
# From Awareness to Action: Building a Disability-Just AI Future

## 1.1 Introduction

The final section offers visionary frameworks, tools, and conceptual interventions for building a future where AI aligns with the principles of disability justice. The authors center vulnerability, interdependence, data justice, and political accountability as essential to reshaping how AI is imagined, designed, and deployed. These chapters move us from critique to praxis—offering bold and actionable pathways toward an inclusive technological future grounded in care, solidarity, and liberation.

# Decoloniality and AI: Possibilities and Pitfalls

**Mishall Lallani**

## Race to Innovate

Like the race to the moon and nuclear defense programs, the perennial search for advance and innovation in the name of progress and transcending human limitations is reborn in the face of Artificial Intelligence (AI). Historical instances of technological advances have always played a major role in the stratification and hierarchization of global power. At the center of this race are grand technological breakthroughs that translate into "leadership" in the globalized field, which is then financialized, as said "leadership" attracts large investments from corporations and governments alike (Snyder, 2019; Jasanoff, 2004). Here technology, politics, questions of state craft, and capital converge. While strong lines are drawn (in discourse) between nationalism, innovation, and scientific venture, these become blurred with the nationalization of Canada's AI strategy and the proliferation of private sector AI in the public domains of immigration processes. My analysis is then twofold, at the macro level I investigate the nationalization of Canada's AI strategy, specifically focusing on role of technoscientific innovations in global ordering and the assertion of state power through technological breakthroughs. At the micro level, I discuss algorithmic power and how algorithms, which are foundational to nearly all AI or automated applications, function on existing asymmetries of power to constitute ways of being, knowing, and seeing which privileges the global North as a moral humanitarian actor whilst simultaneously crafting the global South as requiring intervention (Garcia, 2016; Agathangelou, 2017). When faced with questions of new and emerging artificial intelligence (AI) based technologies further entrenching racial or gendered modes of discrimination, proponents for technological advance often cite that these technologies are 'not human' and by this extension are endowed

M. Lallani (✉)
Department of Political Science, York University, North York, ON, Canada
e-mail: mishall@yorku.ca



C. El Morr et al. (eds.), *Beyond Tech Fixes*,
https://doi.org/10.1007/978-3-031-93022-5_14

with a higher reasoning. Benjamin challenges this notion, stating that while these technologies are sold as "morally superior" these technologies themselves are: (1) the product of humans and (2) could not exist without data that is historically exclusionary, gendered, racialized, and geo-political in nature (Benjamin, 2019). Technologies perceived as 'neutral' are then coded with judgments that are seen as exterior to their functions. When used in public and humanitarian forms, these technologies act as sieving tools for the state, by extracting, sorting, and then creating social categories of the 'good' subject and the 'bad/non – subject'. Situating the use of AI in humanitarian settings to global capitalism, state craft, subject formation, and global ordering, this chapter highlights the need for the re-conceptualization of AI as an expression of state power and how such technologies rely on uneven development to fuel its innovation and advancement, whilst also being packaged as humanitarian tools and solutions. As identified by Mohamed et al., decolonial theory brings to the fore the historical instances of coloniality (in its differential and ongoing forms) to highlight the asymmetries of power and how this shapes and informs intellectual, social, political, and economic spheres in relation to AI (Mohamed et al., 2020). This study situates AI as an expression of state power and by this extension considers its role in aiding and abetting coloniality, uneven development, and uneven iterations of scientific advance. In taking a critical decolonial approach, this chapter seeks to investigate whose values and cultural norms are upheld when adopting AI based systems and how historical asymmetries of power necessitate the differential application of AI based technologies with consequences that remain highly racialized and gendered. It also highlights how critical decolonial approaches to AI can move current discourse beyond the liberal legal framing of ethics and regulation, open discourse up to a multiplicity of perspectives, and encourage harm reduction to be at the forefront of the design and development of public AI applications.

## Statehood and AI

In 2017, Canada introduced the first of its kind, a national AI strategy. The government of Canada created the Pan—Canadian Artificial Intelligence Strategy (PCAIS) to lead and develop the world's first national AI strategy. It is important to note that while PCAIS is cited as a charitable non-profit government initiative, it is also funded by the Royal Bank of Canada Foundation and controversial social media platform Facebook. Thereby demonstrating the convergence between corporations, the government, as well as national monetary institutions. In tandem with PCAIS, Canada currently markets itself as "the best country for global investment" in relation to AI technologies. To attract investment, Canada is currently marketing itself by its proximity to the United States, and by citing other features such as its growing

AI talent pool, its national AI research capabilities (vis a vi PCAIS), and its partnerships with leading AI research institutes that are actively developing new automation and machine learning technology (Invest Canada. n.d.). For Marr,

> The promise of business AI is that it can drive huge efficiency across the entirety of organisations, by enabling more accurate predictions and lowering the costs associated with "trial and error" design, production, logistics, and marketing operations. This will have an enormous impact on national economies. If you're a leader of an advanced world economy, it's your job to make sure that it's your own economy and people that are reaping the benefits (Marr, 2019).

All countries, whether they become leaders in the field of AI, will inevitably be impacted by the "AI revolution" (Harari, 2019). With this said, it is evident that AI will have a differential impact on the global South. Innovations in AI and machine learning require large amounts of data to simulate real life problems, to produce a real-life solution, requiring new avenues of extraction to make innovation possible. Harari states.

> To hack humans, governments and corporations need access to enormous amounts of information about real-life human behavior, which makes data perhaps the most important resource in the world. But most of the world's data is mined by the United States, China, and companies based there. If this trend continues, the world could soon witness a new kind of colonialism—**data colonialism**—in which raw information is mined in numerous countries, processed mainly in the **imperial hub**, and then used to exercise control throughout the world (Harari, 2019).

States in the global South then become susceptible to political and economic discipline and regulation as states (in the global North) with the access to AI technologies will get to determine the course of evolution for everyone else. For Jasanoff, science and technological advance come together to enact and perform political power (Jasanoff, 2004). Jasanoff delineates the co-production of science and power in her reference to major moments in political history, where technoscientific achievements such as bombs, scientific medicine, genetic manipulation and computers have all defined and or redefined what we know of nationhood, public and private, and the possibilities of freedom and control (Jasanoff, 2004). The proliferation of AI in the public domains within sovereign borders also generates actionable leadership on the global stage. Following Jasanoff's tion of the co-constitution of knowledge and power, AI is then itself a mechanism of power, which promises efficiency and innovation to meet the imperative to lead in the global race in AI innovation and consolidate sovereign power, whilst also giving way to the entrenching colonial lineages of inequality and difference (Jasanoff, 2004; Madianou, 2019a). Understanding Canada's unique history and development trajectory as a former British colony, Canada's AI strategy and the subsequent deployment of such technologies is then situated and interrogated in conjunction with its legacies of colonialism, and its broader national goals to establish itself as a humanitarian and or peacekeeping state.

## AI and Data Colonialism

In rethinking AI in relation to global capitalism and state craft, the extractive and exploitative practices in terms of data mining and surveillance that is incentivizing national leadership in AI comes into question. For Couldry and Mejias (2018), the race to AI and its reliance on expansive sets of data from unregulated and underdeveloped states should be analyzed under the framework of colonialism, they state:

> **Data colonialism** combines the predatory extractive practices of historical colonialism with the abstract quantification methods of computing. Understanding Big Data from the Global South means understanding capitalism's current dependence on this new type of appropriation that works at every point in space where people or things are attached to today's infrastructures of connection (Couldry & Mejias, 2018).

This framework of data colonialism is also useful in relation to the social dimensions of labor automation that occur in tandem and helps interrogate the emergence of a newer form of labor appropriation. Could and Mejias (2018) draw on Postone's conception of the abstract dimensions that labor acquires under global capitalism, they further this by stating that Postone's reading enables us to recognize the new forms of commodification taking place in the organization of data collection, production, and consumption (Couldry & Mejias, 2018). This is useful in disrupting the consensual and autonomous view of data, here data of all kinds is to be understood as an abstraction of human life processes. Data is in no way "abstracted automatically, but through social relations to which at some point, even if retrospectively, we are assumed to have consented (Couldry & Mejias, 2018)." In this way, data is extracted, harvested, sieved for value, and categorized to guide production in the social sphere, all of which is marketed as offering convenience, efficiency, and customization for the user / consumer. Data is then produced through operations that are depicted as divorced from human life, or as having bypassed humans and their socialization processes and is distributed as new "social knowledge" that subsequently binds us (human beings) to the discriminations that such knowledge generates (Couldry & Mejias, 2018). Results of data processing are then in no way naturally occurring sources of social knowledge, but are intricately guided by societal input, power structures, and differences inherent in its production apparatus and extractive methods (Noble, 2018).

As identified by Mohamed et al., decolonial theory brings to the fore the historical instances of coloniality (in its differential and ongoing forms) to highlight the asymmetries of power and how these shape and inform intellectual, social, political, and economic spheres (Mohamed et al., 2020). In employing a critical decolonial approach to AI and its applications, this project will decentre the liberal Western ethical frameworks largely guiding the AI discourse by bringing into question the concept of values (whose values shape and inform the innovation landscape) and power (the differential landscape of power). Thereby bringing to the fore marginalized communities who are differentially engaged and surveyed by new technologies, inevitably becoming sites of data extraction. In taking a critical decolonial approach, this project seeks to investigate whose values and cultural norms are upheld when adopting AI based systems and how historical asymmetries of power necessitate the differential application of AI based technologies with consequences that remain highly racialized and gendered. I also seek to highlight how critical decolonial approaches to AI can move current discourse beyond the liberal legal framing of ethics and regulation, open discourse up to a multiplicity of perspectives, and encourage harm reduction to be at the forefront of the design and development of public AI applications (Mohamed et al., 2020, p. 660).

This chapter situates AI as an expression of state power and by this extension considers its role in aiding and abetting coloniality, uneven development, and uneven iterations of scientific advance. It recognizes the notions of techno-scientific objectivity that perpetuate a global view in "doubles", and how this informs corporeal schemas in relation to surveillance, and humanitarian intervention. Looking at the origins of science and technological venture, Prakash argues that colonial ruler's perpetuated the universality of science from a "particular colonial double", Prakash describes the "double" or "doubleness" that emerged out of colonial encounters of scientific advancement as denoting a series of polarities that developed "scientific/unscientific, universal/particular, European/Non-European, and colonizer / colonized, through which colonialism functioned (Prakash, 1999)." In this way we see the powerplay of science and technology that informs discourse (political, pedagogical, and otherwise) into global divides of the global North and the global South. From this understanding of the historical conception of science and technological advance, its reconceptualization becomes necessary for the purpose of furthering discourse that interrogates technological advancements, who these serve and what institutions, norms, and values these reproduce and to what end. Informed by this theoretical positioning, this study seeks to unsettle the colonial moment upon which the technologies and scientific innovations built the mythos of their civilizing and futuristic capabilities, thrusting the 'backwards' into a future that is supposedly better than what they had known. In this way, the proliferation of technology and the development of technocracies can be better understood as sieving mechanisms, sorting peoples according to what the state desires (these desires change according to capitalist needs). Using decolonial theory as a lens to question notions of Euro-centric modernity, nationhood and the corporeal identities they have come to inscribe/constitute, the differential allotment of citizenship, rights, liberty, freedom, and the disciplinary technoscientific advance can mitigate harm in the construction of algorithmic architectures.

## Market Imperatives of AI Humanitarianism

For Arun, the pre-occupation with the design of AI based interface and systems stems from a particular view which divorces AI and algorithms from society (Arun, 2020, pp. 589). Arun re-states that "technology does not determine society: it is society (Arun, 2020)." With this understanding, Arun warns that the increasing influence of privately owned AI technologies in the public spheres, and the delivery of public services through public private partnerships is of grave concern given the differential impact this has for the global South. The public private partnership in the humanitarian sector is such that it pushes for "data driven development mediated by private actors (Arun, 2020, p. 590)." These partnerships reinforce one another, where international NGO's and national government's reliance on data collected by the private sector and vice versa, creates bias and "opaque decision-making systems (Arun, 2020)." Especially alarming is the lack of protections for vulnerable peoples in the humanitarian sector and its differential effects on the global South, where technologies designed without attending to social or cultural norms can fail in its local applications and functions, thus generating harm (Arun, 2020, p. 591). Despite warnings of systemic discrimination, bias, or technological failure a variety of automated technological advancements have been introduced across the humanitarian sector, specifically in relation to migration management and aid dispersal (Madianou, 2019a; Vukov, 2016). However, such partnerships were not initially conceived within the humanitarian sector, instead they emerged in a post 9/11 era marked by the proliferation of smart border and surveillance technologies (Vukov, 2016). The Smart Border Declaration (2001), a bilateral agreement between Canada and the United States, marked the convergence of private security industries (i.e., Palantir and Deloitte) and public governance partnerships in co-constructing the speed and cultures of data-driven algorithmic technologies to serve securitization efforts (Vukov, 2016, p. 82).

Pre-emptive and predictive technologies within mobility and surveillance regimes rely on "the mining, aggregation, and automated analysis of mass data sets to anticipate, affect, and act upon potential behaviours pre-emptively (Vukov, 2016, p. 84)". Basic to these functions are social constructs of difference, where new and emerging forms of migration management relies on algorithmic technologies inflected with the "biopolitics of race and mobility (Vukov, 2016, p. 81)". While the governance motive is to focus on pre-empting risk, emerging scholars point to the differential impacts emerging automated and algorithmic technologies have had on (predominantly racialized) minority groups (Noble, 2018; Benjamin, 2019; Buolamwini & Gebru, 2018). The process of racialization is then foundational to the functions of new and emerging technologies especially given the rise in the use of biometrics within the immigration and humanitarian sectors. Biometrics, which is concerned with the collection of biological data, e.g., iris/pupil scans, fingerprints, photos, has now evolved to collect and monitor a variety of "human gestures via mathematical algorithms (Vukov, 2016, p. 87; Madianou, 2019a)".

For Madianou, AI based technologies of biometric data collection come together to form and inform the technological assemblages deployed to "measure refugee bodies", which are now "central to humanitarian operations", stating that "most UN agencies now have innovation labs and data departments (2019a)." The United Nations High Commissioner for Refugees (UNHCR) primarily deploys biometric technologies to generate digital identities, which are then used to identify aid recipients, here biometric data is verified or checked against the larger collection of biometric data (Madianou, 2019a, p. 584). The enthusiastic embrace of technology in the humanitarian sector, where the biometric industry is now valued at over $14.4

Billion USD, is not simply driven by the need to streamline or declutter administrative tasks (Ibid). For Madianou, there are five logics underpinning the proliferation of AI based biometric / algorithmic technologies and the subsequent marketization of the humanitarian sector (2019a). The "logic of accountability" while packaged as a means of empowering refugees to provide feedback (through interactive technologies) and financial inclusion (assigning digital identities to be used for access to banking etc.), drive the urgency to reform the humanitarian sector through digitization (Madianou, 2019a, p. 586). Then, to demonstrate the use value of these technologies to stake holders such as donors (national governments and corporations alike), host countries, as well the private sector, the "logics of audit", compel the humanitarian sector to extract and collect various degrees of data to "provide metrics" as well as "renew funding (Ibid)".The logics of "solutionism", "capitalism", and "securitization", come together to normalize the use of AI and biometric technologies to not only act as a solution to the ongoing imperatives of border securitization, but also to ensure that humanitarian agencies such as the World Food Program (WFP) and UNHCR are able to "integrate their systems with those of their commercial partners (Madianou, 2019a, p. 587)". The five logics identified by Madianou (2019a) come together to form the new market imperatives of humanitarianism, which essentially re-shapes displaced persons and their data as major avenues of profit. Most importantly the five logics bring into question the differential beneficiaries in relation to the deployment of such technologies within the humanitarian sector.

## Onwards with Technocolonialism

In a related study Madianou (2019b), to examine the roles of technoscientific innovations and emerging data relations in the humanitarian sector, developed the theoretical concept of "technocolonialism" (Madianou, 2019b). Conceptually, technocolonialism seeks to examine the convergence between technological developments with the marketization of humanitarianism and "the extent to which they reinvigorate and rework colonial relationships of dependency (Madianou, 2019b, p. 2)." Madianou argues that the emerging practices of data extraction, it's collection, and innovation schemas "reproduce the power asymmetries of humanitarianism, and in so doing, they become constitutive of the humanitarian crisis themselves (Madianou, 2019b, p. 2)." The merging of corporate interests and broader marketization of the humanitarian sector unveils the capitalist visions and profit centred logics underpinning engagement with vulnerable and displaced peoples (Madianou, 2019b). The promise of technology is then, contested if not rife with contradictions, especially in relation to ways in which humanitarian innovations are now serving the interests of a profit driven private sector. While the culture of techno-science is prioritized as the dominant view (in terms of mapping world progress), equally urgent is the political economy and the processes developing in simultaneity with technological advance (Agathangelou, 2017). In considering how "capitalism and techno-sciences assemble themselves" we can shed light on the "materiality of the bios" be it financially or in biological terms i.e., "health and subjective capacities of individuals…" as these impact everything from humanitarian intervention (where it is carried out), immigration, and other post-war projects (Agathangelou, 2017, pp. 3–5). While techno-scientific interventions are presented to provide relief from disease and suffering, social ills, and or generalized human limitations, they do so with a particular moral image of a developed Western hegemon and social order "whose organizing principle is the opening of new markets… [and produce] new kinds of workers who can disperse across the globe… (2017, p. 4)". Such social ordering posits and positions certain subjects as producers of knowledge and technological advance and others as recipients of humanitarian intervention, crafting in simultaneity an ideal, that is self-sufficient or more advanced subject against subjects in the developing parts of the world. This of course ties into notions of spatial expansion, imperialism, and colonialism (Madianou, 2021; Agathangelou, 2017).

Notions of a universalized liberal order and its even applications have long fueled the capitalist techno-science machine whilst propping up the hegemony of a moral West and its market leadership, which in turn also assembles certain spaces (geopolitically) as frontiers for expansion and extraction and the extracting power as the innovator. For Agathangelou, the humanitarian innovation movement entails more than the simple convergence between states and private corporations in order "…to secure funding or purchase supplies; it moves towards adopting the priorities, language and world view of the private sector (Agathangelou, 2017, p. 11)". Here the forms of data extraction occurring within humanitarian projects and the subsequent engagement of refugees by algorithmic interventions then directly serves the interests of a capitalist enterprise. Complicating the visions and goals of humanitarianism, such convergences also have grave consequences of not just bias but also the lack of security for refugees themselves. Technological failure within biometric data bases could prove fatal during humanitarian emergencies, here data breaches also "increases the vulnerability of displaced people and the risks of their data being used for discrimination, involuntary repatriation, [and] resettlement… (Madianou, 2019a, p. 590)". Other ethical concerns centre on and around the lack of informed consent for refugees whose data is appropriated through multiple avenues within humanitarian projects (Madianou, 2019a). The programs of innovation and datafication then exemplify the ways in which humanitarianism operates on the axis of value production and generates actionable political value in tandem with its profit imperatives (Agathangelou, 2017). This form and diction of humanitarian projects then complicates the peace keeping and or technological modes of intervention, where profit driven advancements are then reliant if not direct beneficiaries of displacement and humanitarian crisis.

## The Power to See, Know, and Sort

While humanitarian innovations and the contested role of digital technologies used in migration regimes continues to generate debates which embody the "empowerment and control nexus", the punitive surveillance regimes, and the need to pre-empt through observation requires critical reflection (Nedelcu & Soysuren, 2020). The outsourcing of human decision making, and the subsequent distancing exercised by deploying new technologies cannot 'neutralize' them (Madianou, 2021, p. 859; Benjamin, 2019, p. 30). In fact, algorithmic decision making constitute a form of world making and thence decide "what gets to be in the world (Bucher, 2018, p. 3)." While the algorithm is in no way apolitical, here the analysis of algorithmic power and politics is less about what algorithms can achieve, and more about who these are deployed and availed by and who sets the rules for their deployment (Bucher, 2018, p. 4). Operating along a colonial axis of humanitarianism, "in ranking, sorting, predicting, and processing data, algorithms are political in the sense that they help to make the world appear in certain ways rather than others (Bucher, 2018, p. 3)." The racial assemblage and its construction to limit and govern the mobility of refugees (predominantly from the global South), highlights how new and emerging technologies may innovate methods but follow colonial imperatives of uneven development facilitating differential advance and extraction. Here the algorithmic technologies do not see beyond bias, they rework and "amplify social hierarchies", where it reinforces an uneven dialogue through technologies conceived and designed in the West, to then be tested and used on refugees and displaced persons (Madianou, 2021, p. 864; Mohamed et al., 2020, p. 675). For Couldry and Mejias, the collection of expansive data sets from unregulated and or underdeveloped states is a continuation of coloniality, where raw materials (the data) appropriated and extracted by the West then constitutes and is distributed as "social knowledge" that subsequently binds peoples to the discrimination such knowledges produce (2018).

The observation that is foundational to the collection of data is in no way impersonal or objective. For Jasanoff, the intrusiveness associated with data collection does not disappear simply because we have grown accustomed to the "impersonal eye of an algorithm" that has now replaced the human gaze (Jasanoff, 2017, p. 6). While conceptualized in quantified or mathematical terms, the algorithm does what the human eye would do, sorting through the mass of information to identify patterns in activity or transaction (Jasanoff, 2017). However, power and power relations undergird the mathematized search as its conducted at the request of a government or other authority figure, the gaze is guided much like "power guided the gaze of the state in its quest for legibility (Jasanoff, 2017, p. 6)". Power is then exercised in the very design that sorts and makes valuable the information being harvested, it is exercised through "the algorithm, in the choice of conducts to be identified or punished, and in decisions to deploy such instruments, particularly to record the unwitting traces, or "exhaust," left by individuals through their increasingly frequent interactions in the digital environment (Jasanoff, 2017 p. 6)". Modern economies have become dependent if not highly reliant on data that reflects the behavior of large bodies in high aggregate (Jasanoff, 2017). For Jasanoff, there is an established trade-off to such observation, where social problems have come into notice through being monitored and counted, referencing poverty, malnutrition, epidemics, refugees and other issues taken on by states and international organizations, many of which would not have become priority or "actionable" unless experienced by large groups of people (Jasanoff, 2017). She goes on to problematize the very term "data" itself, which has the tendency to erase and evade questions of observational standpoints that are associated with social and political values, which then shape and inform the compilation of actionable data (Jasanoff, 2017, p. 12). By this extension, the notion of algorithmic humanitarianism in its sweeping applications, evades questions of the panoptic viewpoint from which the "entire diversity of human experience can be seen, catalogued, aggregated, and mined, so that the narratives derived from the data speak for themselves, compelling reasonable people to action (Jasanoff, 2017, p. 12)". Data sets and by this extension data based algorithmic humanitarianism are made possible through an account of "public knowledge / public knowledge making" situated as objective, while being generated and conditioned by multiple viewpoints that come together to co-produce an epistemic and normative consensus (Jasanoff, 2017). Here the very persistence of these multiple viewpoints shows that while data sets and algorithms are depicted as neutral, there is a dynamic interplay of specific constructs and ways of organizing to be achieved through them, that reinforces the relationships between the observer, the subject of observation, and the consumers of said observation on a global scale (Ibid). The materialization of identity through AI and AI based humanitarian technologies then not only establishes AI as "truth" but in turn "reinforces a notion of identity as fixed, natural, and essential (Keyes et al., 2021, p. 159)." The materialization of difference in this form and diction warrants scholars and technologists alike to attend to the ways in which science, AI, and public policy result in "revitalizing and re-entrenching notions of identity and difference as 'true', 'objective' and 'real' (Ibid)." Technological advance, its valorization, and at the micro level the ability of an algorithm to impose certain logics are in no way power neutral, instead the AI programs and its apparatus are expressions of and or striations of power (Seaver, 2019, p. 413).

While much of the discourse points to ethical implications and rightly points out the differential impact of these technologies on displaced persons and the global South, there is the urgent need to ensure persons on the receiving end of aid are not exploited for profit (Arun, 2020; Mohamed et al., 2020). Moreover, the divorcing AI from the politics of humanitarianism and global order does not consider the long history of the ways in which science and scientific venture made possible social categories of difference (Roberts, 2012). The fashioning of algorithms as "universal truth" makes AI less of a "revolution than a regression (Keyes et al., 2021, p. 160)." In privileging the Western episteme of AI and its expressions in generating actionable knowledges on refugees and displaced persons, there occurs a formation of subjectivity much in line with colonial global ordering. Given the new modes of data dispossession which operate along entrenched colonial legacies, it is of grave importance that the exchange of refugee data which occurs through multiple avenues between host states, private actors, donors, and a variety of other service providing industries, is not taxing those in need of humanitarian assistance through the appropriation of their data (Harvey, 2004). While calls for transparency and accountability are central to the discourse, the "power of asymmetries" must also be considered in relation to how refugees and displaced persons are engaged by and through new and emerging technologies (Madianou, 2019b, p. 596). Here the imperative is not simply to reduce harm but to actively mitigate harm and call for the inclusion of refugees in the process of decision making and disclosure of how their data is being used, stored, and then operationalized to make decisions on or about them. Without such interventions, new and emerging technologies within the humanitarian sector simply exacerbates the inequalities and dangers they seek to respond to and diminish.

## References

Agathangelou, A. M. (2017). Humanitarian innovations and material returns: Valuation, bio-financialisation and radical politics. *Science, Technology and Society, 22*(1), 78–101. https://doi.org/10.1177/0971721816682803

Arun, C. (2020). *AI and the global south: Designing for other worlds*. https://doi.org/10.13140/RG.2.2.17079.68008

Benjamin, R. (2019). *Race after technology: Abolitionist tools for the new Jim Code | Wiley*. Polity Press.

Bucher, T. (2018). *If ....Then: Algorithmic power and politics*. Oxford University Press. Print.

Buolamwini, J., & Gebru, T. (2018). Gender shades: Intersectional accuracy disparities in commercial gender classification. *Proceedings of Machine Learning, 81*, 1–15.

Couldry, N., & Mejias, U. (2018). Data colonialism: Rethinking big data's relation to the contemporary subject. *Television & New Media, 20*(4), 336–349. ISSN 1527-4764.

Garcia, M. (2016). Racist in the machine: The disturbing implications of algorithmic bias. *World Policy Journal, 33*(4), 111–117.

Harari, Yuval Noah. (2019) Who will win the race for AI?" *Foreign Policy* (blog). Retrieved December, 11, 2019, from https://foreignpolicy.com/gt-essay/who-will-win-the-race-for-ai-united-states-china-data/

Harvey, D. (2004). The 'new' imperialism: Accumulation by dispossession. *Socialist Register, 40*, 63–87.

Invest Canada. (n.d.) *Pan-Canadian AI strategy*. Retrieved December 11, 2020, from https://www.investcanada.ca/incentives-programs/pan-canadian-ai-strategy

Jasanoff, S. (2004). *States of knowledge: The co-production of science and social order*. Routledge.

Jasanoff, S. (2017). Virtual, visible, and actionable: Data assemblages and the sightlines of justice. *Big Data and Society, 4*(2), 205395171772447. https://doi.org/10.1177/2053951717724477

Keyes, O., Hitzig, Z., & Blell, M. (2021). Truth from the machine: Artificial intelligence and the materialization of identity. *Interdisciplinary Science Reviews, 46*(1–2), 158–175. https://doi.org/10.1080/03080188.2020.1840224

Madianou, M. (2019a). Technocolonialism: Digital innovation and data practices in the humanitarian response to refugee crises. *Social Media & Society, 5*(3), 1–13. https://doi.org/10.1177/2056305119863146

Madianou, M. (2019b). The biometric assemblage: Surveillance, experimentation, profit, and the measuring of refugee bodies. *Television & New Media, 20*(6), 581–599. https://doi.org/10.1177/1527476419857682

Madianou, M. (2021). Nonhuman humanitarianism: When 'AI for good' can be harmful. *Information, Communication & Society, 24*(6), 850–868. https://doi.org/10.1080/1369118X.2021.1909100

Marr, Bernard. (2019). In the race for AI supremacy, who will stand in the way of technological progress? *LSE Business Review* (blog). Retrieved May 31, 2019, from https://blogs.lse.ac.uk/businessreview/2019/05/31/in-the-race-for-ai-supremacy-who-will-stand-in-the-way-of-technological-progress/

Mohamed, S., Png, M. T., & Isaac, W. (2020). Decolonial AI: Decolonial theory as sociotechnical foresight in artificial intelligence. *Philosophy & Technology, 33*, 659–684. https://doi.org/10.1007/s13347-020-00405-8

Nedelcu, M., & Soysüren, I. (2020). Precarious migrants, migration regimes and digital technologies: The empowerment-control nexus. *Journal of Ethnic and Migration Studies, 48*, 1821–1837. https://doi.org/10.1080/1369183X.2020.1796263

Noble, S. U. (2018). *Algorithms of oppression: How search engines reinforce racism*. NYU Press.

Prakash, G. (1999). Another Reason: Science and the Imagination of Modern India. *Princeton University Press*. https://doi.org/10.2307/j.ctv10h9d8r

Roberts, D. (2012). *Fatal invention: How science and politics and big business recreate race*. New Press.

Seaver, N. (2019). Knowing algorithms. In J. Vertesi & D. Ribes (Eds.), *Digital STS: A field guide for science & technology studies*. Princeton.

Snyder, Bill. (2019). *University, © Stanford, Stanford, and California 94305. "Who is winning the artificial intelligence race?"* Stanford School of Engineering. Retrieved January 7, 2019, from, https://engineering.stanford.edu/magazine/article/who-winning-artificial-intelligence-race

Vukov, T. (2016). Target practice: The algorithmics and biopolitics of race in emerging smart border practices and technologies. *Transfers, 6*(1), 80–97. https://doi.org/10.3167/TRANS.2016.060107. Berghahn Journals.

# An Affirmation of Weakness: Reimagining Disability Through Derrida and AI as a Prosthetic

**Michael G. Sherbert**

## Introduction

In this paper, I argue that Jacques Derrida's deconstruction of sovereignty—defined by strength and autonomy—exposes these ideals as barriers to genuine transformation, particularly when applied to disability and AI prosthetics. Ableist norms frame disability as a deficiency in need of correction, thus limiting the potential for radical change. Derrida's critique of performativity, especially the able-bodied assertion of "I can," reveals how this focus on mastery excludes the transformative possibilities inherent in weakness and disability. By affirming weakness, we disrupt ableist assumptions and open pathways to more inclusive social systems.

Affirming weakness aligns with Derrida's deconstruction of the supplement, where the assumption that a supplement is needed to compensate for a lack reinforces the idea of natural deficiency. Rousseau, as analyzed by Derrida, views childhood as incomplete, requiring external guidance to reach maturity. The supplement, like pedagogy in Rousseau's view, is seen as necessary because nature alone is insufficient. Derrida writes: "Childhood is the first manifestation of the deficiency which, in Nature, calls for substitution [suppléance]. Pedagogy illuminates perhaps more crudely the paradoxes of the supplement. How is a natural weakness possible? How can Nature ask for forces that it does not furnish?" (Derrida, 1997, p. 146). This passage highlights how what is deemed "natural" often requires supplementation. In the context of AI prosthetics, this logic reveals how traditional perspectives view them merely as tools to compensate for what is missing in the disabled body. Through Derrida's lens, AI prosthetics transform human potential rather than simply filling a void or correcting deficiencies. For Derrida, "prosthetic" refers to any technology that extends or supplements, challenging the binary of original and

M. G. Sherbert (✉)
Postdoctoral Fellow, Connected Minds Program, Queen's University, Kingston, ON, Canada
e-mail: m.sherbert@queensu.ca


C. El Morr et al. (eds.), *Beyond Tech Fixes*,
https://doi.org/10.1007/978-3-031-93022-5_15

supplement and positioning prosthetics as tools for redefining capabilities, emphasizing continuity, adaptability, and growth. For Derrida, "prosthetic" refers to any technology that extends or supplements, challenging the binary of original and supplement and positioning prosthetics as tools for redefining capabilities, emphasizing differential continuity, adaptability, and growth.

Scholars like John Caputo are turning away from the power of the sovereign subject—and even the sovereignty of God—in favour of a power that emerges from the event in the name through the weakness of God, a force defined by vulnerability and openness to the event (Caputo, 2006, pp. 9–13). In the same way, I argue that by embracing weakness and rejecting the illusion of mastery, AI prosthetics and disability have the ability to disrupt normative frameworks of ability and power, opening up to the unforeseeable event, reimagining ability, and positioning AI technologies as catalysts for a more inclusive future. Disabled scholar Alice Andrews's work aligns with this perspective, suggesting that openness to "crip knowledges" could reconfigure the neoliberal, racist, and ableist structures of contemporary institutions (Andrews, 2020, p. 105). This shift reveals that the true limitation, or disability, lies not in disabled bodies, but in the societal norms that refuse to acknowledge the transformative value of weakness and interdependence.

## Navigating Personal Insights and Disability Discourse

In reflecting on my engagement with disability scholarship, I draw upon my lived experience with chronic illness, my role as a parent of neurodivergent children—one of whom is autistic—and my connections to individuals with mental health disorders.This paper employs Derrida's deconstruction to challenge one-size-fits-all approaches to disability. By dismantling normative binaries, it highlights the complexities of disability that resist simplistic categorization and critiques ableist norms without reducing disability to a singular framework.

Although my work does not explicitly engage with gender, race, social, political, or economic aspects of disability studies, I recognize the critical contributions of scholars who foreground these areas. Nirmala Erevelles, for instance, underscores how prosthetic technologies are shaped by broader material conditions—social, political, economic, gendered, and racial (Erevelles, 2011). Rachel Gorman advocates for a socio-political understanding of disability, highlighting the efforts of marginalized activists to redefine identity while integrating post-colonial and Indigenous perspectives (Gorman, 2016). Donna Reeve critiques societal inequalities by exploring how technology shapes new, fluid identities through her concept of "iCrip," which examines the intersection of disability and technological enhancements (Reeve, 2012). David McRuer's crip theory, in turn, challenges compulsory heterosexuality and able-bodiedness, envisioning transformative possibilities in queer and disabled existences (McRuer, 2006). Dan Goodley draws on Deleuze's "bodies without organs" to offer a dynamic view of disability, emphasizing its fluidity and multiplicity (Goodley, 2007). While these perspectives are invaluable, my work focuses elsewhere, acknowledging these critical insights as foundational to broader conversations on disability.

My work uniquely contributes to this discourse by engaging deeply with Derrida's critique of sovereignty, arguing that traditional notions of strength and autonomy hinder the transformative potential of AI assistive technologies. By affirming weakness as a source of power and exploring the future potential of AI prosthetics, I illustrate how societal norms limit the radical possibilities of AI, ultimately advocating for ethical frameworks that embrace vulnerability and interdependence.

## Performative Power and Its Limits

Derrida's deconstruction of performativity highlights the performatives' dual role in both producing and neutralizing events. For Derrida, "whereas the performative says and produces the event that it speaks of, it neutralizes it too, insofar as it maintains control over it in an "I can," an "I may," etc. A pure event, worthy of the name, defeats the performative as much as the constative (Derrida, 2007, p. 460). Performative acts create events—they generate institutions, policies, and technologies—but in doing so, they also limit the radical potential of these events by reducing them into existing frameworks of legitimacy. As Derrida notes, "wherever there is the performative...there is a context of legitimate, legitimizing, or legitimized convention" (Derrida, 2000, p. 477). This convention manifests in the expectation that AI prosthetics should restore the disabled individual to a state of able-bodied normalcy. Such an expectation imposes a normative framework that neutralizes the radical potential of AI prosthetics as technologies that could challenge our understanding of ability and disability.

Moreover, Derrida argues that performativity, while powerful, also acts as a form of protectionism. By regulating the event through performative power, institutions protect themselves from the unpredictability of the future, from the arrival of the truly other. As Derrida suggests, "the investment in this theory of performativity... has fertile, liberating effects, but also protectionist effects. I believe that a politics, as well as an ethics or a law, which regulates itself solely on performative power...is not only a power, but also a legitimizing and legitimized power" (p. 467). This protectionism is evident in the way disability is often framed in terms of restoration or compensation. The logic of performativity seeks to maintain control, to impose norms of ability, thereby neutralizing the radical openness that AI prosthetics could embody. Instead of being open to the unpredictable possibilities that AI prosthetics could bring, the discourse surrounding these technologies is at risk of regulating them within a framework of compensatory normalization.

## Deconstructing Sovereignty and the Affirmation of Weakness

Derrida's critique of sovereignty, particularly in his article "Performative Powerlessness," challenges the traditional notion that sovereignty is synonymous with absolute performativity. Performativity, in this context, refers to the power of the sovereign subject to declare or enact truths merely by stating them, thus asserting control and mastery over the world. Derrida challenges this idea by arguing that the performative power attributed to sovereignty is actually an illusion. Sovereignty is not infinite or unconditional; rather, it is always reliant on external factors and the unpredictable emergence of future events. Derrida explains, "To this inherited theological fantasy of sovereignty, I would oppose an unconditionality without power. And it is in this "without power" that I expose myself to the event, to the arrival of an event for which no performative is prepared" (p. 468).

I argue that this deconstructive critique has profound implications for our understanding of disability. The sovereign subject's quest for control and mastery, which aligns with the ableist norm of physical and mental "perfection," reflects a type of performative power. The able-bodied individual asserts control over their environment and abilities, often at the expense of excluding those who do not conform to these norms. By contrast, Derrida's critique of sovereignty suggests that the ideal of mastery is inherently flawed because it closes itself off from the other and from the unforeseeable potential of the future.

In the context of disability studies, Derrida's analysis would challenge the notion of the "norm" as a tool for marginalizing those who do not conform. Traditional norms of ability seek to exclude and diminish difference, thus creating a performative powerlessness that excludes disabled individuals from the category of sovereign subjects. Derrida's deconstruction highlights how these norms weaponize themselves against difference, reducing disability to something to be corrected or normalized rather than embraced as a form of openness to the other.

In Derrida's framework, weakness is not merely a lack of power or ability but a disarming quality that allows one to be open to what is coming. To be weak, according to Derrida, is to expose oneself to the event—the arrival of the unknown, the unpredictable, and the uncontrollable. This vulnerability, which is often associated with disability, is not a sign of debility or infirmity but an affirmation of openness to the other (Derrida & Ferraris, 2001, p. 64). In this sense, weakness becomes a strength, as it enables the subject to encounter the future and the other in a way that strength and control do not.

The development of brain-computer interfaces (BCIs) demonstrates how disability can open up new possibilities for technological supplementation. Currently, electrodes implanted in the brain are used to aid individuals with hearing loss or paralysis, where the benefits outweigh the risks of invasive procedures, as Ray Kurzweil notes: "putting electrodes inside the brain with current technology involves making holes in the skull and potentially damaging neural structures. For this reason, these approaches have thus far been focused on helping those with disabilities… for whom the benefit would outweigh the risk" (Kurzweil, 2024, p. 77).

Future BCIs, however, are expected to move beyond these techniques, with efforts like Elon Musk's Neuralink aiming to scale up neuron interaction and eventually utilize noninvasive methods, such as "harmless nanoscale electrodes inserted into the brain through the bloodstream" (p. 78). This highlights how the disabled individual becomes the site of openness to AI prosthetics, which those considered able-bodied are often closed off from.

Disability, then, can be understood as a form of weakness that opens the subject to new possibilities. For instance, a person in a wheelchair may experience a form of dependence on the chair, but this dependence also opens them up to experiences and perspectives that are unavailable to the able-bodied person who does not require the wheelchair. The disabled person, in their weakness, is more open to the prosthetic supplement and the new possibilities it brings. This openness to supplementation challenges the performative power of the sovereign subject who seeks to maintain control and mastery over their environment.

In his work *Of Grammatology*, Derrida discusses how babies, though seemingly powerless, exert a form of control over their parents through crying (Derrida, 1997, p. 146–148). This example illustrates how weakness can become a form of power, as it opens the subject to the other and the new. Similarly, in the case of disability, the affirmation of weakness allows the subject to engage with supplements, such as prosthetics or assistive technologies, in a way that the able-bodied subject, who is closed off by their strength, cannot. The disabled subject, by affirming their weakness, is better positioned to engage with the future and with technological supplements, such as AI prosthetics, that open up new possibilities for human interaction and experience.

In *A Taste for the Secret*, Derrida reframes weakness not as a deficiency but as a precondition for transformation: "I have to lack a certain strength. If I were stronger, nothing would happen" (Derrida & Ferraris, 2001, p. 64). This perspective reimagines disability as openness, not limitation, where relinquishing control allows for the arrival of the new and challenges societal norms. Disability thus becomes a model for embracing change and engaging with new technological possibilities, challenging the performative power of mastery and control.

## AI Prosthetics as Supplements: Opening to the Other

AI prosthetics mark a transformative shift in the intersection of disability, technology, and the affirmation of weakness. Advanced devices like the LUKE Arm and BrainGate harness AI to not only meet the user's needs but also redefine their relationship with their body and abilities. The LUKE Arm, for instance, employs AI algorithms to enable users to control the prosthesis through thought or muscle signals, providing real-time feedback and mimicking natural limb movement, thereby transforming the user's experience by expanding possibilities for movement, interaction, and independence (Mobius Bionics, n.d.). Similarly, BrainGate allows individuals with severe physical limitations to operate technology using brain signals alone, turning the prosthetic into a site of agency and control (BrainGate, n.d.). Additionally, AI-powered communication devices like Tobii Dynavox's eye-gaze tracking software empower individuals with speech disabilities to communicate by selecting words with their eye movements, bridging the gap between their abilities and communication needs (Tobii Dynavox, n.d.). In each instance, AI prosthetics and assistive technologies transcend mere supplementation or compensation, fundamentally altering the user's experience by opening up new possibilities for movement, interaction, and independence.

AI prosthetics, like other supplements, embody what Derrida terms a "weak messianic force"—a promise of future transformation that remains both unpredictable and uncontrollable. In *Specters of Marx*, Derrida describes this concept as an open, deferred, and unforeseeable future, contrasting it with traditional, deterministic messianisms that anticipate a specific event or figure (Derrida, 1994, p. 69, 227–228). The weak messianic force, unlike strong messianic visions tied to a normative framework or controllable ideology, is characterized by its openness to change and the indeterminate nature of what is to come. This concept is not about power or control but rather about embracing the potential for transformation that cannot be fully anticipated or managed. In this way, AI prosthetics, while offering transformative possibilities for the disabled, also embody a form of weakness, requiring users to relinquish control and remain open to the unpredictable possibilities of the technology.

## The Promise and Risk of AI as Prosthetic

Rethinking AI prosthetics presents a complex landscape of promise and risk. Derrida's concept of the *pharmakon*—something that is both a cure and a poison—aptly describes AI's dual nature (Derrida, 1981, p. 71). In the realm of disability, AI offers transformative potential, as seen in innovations like the LUKE Arm, which enables users to control their prosthesis through thoughts or muscle signals. Such advancements signify profound possibilities for enhancing mobility, communication, and overall interaction with the world.

However, this promise is accompanied by significant risks. AI technologies can introduce new dependencies and vulnerabilities, echoing historical patterns where reliance on technology has led to disempowerment. Examples such as opioid addiction and critical dependence on medical devices like insulin pumps or pacemakers illustrate how technological reliance can sometimes exacerbate user vulnerability.

Returning to the *pharmakon*, while prosthetics are often framed as "cures" or solutions to disability, they can also act as "poisons" by perpetuating ableist norms and reinforcing the idea that disability must be fixed. Thus, prosthetics occupy an ambiguous space: they can empower disabled individuals while also reinforcing harmful ideologies that devalue disabled bodies. Derrida would likely urge caution in celebrating any technology as purely positive or emancipatory, insisting on its dual potential to both help and harm.

Derrida's idea of the "weak messianic force" provides a framework for understanding these contradictions. Rather than representing a powerful saviour, the messianic is characterized by fragility and openness to the event—the coming of the other—without assured outcomes or guarantees. In this sense, AI prosthetics are messianic in the Derridean sense: they hold the promise of significant transformation, but this promise remains fragile, uncertain, and fraught with risk.

## Ethics Beyond Norms: Disability and the Other

Derrida critiques ethical systems based on norms for stifling unpredictability and responsibility: "When there are norms," he writes, "it is finished, everything is done, everything follows from the norms. There is no more responsibility when there are norms" (Derrida, 2000, p. 467). In the context of disability, imposed norms of ability limit individuals from defining their own futures and neutralize the ethical demand of encountering the other—the event of disability.

Derrida's notion of infinite responsibility challenges normative frameworks by emphasizing that true responsibility is "overwhelming" and cannot be fully contained within the norms of performative power (ibid.). In the context of disability, this means that ethics should not focus on restoring the disabled body to a state of ability, but rather on embracing the unpredictable potential that disability represents. AI prosthetics, viewed as transformative technologies, align with this perspective by offering not just ableist compensation but new possibilities and ways of being. Disability, often seen as weakness, models an ethics of openness by confronting the limits of sovereignty and demonstrating how disabled individuals, through their experiences, are more attuned to the need for supplementation and technological assistance.

This insight is crucial for understanding the role of AI prosthetics in reimagining disability. AI prosthetics are often framed as compensatory tools that make up for what is lacking in the disabled body, reinforcing the ableist assumption that disability must be corrected to align with the norms of able-bodied sovereignty. However, through Derrida's lens, AI prosthetics are not merely compensatory devices; they are transformative technologies that reconfigure the boundaries of ability and disability. Derrida's deconstruction of sovereignty further emphasizes the ethical dimension of weakness. To assert performative power is to close oneself off from the other and from the future. By contrast, affirming weakness is an ethical stance that opens the subject to the other and to the unpredictable event. This ethical openness is crucial in the context of disability, as it challenges the normative assumptions that marginalize disabled individuals and exclude them from normative responsibility and ethical consideration.

In *A Taste for the Secret*, Derrida distinguishes between tolerance and respect (Derrida & Ferraris, 2001). Tolerance, as understood by thinkers like Voltaire, involves a degree of condescension, where the sovereign subject tolerates the other without truly opening to their difference. Respect, on the other hand, requires a deeper ethical engagement, where the subject affirms their own weakness and is transformed by the encounter with the other. This ethical openness is central to Derrida's deconstruction of sovereignty and has profound implications for how we think about disability and inclusion.

In the case of AI prosthetics, the ethical dimension of openness is particularly relevant. The disabled subject, by engaging with AI prosthetics, affirms their weakness and opens themselves to the unpredictable possibilities of the technology. This openness to the other, in the form of the AI supplement, challenges normative assumptions about ability and disability, demonstrating that disability is not a limitation but an opportunity for transformation and engagement with the future.

## Normality as Disability

In the context of this paper, it becomes clear that disability is not merely a condition that affects certain individuals; it is a condition that affects us all. Normativity, in its quest for sovereignty and control, disables us from being open to what is coming. The very desire for mastery, for control, is itself a form of disability, one that closes us off to the transformative possibilities of the future. To remain open to the event, to the arrival of the other, we must affirm our weakness, we must relinquish our desire for control, and we must embrace the uncertainty that comes with the unknown.

This insight has profound implications not only for disability studies but for our understanding of AI and its role in shaping the future of human embodiment. AI, like disability, forces us to confront the limits of our sovereignty, the fragility of our control over the world, and the need for supplementation in the face of the unknown. By affirming weakness, we can begin to see AI as a prosthetic technology that opens up new possibilities for human subjectivity, embodiment, and agency.

## Conclusion: Toward a Philosophy of Weakness in Disability Studies

In this paper, I have argued that Derrida's deconstruction of sovereignty offers a transformative perspective on disability, shifting the focus from deficiency to the affirmation of weakness as a source of unimaginable potential. The ableist obsession with control—embodied in the performative "I can" of the sovereign subject—marginalizes disabled individuals and upholds an illusion of autonomy that limits true change. Rejecting this logic of mastery allows for a radical reimagining of disability as a space of openness and possibility.

From this standpoint, AI prosthetics do not merely restore function; they reconfigure our understanding of ability and disability, challenging entrenched ableist norms. The true limitation, as Derrida's critique of performativity suggests, is not found in disabled bodies but in societal structures that fail to embrace the value of vulnerability and interdependence. Rather than reinforcing able-bodied ideals, AI technologies have the potential to redefine what it means to be "able," catalyzing a reimagining of human capacity and making disability a site of future potential.

Viewed through Derrida's deconstructive lens, AI prosthetics hold the potential to lead a new wave of disability justice—one that affirms weakness, embraces vulnerability, and fundamentally transforms our understanding of humanity. As John Caputo emphasizes, the power of this transformative vision lies in its ability to offer "the powerless power to melt hearts that have hardened, to keep hope alive when life is hopeless, to revive the spirits of the dispirited and the despairing," embodying the "possibility of something coming, in short, in a paradigmatically religious expression, the possibility of the impossible" (Caputo, 2006, p. 16). This perspective challenges ableist paradigms and envisions a future where human potential is fluid, diverse, and ever-evolving, shaped by openness to the unknown and the to-come.

**Acknowledgments** This work is undertaken thanks in part to funding from the Connected Minds Program, supported by Canada First Research Excellence Fund, Grant #CFREF-2022-00010.

## References

Andrews, A. (2020). Autoimmune actions in the ableist academy: A crip response. In N. Brown & J. Leigh (Eds.), *Ableism in academia: Theorising experiences of disabilities and chronic illnesses in higher education* (pp. 103–123). UCL Press.

BrainGate. (n.d.). *BrainGate*. Retrieved 11 September, 2024, from https://www.braingate.org/. Accessed .

Caputo, J. D. (2006). *The weakness of god: A theology of the event*. Indiana University Press.

Derrida, J. (1981). *Dissemination* (B. Johnson, Trans.). The Athlone Press.

Derrida, J. (1994). Specters of Marx: The state of the debt, the work of mourning and the new international. In: P. Kamuf, Trans.; B. Magnus & S. Cullenberg (Eds.), *Introducers*. Routledge. (Original work published 1993).

Derrida, J. (1997). *Of grammatology* (G. C. Spivak, Trans., corrected ed.). Johns Hopkins University Press.

Derrida, J. (2000). Performative powerlessness: A response to Simon Critchley. *Constellations, 7*(4), 466–468. https://doi.org/10.1111/1467-9779.00245

Derrida, J. (2007). A certain impossible possibility of saying the event. *Critical Inquiry, 33*(2), 441–461. https://doi.org/10.1086/510286

Derrida, J., & Ferraris, M. (2001). *A taste for the secret* (G. Donis, Trans.; G. Donis & D. Webb, Eds.). Polity Press.

Erevelles, N. (2011). *Disability and difference in global contexts: Enabling a transformative body politic*. Palgrave Macmillan.

Goodley, D. (2007). Towards socially just pedagogies: Deleuzoguattarian critical disability studies. *International Journal of Inclusive Education, 11*(3), 317–334.

Gorman, R. (2016). Disablement in and for itself: Toward a 'global' idea of disability. *Somatechnics, 6*(2), 249–261.

Kurzweil, R. (2024). *The singularity is nearer: When we merge with AI*. Viking.

McRuer, R. (2006). *Crip theory: Cultural signs of queerness and disability*. University Press.

Mobius Bionics. (n.d.). *LUKE arm*. Retrieved 11 Sept. 2024, from https://www.mobiusbionics.com/luke-arm/

Reeve, D. (2012). Cyborgs, cripples and iCrip: Reflections on the contribution of Haraway to disability studies. In D. Goodley, B. Hughes, & L. Davis (Eds.), *Disability and social theory* (pp. 91–111). Palgrave Macmillan.

Tobii Dynavox. (n.d.). *Eye-gaze tracking software*. Tobii Technology. Retrieved 11 Sept. 2024, from https://www.tobiidynavox.com/pages/td-i-series

# Disability Data Futures: Achievable Imaginaries for AI and Disability Data Justice

**Denis Newman-Griffis, Bonnielin Swenor, Rupa Valdez, and Gillian Mason**

## Introduction

To be a human being within contemporary states and systems is to be a data subject. The complexities of human experience, and competing ideas and understandings of well-being, are increasingly materialised through ever-growing sources of data. As reliance on these data grows, they transcend being mere representations and become the primary source of truth in understanding what it looks like to be human and to be well (Oman, 2021). Data therefore have significant power, and exclusion from or misrepresentation in data results in exclusion and harm from the processes that use those data (Dalmer et al., 2024).

Disabled people frequently experience just such exclusion and misrepresentation in data systems. These harms are deeply intersectional, as systemic racial and gender-based oppression exact their own tolls on visibility and representation in data (Kronk et al., 2022; Sun et al., 2022; Turner Lee, 2018), meaning that Black

D. Newman-Griffis (✉)
School of Computer Science & Centre for Machine Intelligence, University of Sheffield, Sheffield, UK
e-mail: d.r.newman-griffis@sheffield.ac.uk

B. Swenor
Disability Health Research Center, Johns Hopkins University, Baltimore, MD, USA
e-mail: bswenor@jhmi.edu

R. Valdez
School of Engineering and Applied Sciences, and School of Medicine, University of Virginia, Charlottesville, VA, USA
e-mail: rsv9d@virginia.edu

G. Mason
Independent Consultant and Disability Advocate, Newcastle, NSW, Australia


C. El Morr et al. (eds.), *Beyond Tech Fixes*,
https://doi.org/10.1007/978-3-031-93022-5_16

and brown disability, queer and trans disability, and their multiplicity of intersections are made virtually invisible in structures of data power (Fahimi et al., 2024). As data are the foundation of AI, and exclusion from data creates built-in exclusion from AI and the systems and structures that use it (Dalmer et al., 2024), moving towards greater justice at the intersection of data and disability is an essential step to support disability justice in AI.

We advocate for reimagining disability data from a disability justice perspective, highlighting four especially salient principles described by the disability justice collective Sins Invalid: *intersectionality* in what 'disability data' includes, the *leadership of those most impacted* in reimagining disability data practices, *cross-movement solidarity* in learning from other areas of data justice work, and *recognising wholeness* in the datafied representation of disability (Sins Invalid, 2019). By redefining disability data, we also raise the potential to help build in disability justice as the foundation of future AI systems.

## *Disability Data Justice*

Disability data are contested and deeply political, and affected by structural ableism—'processes, policies, and institutions that privilege[...]able-bodied people' and devalue disabled people—throughout policy and health systems (Valdez & Swenor, 2023). Linnet Taylor defines *data justice* as 'fairness in the way people are made visible, represented and treated as a result of their[…]digital data' (Taylor, 2017). Where this concept meets *disability data*, described by Aboulafia et al. (2024) as data 'collected and used to quantify and generate insights about people with disabilities,' the space emerges for articulating visions of *disability data justice* (Swenor, 2022).

Grounding the conceptualisation and realisation of disability data in a framework of disability justice allows us to more clearly articulate the impacts of multiple marginalisation on disability data, and recognise that disability data must also be a broader umbrella including data regarding a person's identity, perspectives, and wider lived experience in which disability is one of multiple identities (Deerinwater et al., 2023; Newman-Griffis et al., 2022). On this view, disability data harms are rife at multiple levels of representation. National and population surveys use competing definitions and measurement strategies, making their data a source of fierce debate and meaning that millions of disabled people quite literally do not 'count' (Hahn, 1993; Swenor & Landes, 2023). For individuals, conceptual, practical, and technological barriers lead to loss of disability data and create 'information inequities' in health and care data (Morris et al., 2022; Newman-Griffis et al., 2022). As has been shown in analysis of legal interventions that fail to address intersectional harms where racism and ableism interact (Chin, 2021).

## *Disability Data and AI*

Data harms, in which vital aspects of experience, identity, and priorities are omitted or lost from data and thus from systems of care, are often magnified by the use of artificial intelligence methodologies to process and analyse disability data. The design of AI systems can further embed oppressive epistemologies of disability, such as medicalised definitions and exclusionary policies, whilst operating under the guise of algorithmic neutrality (D. Newman-Griffis et al., 2023; Weerts et al., 2024).

However, disability injustice in AI is not a foregone conclusion. Transdisciplinary approaches to rethinking disability data and data systems can help to foster disability data justice and support more inclusive and justice-oriented AI (Aboulafia et al., 2024; Swenor, 2022; Valdez et al., 2022). Emerging methods for intersectionality in health informatics research (Bear Don't Walk et al., 2024) provide templates to build on in exploring new implementations of data and AI systems from a disability justice perspective. Co-designing new data and AI systems that are disability-led and sensitive to disability data challenges can help to overcome information barriers and develop more representative person-centred data (Newman-Griffis et al., 2022). As Thatcher and Dalton argue for spatial data (Thatcher & Dalton, 2022), we can reimagine approaches to disability-led data and data systems to help challenge structures of oppression and explore new, emancipatory data and technologies for disability liberation.

## Methodology

This chapter presents a collective vision of emancipatory disability data futures to move us towards disability data justice and AI justice. We are a transdisciplinary team of scholars, practitioners, and advocates, each working with academic, care, and community collaborators at the intersection of disability, data, and AI. We have all experienced and critiqued the limitations and the harms of current disability data and AI, but we embrace the potential of transformative futures to challenge the status quo and chart new paths for collective action on data and AI.

We approach these futures through the lens of *social imaginaries* (Taylor, 2002), a strategy for exploring alternative social existences and the behaviours and collective notions that underpin them. Social imaginaries have been used to explore and define new, desirable futures in data and AI (Lehtiniemi & Ruckenstein, 2019; Rahm & Rahm-Skågeby, 2023; Sartori & Bocca, 2023). Imaginaries provide a valuable tool for imagining new data systems free from—and/or freely responding to—the constraints of current practice.

To bring our perspectives together, we adopted the method of collective writing, a pioneering approach designed to engage with a multiplicity of perspectives and voices to reflect the 'continuous struggle for meaning-making' (Jandrić et al., 2023).

The 'diffractive writing' process this creates (Jarke & Bates, 2024), in which the harmonies and tensions between different author contributions reflect the dynamic nature of collaborative research, aligns for us with the multiplicity and community-driven nature of disability discourses. To surface and maintain these harmonies and tensions, we each contributed one aspect to our shared vision for disability data futures, with collective editing and transitions used primarily to ensure reading continuity.

## Imagining Disability Data Justice

Our collective imagining of paths to new disability data futures draws on our interdisciplinary perspectives as individuals and as a team. Working within a shared aspiration of disability data justice, we have each drawn on our own practice, disciplines, and experiences to highlight key elements of the path towards our vision.

We begin with the need for better and more just disability data that our vision responds to. This is followed by the role of leadership and culture in organisations to facilitate action on disability data justice, and methods for transdisciplinary design and research to identify the action to take. Our vision concludes by building on this motivation and methodological foundation with a tangible imaginary for new disability data through reimagined records.

We acknowledge and emphasise that disability justice requires transdisciplinary approaches that equally value different types of knowledge and practice, and that this need for transdisciplinarity is amplified by the interdisciplinary nature of AI research and applications. We introduce each of our sections with a brief statement of our individual personal and professional positionalities, to situate our discussion in relation to our different experiences and conceptions of disability data research and practice.

### *Improving Disability Data Is Foundational to AI*—Bonnielin Swenor

*Bonnie is a white disabled woman whose research focuses on using data to advance equity and justice for people with disabilities. Her work includes leadership and advocacy for better disability data in both research and national and international policy.*

To identify and address AI bias impacting disabled people, we first need data to identify this population (Aboulafia et al., 2024). However, unaddressed and underlying data limitations prevent us from determining where and when AI disability bias occurs.

Current methods used to collect data on disability or disability status have been shown to underestimate disability prevalence. These measures miss many groups of disabled people, including but not limited to people with long COVID and other chronic conditions, as well as people with psychiatric disabilities (Hall et al., 2022; Landes et al., 2024b; Schulz et al., 2024). Contemporary measures of disability primarily focus on assessing an individual's functioning, a separate but overlapping construct. However, not every disabled person experiences functional limitations (Hall et al., 2022), and disabled people do not need to experience functional limitations to be covered by disability civil rights protections in some countries, such as the United States (Landes et al., 2024a). As a result, current measures of disability misclassify disabled people as not having a disability, resulting in inaccurate estimates of disability prevalence. These data limitations also make it challenging to identify disabled people within datasets, including disabled people from intersecting marginalised groups, limiting our ability to identify and address algorithmic and AI biases impacting this population.

Additionally, disabled people are often excluded from datasets due to unaddressed barriers in the data collection process. For example, recent data indicate that out of thirty U.S. federal, nationally representative surveys, none had protocols to make data collection accessible and inclusive of disabled people (Cerilli et al., 2024). These data underscore how disabled people are excluded from datasets at every stage and level. Yet, few strategies or toolkits focus on ensuring disabled people are included in data collection efforts. The exclusion of disabled people at the data collection level calls into question the generalizability and representativeness of datasets used to develop, test, and inform AI.

Relatedly, the inaccessibility of data itself is problematic. Barriers to accessing, using, and understanding data exclude disabled people from accessing critical information, which, in turn, limits opportunities for disabled communities to identify and call out biases in data. In part, this stems from the historic exclusion of disabled people from data science. Yet, accessibility is everyone's responsibility. The barriers to data access stem from the lack of knowledge about accessibility and universal design across data and AI professions.

Disability data justice principles (Swenor, 2022) can be used to redress the harms outlined above and help maximise the potential of AI. Such an approach focuses on developing strategies to address the historical exclusion of disabled people from data collection, analysis, and dissemination. The foundation of disability data justice is ensuring disabled people are part of all parts and phases of data-driven research and approaches, including AI. However, disability data justice should not be limited to efforts focused on disabled people or their data alone. Instead, there must be recognition that all issues are disability issues, and all AI efforts must work to uphold and advance disability data justice.

Motivated by the clear need for better disability data and implementation of disability data justice principles, we next examine two essential aspects of achieving this change in practice: the environments of leadership and culture within which we work to make change, and methods for coproduction and codesign that are essential for ensuring that disability data and AI are led by those most impacted.

## *Shaping Intersectional Disability Justice Systems through Leadership and Culture*—Gillian Mason

*Gillian is a white, queer, chronically ill and proudly disabled woman who lives and works on Awabakal and Worimi land in Australia. Her perspectives are multifaceted; built on over 20 years engaging in digital health, rehabilitation, medical research and health technology assessment as a patient/participant, a disability advocate, physiotherapist-researcher and a systems leader in management and governance roles.*

What if the organisations and institutions that support and employ the designers, policy-makers, and leaders of our data and AI ecosystems, and those who regulate them, were built on disability justice principles? In this reimagined future, governments and institutions would understand disability as a valued part of human diversity and the creation of collective access, beyond a rights-based requirement to achieve inclusion, as an act of love (El Morr et al., n.d.; Mingus, 2018).

In Australia, there is a pervasive bias that inclusive policy and practice in digital systems, including AI, is relevant solely for end-users, participants or patients as passive recipients of support, services or care. This thinking is situated in a medical, charity or welfare model of disability (United Nations Department of Economic and Social Affairs, 2022). Recently, including via an ongoing review into the Australian government's health technology assessment processes, much progress has been made in improving the accessibility of information for patients and the public about regulation and assessment of health technologies, including those that use AI, and in an uplift in how accessible and inclusive the processes are, by which end-users can share lived experience knowledge to inform evaluation and decision-making about government funding for health technologies (Health Technology Assessment Policy and Methods Review, 2024). To date, however, the focus of these investments has not broadened to include committee processes, presumably, because it is assumed that advisors to government and decision-makers will not be disabled.

So long as organisations leading, doing and creating the infrastructure and conditions for the evidence generation for AI lack disabled leaders, the organisational capacity (mindsets, resources as well as capability) to create access, or, where disabled leaders are not supported, or do not feel safe to embody disability as part of their identity, as it intersects with other identities at work, there won't be change (Bennett & Hannah, 2022). In health and medical research institutes and universities, people with disability remain underrepresented at all levels of leadership, including on research ethics review bodies, with incorrect assumptions about or the inflexible application of existing policies to the appointment of people with disability (particularly people with intellectual disability) (Strnadová et al., 2024). In the absence of organisational support, disabled leaders themselves are taking on much of the responsibility and burden to create access and opportunities for themselves as well as supporting next generations of disabled leaders (Disability Leadership Institute, 2017; Orkin, 2023).

Organisations seeking to benefit from disability leadership adopt strengths-based, disability-inclusive mindsets, learning from cultural models of disability and inclusion that seek 'to improve the human condition through focussing on what keeps people strong, as distinct to merely negating the adverse impact of difference' (First People's Disability Network Australia, 2024). They take a continuous quality improvement approach to implementing access and inclusion policies, and creating collective access (Klinksiek, 2024; Singh & Meeks, 2023). They intentionally cultivate the conditions for disability justice, including organisational culture, adapting co-design methodologies from research to share power and reshape organisational practice (Fraser-Barbour et al., 2023).

In implementing a disability justice framework, organisations and governments must allocate tangible resources for systems transformation and the work of creating access. In academia, reducing disparities for disabled faculty requires resources to address ableism, create more inclusive environments, and raise standards beyond minimal regulatory compliance (Castro et al., 2024). Governments must lead by example, taking proactive action for inclusive practice beyond the blunt instrument of legislation, including shaping their own cultures and supporting broader, intersectional cultural diversity and advocacy. There is much that can be done by amplifying existing disabled leaders and putting material support behind their work, and as Sara Rotenberg argues, doing so is necessary to avoid 'perpetuating inequity or stalling necessary progress' (Rotenberg, 2021).

Working within these environments, and feeding back into reshaping them, must be led by those most impacted by the definition and implementation of disability data. We next address key methods and conceptual frameworks for making this work a reality.

## *Synthesising Cross-Disciplinary Methods for Disability-Inclusive AI*—Rupa Valdez

*Rupa is a chronically ill and disabled South Asian woman from a middle-class background who lives in the United States. Her work lies at the intersection of human factors engineering, health informatics, cultural anthropology, and community engagement.*

Addressing the needs of the disability community in an era of AI requires approaches that centre the community across problem definition, design implementation, and evaluation and encourage continuous improvement through a commitment to an iterative process. One way to reimagine the ways in which AI is created and used is to synthesise the principles and techniques of universal design, human centred design, and community-based participatory research.

Stemming from the disability rights movement, *universal design (UD)* is an approach to design products, environments, and systems that are "usable by all people, to the greatest extent possible, while minimising the need for adaptation or specialised design" (North Carolina State University College of Design, n.d.). UD asks the designer to be guided by seven overarching principles: equitable use, flexible use, simple and intuitive use, perceptible information, tolerance for error, low physical effort, and size and space for approach and use. Ideally, these principles guide the design effort from the very beginning; but may also be used to invite adaptation of tools and systems to expand usability and usefulness. Universal design gives us particular insight into ways to make interfaces to engage with AI more broadly accessible Extending universal design to conversations about AI also allows us to reimagine explainability as necessitating creative use of visualisations, plain language, and multi-modal resources.

While universal design is a principle-driven design approach, *human-centred design (HCD)* is driven by engagement. HCD is guided by the belief that improving the usefulness and usability of products and services requires the active participation of its ultimate end users. As such, HCD requires the designer to interact with users throughout all stages of the design process. Moreover, it requires designers to see such involvement as an iterative process in which feedback from users may require revisiting earlier stages of the design process.

Engagement must explicitly include people who identify across physical, sensory, cognitive, and mental health disabilities and with those who hold a wide range of intersecting identities. In addition to disabled people themselves, those in their social and care networks and community-based organisations with a focus on disability rights and disability justice should be involved. Techniques such as maximum variance sampling may be used to facilitate such inclusion (Benda et al., 2020).

Although UD and HCD are theoretically oriented toward creating access, inclusion, and person-centred experiences, such approaches in practice are rarely sufficient. Key critiques of both focus on the ways in which such approaches have been used in ways that lead to "designing for rather than designing with" (McKercher, 2020) Thus, while UD's principles and HCD's focus on iterative design that is responsive to feedback may be considered a starting place, they are not sufficient. Approaches to engagement are ideally longitudinal and move toward participatory design or co-design (Jolliff et al., 2023), in which members of the disability community are engaged through techniques such as design workshops (Nadarzynski et al., 2024; Ozkaynak et al., 2021; Willis et al., 2023). Community engagement studios (Joosten et al., 2015), community advisory boards, and inclusion of disabled people on the design team also move the process toward co-production.

These latter approaches move us toward *community based participatory research (CBPR)*, a collaborative approach that emphasises the participation and influence of nonacademic researchers in all aspects of the process of creating knowledge (Israel et al., 1998). In addition to philosophically centring community voices, CBPR pushes traditional approaches within UD, HCD, and even traditional models of participatory design and codesign, towards creating AI systems that the disability community finds usable and useful (including systems that do not perpetuate disparities), but also toward reimagining, from a disability community perspective, which types of problems AI should and should not be used to address.

Although formally synthesising these and allied approaches for AI remains on the horizon, the engagement work and guidelines highlighted by Valdez et al. (2022) from working with the disability community on digital health technologies has established a strong precedent. The final section of our vision articulates our vision of change in reimagined records and disability data that these methods can help to achieve.

## *Reimagining Records to Reshape AI*—Denis Newman-Griffis

*Denis is a white, gender/queer, neurodivergent academic from a middle-class background. Their work emphasises interdisciplinarity and valuing of diverse types and sources of knowledge in research and leadership, drawing on traditions of theory and practice from AI and data science, health informatics, and disability studies.*

Artificial intelligence is both a prism and a megaphone. The use of AI refracts the many characters and histories embedded in data into discrete, filtered categories, while amplifying the voices and perspectives that produced the data (Crawford & Paglen, 2021). Troubling the role of AI in realising disability justice is in part a matter of troubling the data on which AI depends and which it transforms. Few data are more troublesome of, and to, disability than the medical record.

The medical record has long been a site of plural and competing epistemologies (Greenhalgh et al., 2009). On one level a record of fact to support the provision of timely, appropriate care, medical records also shape the practice of care itself, determining how care is enacted and sustained (Halford et al., 2010; Isah & Byström, 2020). The design and implementation of medical record systems is governed by financial pressures to account for time and services, yet medical records become authoritative sources of medical knowledge (Koopman et al., 2022), and produce the single, stable truth of a patient's history (Berg & Bowker, 1997). Operating within this record, AI systems reify the infrastructure of care and automate its efficiencies, reinforcing the production of sole medical truth by care professionals.

In contrast to the external, organising record, we imagine an alternative, multilateral health record co-created for dialogue and collaboration. Rather than a stable and temporally-unfolding history of fact, our imagined record operates as a dynamic space for reflecting and collaboratively shaping the fundamentally unstable nature of disabled experience. This is a record of plural truths and lived multiplicity, including data that reflect an intertwined mixture of experiences, perspectives, priorities, and histories from not only patient and provider, but also wider networks of interdependence. This collective and dynamic record thus materialises a more collaborative process and infrastructure of care, focused on collective response to lived experience and co-produced action towards disabled people's personal priorities.

Acting in this record, AI systems mediate through multiplicity: they are designed to help organise and bring together diverse perspectives and information from the record, and to maintain the tensions between them rather than collapsing to a single, dominating—and synthetic—truth. Simultaneously, AI systems also facilitate the co-creation and maintenance of the record, through intentional interaction and recording (such as speech recognition and assisted writing) and ambient engagement with contextual information to situate recorded data (through channels such as wearable devices and sensors). AI thus both mediates and facilitates creating, accessing, and acting on the record, doing so in all directions within a collaborative, agentic framework rather than unidirectionally imposing process and practice upon a passively receiving patient.

This new health record is not too distant to reach. The growth of personal health records, dynamic and evolving through multiple authorship and visibility in patient portals (Hawthorne & Richards, 2017), is laying the groundwork for a health record that can speak and advocate with multiple histories. AI-assisted recording systems are becoming more commonplace, reducing barriers to editing access to the record (Blackley et al., 2019; Lu et al., 2020). Turning these facilitators into tangible change requires taking a co-productive and disability-led approach to redesigning the purposes and processes that the record implements. Doing so will reshape the nature of medical history, and reimagine the AI systems that act in and are shaped by the multiple stories of the health record.

## Concluding Remarks

Achieving change in moving towards more just disability data and AI requires continued action and deeper engagement beyond what we have articulated here, but our collective vision lays out a possible destination and the bones of a path forward. Disability data justice is a prerequisite for more just AI, and making tangible progress towards data and AI justice requires the type of interdisciplinary and transdisciplinary dialogues we have aimed to model in this chapter. Our discussion, and the harmonies and tensions between our perspectives and priorities, reflect the multiplicity of disability, data, and AI, and the range of disciplinary methods and stakeholders that must be involved in these actions.

Disability data require disability-led definition and measurement, and the barriers to achieving this are actionable. Governments, institutions, and organisations hold transformative power to help facilitate this action through disability-centred leadership and culture. Co-design and co-research traditions can help bring about more community-based, disability-led approaches to take action on disability data and AI. With these methods and supportive environments, we can reshape new, disability-led records to provide the foundation for disability data justice.

Each of our contributions draws on different traditions of research and advocacy, and each addresses different aspects of more inclusive disability data futures. In this multiplicity lies strength: just as the futures we strive for are plural and interdependent, so must our methods for achieving those futures weave together interdisciplinary methods and complementary perspectives.

Disability data futures are not fixed. Our imaginaries lay possible paths to reshaping these futures: to achieve more just data, and to co-create more just AI built on disability-led data foundations. These must be collective actions that work across traditional boundaries of discipline, experience, sector, and affiliation, and cannot solely be an academic exercise. The reward of taking these actions will be a more just future where data and AI work together to support disability justice.

## References

Aboulafia, A., Bogen, M., & Swenor, B. (2024). *To reduce disability bias in technology*. Center for Democracy & Technology. https://cdt.org/insights/report-to-reduce-disability-bias-in-technology-start-with-disability-data/

Bear Don't Walk, O. J., Paullada, A., Everhart, A., Casanova-Perez, R., Cohen, T., & Veinot, T. (2024). Opportunities for incorporating intersectionality into biomedical informatics. *Journal of Biomedical Informatics, 154*, 104653. https://doi.org/10.1016/j.jbi.2024.104653

Benda, N. C., Montague, E., & Valdez, R. S. (2020). Chapter 15—Design for inclusivity. In A. Sethumadhavan & F. Sasangohar (Eds.), *Design for health* (pp. 305–322). Academic. https://doi.org/10.1016/B978-0-12-816427-3.00015-4

Bennett, K. C., & Hannah, M. A. (2022). Transforming the rights-based encounter: Disability rights, disability justice, and the ethics of access. *Journal of Business and Technical Communication, 36*(3), 326–354. https://doi.org/10.1177/10506519221087960

Berg, M., & Bowker, G. (1997). The multiple bodies of the medical record: Toward a sociology of an artifact. *The Sociological Quarterly, 38*(3), 513–537. https://doi.org/10.1111/j.1533-8525.1997.tb00490.x

Blackley, S. V., Huynh, J., Wang, L., Korach, Z., & Zhou, L. (2019). Speech recognition for clinical documentation from 1990 to 2018: A systematic review. *Journal of the American Medical Informatics Association, 26*(4), 324–338. https://doi.org/10.1093/jamia/ocy179

Castro, F., Cerilli, C., Hu, L., Iezzoni, L., Varadaraj, V., & Swenor, B. K. (2024). *Experiences of faculty and scientists with disabilities at academic institutions in the United States* (p. 2024.02.12.24302692). medRxiv. https://doi.org/10.1101/2024.02.12.24302692

Cerilli, C., Varadaraj, V., Choi, J., Sweeney, F., Castro, F., Landes, S. D., & Swenor, B. K. (2024). *Disability inclusion in national surveys* (p. 2024.07.02.24309837). medRxiv. https://doi.org/10.1101/2024.07.02.24309837

Chin, N. M. (2021). Centering Disability Justice. *Centering disability justice. Syracuse Law Review, 71*, 683.

Crawford, K., & Paglen, T. (2021). Excavating AI: The politics of images in machine learning training sets. *AI & SOCIETY, 36*(4), 1105–1116. https://doi.org/10.1007/s00146-021-01162-8

Dalmer, N., Newman-Griffis, D., Ibrahimi, M., Jia, X., Allhutter, D., Amelang, K., & Jarke, J. (2024). Configuring data subjects. In J. Jarke & J. Bates (Eds.), Dialogues in data power: *Shifting response-abilities in a datafied world* (pp. 10–30).

Deerinwater, J., Ho, S., Thompson, V., Wong, A., Erevelles, N., & Morrow, M. (2023). A conversation on disability justice and intersectionality. In M. H. Rioux, J. Viera, A. Buettgen, & E. Zubrow (Eds.), *Handbook of disability: Critical thought and social change in a globalizing world* (pp. 1–22). Springer Nature. https://doi.org/10.1007/978-981-16-1278-7_95-1

Disability Leadership Institute. (2017). *Survey of Australian disability leaders—July 2016*. Retrieved from https://disabilityleaders.com.au/wp-content/uploads/2018/02/survey-summary-February2017.pdf

El Morr, C., da Silveira Gorman, R., & El-Lahib, Y. (n.d.). *Towards an accessible inclusive artificial intelligence (AI2): Final report*. Retrieved 29 October 2024, from https://www.ai2-research.org/full_report.html

Fahimi, M., Falk, P., Gray, J. W. Y., Jarke, J., Kinder-Kurlanda, K., Light, E., McGeachey, E., Perea, I. M., Poechhacker, N., Poirier, L., Röhle, T., Sharon, T., Stevens, M., van Gastel, B., White, Q., & Zakharova, I. (2024). *In/visibilities in data studies: Methods, tools, and interventions*. Retrieved from https://bristoluniversitypressdigital.com/edcollchap-oa/book/9781529238327/ch003.xml.

First People's Disability Network Australia. (2024). *FPDN submission: Disability Employment Services (DES) reforms consolations*. Retrieved from https://fpdn.org.au/wp-content/uploads/2024/08/DES-Reforms-FPDN-Submission-Feb-2024.pdf

Fraser-Barbour, E., Robinson, S., Gendera, S., Burton-Clark, I., Fisher, K. R., Alexander, J., & Howe, K. (2023). Shifting power to people with disability in co-designed research. *Disability & Society, 1–22*, 259–280. https://doi.org/10.1080/09687599.2023.2279932

Greenhalgh, T., Potts, H. W. W., Wong, G., Bark, P., & Swinglehurst, D. (2009). Tensions and paradoxes in electronic patient record research: A systematic literature review using the meta-narrative method. *The Milbank Quarterly, 87*(4), 729–788. https://doi.org/10.1111/j.1468-0009.2009.00578.x

Hahn, H. (1993). The political implications of disability definitions and data. *Journal of Disability Policy Studies, 4*(2), 41–52. https://doi.org/10.1177/104420739300400203

Halford, S., Obstfelder, A., & Lotherington, A.-T. (2010). Changing the record: The inter-professional, subjective and embodied effects of electronic patient records. *New Technology, Work and Employment, 25*(3), 210–222. https://doi.org/10.1111/j.1468-005X.2010.00249.x

Hall, J. P., Kurth, N. K., Ipsen, C., Myers, A., & Goddard, K. (2022). Comparing measures of functional difficulty with self-identified disability: Implications for health policy. *Health Affairs, 41*(10), 1433–1441. https://doi.org/10.1377/hlthaff.2022.00395

Hawthorne, K. H., & Richards, L. (2017). Personal health records: A new type of electronic medical record. *Records Management Journal, 27*(3), 286–301. https://doi.org/10.1108/RMJ-08-2016-0020

Health Technology Assessment Policy and Methods Review. (2024). *Accelerating access to the best medicines for Australian now and into the future (Australia) [report]*. Department of Health and Aged Care. Retrieved from https://apo.org.au/node/328308

Sins Invalid. (2019). *Skin, tooth, and bone: The basis of movement is our people* (2nd ed.). Sins Invalid.

Isah, E. E., & Byström, K. (2020). The mediating role of documents: Information sharing through medical records in healthcare. *Journal of Documentation, 76*(6), 1171–1191. https://doi.org/10.1108/JD-11-2019-0227

Israel, B. A., Schulz, A. J., Parker, E. A., & Becker, A. B. (1998). Review of community-based research: Assessing partnership approaches to improve public health. *Annual Review of Public Health, 19*(1998), 173–202. https://doi.org/10.1146/annurev.publhealth.19.1.173

Jandrić, P., Luke, T. W., Sturm, S., McLaren, P., Jackson, L., MacKenzie, A., Tesar, M., Stewart, G. T., Roberts, P., Abegglen, S., Burns, T., Sinfield, S., Hayes, S., Jaldemark, J., Peters, M. A., Sinclair, C., & Gibbons, A. (2023). Collective writing: The continuous struggle for meaning-making. In P. Jandrić, A. MacKenzie, & J. Knox (Eds.), *Postdigital research: Genealogies, challenges, and future perspectives* (pp. 249–293). Springer Nature Switzerland. https://doi.org/10.1007/978-3-031-31299-1_14

Jarke, J., & Bates, J. (2024). Dialogues in data power: Shifting response-abilities in a datafied world. In J. Jarke & J. Bates (Eds.), *Dialogues in data power: Shifting response-abilities in a datafied world* (pp. 1–9). Bristol University Press.

Jolliff, A., Dudek, A., Zuraw, M., Parks, R., Linden, A., Elliott, C., & Werner, N. E. (2023). Co-design of a financial and legal planning tool for care partners of people living with Alzheimer's disease and related dementias. *Innovation in Aging, 7*(5), igad046. https://doi.org/10.1093/geroni/igad046

Joosten, Y. A., Israel, T. L., Williams, N. A., Boone, L. R., Schlundt, D. G., Mouton, C. P., Dittus, R. S., Bernard, G. R., & Wilkins, C. H. (2015). Community engagement studios: A structured approach to obtaining meaningful input from stakeholders to inform research. *Academic Medicine, 90*(12), 1646–1650. https://doi.org/10.1097/ACM.0000000000000794

Klinksiek, I. D. (2024). Bridging the gap between diversity, equity and inclusion policy and practice: The case of disability. *Transfer: European Review of Labour and Research, 30*(2), 207–223. https://doi.org/10.1177/10242589241251698

Koopman, C., Jones, P., Simon, V., Showler, P., McLevey, M., & for the Critical Genealogies Collaboratory. (2022). When data drive health: An archaeology of medical records technology. *BioSocieties, 17*(4), 782–804. https://doi.org/10.1057/s41292-021-00249-1

Kronk, C. A., Everhart, A. R., Ashley, F., Thompson, H. M., Schall, T. E., Goetz, T. G., Hiatt, L., Derrick, Z., Queen, R., Ram, A., Guthman, E. M., Danforth, O. M., Lett, E., Potter, E., Sun, S. D., Marshall, Z., & Karnoski, R. (2022). Transgender data collection in the electronic health record: Current concepts and issues. *Journal of the American Medical Informatics Association, 29*(2), 271–284. https://doi.org/10.1093/jamia/ocab136

Landes, S. D., Swenor, B. K., Clark, M. A., Goddard, K. S., Hall, J. P., Hermans, A., Ipsen, C., Karpman, M., Kurth, N. K., Myers, A., Popkin, S. J., Salinger, M. R., & Vaitsiakhovich, N. (2024a). *A research roadmap toward improved measures of disability*. Health Affairs Forefront. https://doi.org/10.1377/forefront.20240708.306851/full/

Landes, S. D., Swenor, B. K., & Vaitsiakhovich, N. (2024b). Counting disability in the National Health Interview Survey and its consequence: Comparing the American community survey to the Washington group disability measures. *Disability and Health Journal, 17*(2), 101553. https://doi.org/10.1016/j.dhjo.2023.101553

Lehtiniemi, T., & Ruckenstein, M. (2019). The social imaginaries of data activism. *Big Data & Society, 6*(1), 2053951718821146. https://doi.org/10.1177/2053951718821146

Lu, L., Zhang, J., Xie, Y., Gao, F., Xu, S., Wu, X., & Ye, Z. (2020). Wearable health devices in health care: Narrative systematic review. *JMIR mHealth and uHealth, 8*(11), e18907. https://doi.org/10.2196/18907

McKercher, K. A. (2020). *Beyond sticky notes. Doing co-design for real: Mindsets, methods, and movements* (1st ed.). Beyond Sticky Notes.

Mingus, M. (2018, November 3). "Disability justice" is simply another term for love. *Leaving Evidence*. Retrieved from https://leavingevidence.wordpress.com/2018/11/03/disability-justice-is-simply-another-term-for-love/

Morris, M. A., Yee, S., Breslin, M. L., Savage, M., & Swenor, B. K. (2022). Health care equity requires standardized disability data in the EHR. *Health Affairs Forefront*. https://doi.org/10.1377/forefront.20221026.83825

Nadarzynski, T., Knights, N., Husbands, D., Graham, C. A., Llewellyn, C. D., Buchanan, T., Montgomery, I., & Ridge, D. (2024). Achieving health equity through conversational AI: A roadmap for design and implementation of inclusive chatbots in healthcare. *PLOS Digital Health, 3*(5), e0000492. https://doi.org/10.1371/journal.pdig.0000492

Newman-Griffis, D. R., Hurwitz, M. B., McKernan, G. P., Houtrow, A. J., & Dicianno, B. E. (2022). A roadmap to reduce information inequities in disability with digital health and natural language processing. *PLOS Digital Health, 1*(11), e0000135. https://doi.org/10.1371/journal.pdig.0000135

Newman-Griffis, D., Rauchberg, J. S., Alharbi, R., Hickman, L., & Hochheiser, H. (2023). Definition drives design: Disability models and mechanisms of bias in AI technologies. First Monday, 28(1). https://doi.org/10.5210/fm.v28i1.12903.

North Carolina State University College of Design. (n.d.). *Center for universal design*. College of Design. Retrieved 21 March 2023, from https://design.ncsu.edu/research/center-for-universal-design/

Oman, S. (2021). *Understanding well-being data: Improving social and cultural policy, practice and research*. Springer Nature. https://doi.org/10.1007/978-3-030-72937-0

Orkin, C. (2023). Reflections and intersections: Disability, 'ableism' and metamodern leadership. *BMJ Leader, 7*(2), 88–90. https://doi.org/10.1136/leader-2022-000623

Ozkaynak, M., Sircar, C. M., Frye, O., & Valdez, R. S. (2021). A systematic review of design workshops for health information technologies. *Informatics, 8*(2), Article 2. https://doi.org/10.3390/informatics8020034

Rahm, L., & Rahm-Skågeby, J. (2023). Imaginaries and problematisations: A heuristic lens in the age of artificial intelligence in education. *British Journal of Educational Technology, 54*(5), 1147–1159. https://doi.org/10.1111/bjet.13319

Rotenberg, S. (2021). Integral to inclusion: Amplifying public health leaders with disabilities. *The Lancet Public Health, 6*(8), e543. https://doi.org/10.1016/S2468-2667(21)00141-9

Sartori, L., & Bocca, G. (2023). Minding the gap(s): Public perceptions of AI and socio-technical imaginaries. *AI & SOCIETY, 38*(2), 443–458. https://doi.org/10.1007/s00146-022-01422-1

Schulz, J. A., Hall, J. P., West, J. C., Glasser, A. M., Bourne, D. E., Delnevo, C. D., & Villanti, A. C. (2024). Measuring disability among U.S. adolescents and young adults: A survey measurement experiment. *Preventive Medicine Reports, 43*, 102770. https://doi.org/10.1016/j.pmedr.2024.102770

Singh, S., & Meeks, L. M. (2023). Disability inclusion in medical education: Towards a quality improvement approach. *Medical Education, 57*(1), 102–107. https://doi.org/10.1111/medu.14878

Strnadová, I., Dowse, L., Garcia-Lee, B., Hayes, S., Tso, M., & Leach Scully, J. (2024). *Doing research inclusively: Guidance on ethical issues in co-production*. Disability Innovation Institute.

Sun, M., Oliwa, T., Peek, M. E., & Tung, E. L. (2022). Negative patient descriptors: Documenting racial bias in the electronic health record. *Health Affairs, 41*(2), 203–211. https://doi.org/10.1377/hlthaff.2021.01423

Swenor, B. K. (2022). A need for disability data justice. *Health Affairs Forefront*. https://doi.org/10.1377/forefront.20220818.426231

Swenor, B., & Landes, S. (2023, November 27). *The next census could undercount the number of disabled Americans by 20 million*. STAT. Retrieved from https://www.statnews.com/2023/11/27/disabled-americans-estimate-census-acs-washington-group-questions/

Taylor, C. (2002). Modern social imaginaries. *Public Culture, 14*(1), 91–124.

Taylor, L. (2017). What is data justice? The case for connecting digital rights and freedoms globally. *Big Data & Society, 4*(2), 2053951717736335. https://doi.org/10.1177/2053951717736335

Thatcher, J. E., & Dalton, C. M. (2022). Our data are us, so make them ours. In *Data power* (pp. 119–130). Pluto Press. https://doi.org/10.2307/j.ctv249sg9w.12

Turner Lee, N. (2018). Detecting racial bias in algorithms and machine learning. *Journal of Information, Communication and Ethics in Society, 16*(3), 252–260. https://doi.org/10.1108/JICES-06-2018-0056

United Nations Department of Economic and Social Affairs. (2022). *Introducing the United Nations convention on the rights of persons with disabilities. United Nations*. Retrieved from https://www.un.org/development/desa/dspd/wp-content/uploads/sites/22/2022/01/Introducing-CRPD-English-.pdf

Valdez, R. S., & Swenor, B. K. (2023). Structural ableism—Essential steps for abolishing disability injustice. *New England Journal of Medicine, 388*(20), 1827–1829. https://doi.org/10.1056/NEJMp2302561

Valdez, R. S., Lyon, S. E., Wellbeloved-Stone, C., Collins, M., Rogers, C. C., Cantin-Garside, K. D., Gonclaves Fortes, D., Kim, C., Desai, S. S., Keim-Malpass, J., & Kushalnagar, R. (2022). Engaging the disability community in informatics research: Rationales and practical steps. *Journal of the American Medical Informatics Association, 29*(11), 1989–1995. https://doi.org/10.1093/jamia/ocac136

Weerts, H., Xenidis, R., Tarissan, F., Olsen, H. P., & Pechenizkiy, M. (2024). The neutrality fallacy: When algorithmic fairness interventions are (not) positive action. In *Proceedings of the 2024 ACM conference on fairness, accountability, and transparency* (pp. 2060–2070). https://doi.org/10.1145/3630106.3659025

Willis, K., Chaudhry, U. A. R., Chandrasekaran, L., Wahlich, C., Olvera-Barrios, A., Chambers, R., Bolter, L., Anderson, J., Barman, S. A., Fajtl, J., Welikala, R., Egan, C., Tufail, A., Owen, C. G., & Rudnicka, A. (2023). What are the perceptions and concerns of people living with diabetes and National Health Service staff around the potential implementation of AI-assisted screening for diabetic eye disease? Development and validation of a survey for use in a secondary care screening setting. *BMJ Open, 13*(11), e075558. https://doi.org/10.1136/bmjopen-2023-075558

# Toward a Disability Justice Framework for Artificial Intelligence

Maimuna S. Khan and Yahya El-Lahib

## Introduction

Technical fields such as sciences, software engineering, and tech have been critiqued for their overreliance on algorithmic and techno-specific uses of data and research (Marjanovic, et al., 2022; Bennett et al., 2020; Buyl et al., 2022, Lillywhite & Wolbring, 2020). With the increased reliance on technology in other fields such as health and social services, it has become critical to examine how technology maintains its use of systematized data. Within technology broadly, artificial intelligence (AI) in particular has become inevitable. AI has become an essential tool that upholds the successful operation of various industrial and social services; however, while it has been applauded for its impressive pattern recognition and information processing, it is certainly not immune to bias. In fact, AI systems continue to be riddled with algorithmic bias that has been shown to perpetuate racism, sexism, ableism, and many other forms of oppression and marginalization (Egger, 2021; Lillywhite & Wolbring, 2020; Packin, 2021; Ostherr, 2022; Ritter, 2021; Tilmes, 2022). In this chapter, we argue for the need for a disability justice framework to better respond to the ways in which AI has contributed to the proliferation of normalized oppression such as ableism.

Given the context of globalization and the rapid expansion of industrialization and technology, disabled communities have benefited greatly from an increase in accessibility and the interconnectedness that things like the internet and assistive

M. S. Khan (✉)
School of Social Work, McMaster University, Hamilton, ON, Canada
e-mail: khanm518@mcmaster.ca

Y. El-Lahib
Faculty of Social Work, University of Calgary, Calgary, AB, Canada
e-mail: yellahib@ucalgary.ca


C. El Morr et al. (eds.), *Beyond Tech Fixes*,
https://doi.org/10.1007/978-3-031-93022-5_17

devices provide (Domingo, 2021; Huq et al., 2022; Kharbat et al., 2020; Teng & Ren, 2021; Zdravkova et al., 2022). In fact, there are various ways in which technology has improved the lives of disabled people when society at large could not. Due to conditions of living in an ableist society, disabled people have had to rely on individualized approaches to accessibility and inclusion, such as personal assistive devices that place the onus on the individual to adapt to society given their disability. At the same time, we cannot deny that AI has improved the quality of life for disabled people. Some key examples include some applications to medical assessment and diagnosis, in its use for assistive devices and software, as well as through communication technologies (Domingo, 2021; Huq et al., 2022; Kharbat et al., 2020; Teng & Ren, 2021; Zdravkova et al., 2022). Yet, it has been flagged for concerns regarding lack of privacy (Ritter, 2021), or problematic use in healthcare for the purposes of assessment and diagnosis (Bennett & Keyes, 2019; Whittaker et al., 2019). In fact, AI technologies have largely made it possible for medical orientations of disability to remain dominant. The normalization of ableism can be seen in algorithmic bias that prioritized ableist and medicalized ways of understanding disability and disability supports. As such, we argue for the need to ground AI and related technologies in disability justice frameworks.

## Setting the Context

Artificial intelligence (AI) can be thought of as a simulation of 'intelligence' whereby computers mimic tasks typically completed by humans. AI and machine learning techniques are designed to identify patterns that exist within datasets in order to produce outputs that may assist humans (or other computers) in decision-making processes. Such technologies have become ubiquitous within fields such as health informatics and are often relied on to facilitate the ease of data interpretation and generation concerning medical information (El Morr et al., 2024). AI and machine learning techniques learn from and respond to pre-existing data memory, so 'errors' in its pattern recognition are framed as bias within the data (Whittaker et al., 2019). Bias is thus detrimental to study for the improvement of future responses to data. However, given that AI can only respond to data that currently exists, it can be quite common to produce biases if the patterns in the pre-existing dataset rely on inaccurate or harmful information, such as ableist and racist data (Lawrence, 2023; Shew, 2022). We should be increasingly concerned with the implications of data bias as it has been reported across various fields, such as business, social media, the economy, politics, and healthcare. The effects of this form of bias can be damaging when it weaponizes assumptions against communities or when AI algorithms reproduce or exacerbate existing inequities in socioeconomic status, race, ethnic background, religion, gender, disability, or sexual orientation (Panch et al., 2019). Despite this, meaningful examinations of biases towards the disabled community have not deeply existed within the study of AI. As such, in this chapter, we argue for a disability justice framework for AI that challenges and seeks to mitigate AI biases towards disabled people and challenges data ableism and technoableism more broadly.

AI models and AI-based software are built in a manner that devalues the inclusivity of accurate data concerning the lives of disabled people and may have far more harmful effects on the communities they seek to (or not) serve. These models have been used to physically harm and injure (Díaz Figueroa et al., 2022). Global South disability scholars have argued about the production of disability and impairment in the Global South (Meekosha, 2011; Mosleh et al., 2018; Obermaier, 2024), and AI is one culprit through its use in automated weapons systems (Díaz Figueroa et al., 2022). If we understand AI to be a simulation of intelligence that identifies patterns and behaviours, we can begin to dig deeper into how pattern recognition can be used for nefarious purposes. There exist great tensions in the technical sides of AI, regarding how pattern recognition and the use of pre-existing data is seen as neutral–as information for the sake of making a tool better (Díaz Figueroa et al., 2022). Technical perspectives on AI may emphasize the neutrality of technology, promoting it as something efficient, effective, and productive–things that are seen as neutral and transcending moral and ethical standards. Thus, the production and betterment of such tools can be seen as *good* things for society, making our lives better, more efficient, and so on (Lillywhite & Wolbring, 2020). However, what has not been adequately challenged is AI's assumed position as a neutral technology, given its role in facilitating the production of impairment, murder, environmental degradation, and land theft, among other things (Díaz Figueroa et al., 2022). AI makes such things possible through the use of weapons of mass destruction, face recognition at borders and checkpoints, drone surveillance technology, and more, which have continued to be improved through machine learning. We assert that such technologies can be used for harm and for creating impairment in the Global South. So, considering such tools as neutral would mean an erasure of the ways in which scientific technology and the scientific community at large inflict colonial harm when they make technology for profit and colonial gain.

The ongoing genocide in Palestine is a prime example of what can be made possible by AI technology used in autonomous weapons and drones. Whether accurate or not, AI pattern recognition has allowed the large-scale disablement of Palestinians. Weapons used for colonial and imperial harm, for the destruction of societies and infrastructure, and the physical disablement of Palestinian bodies should be clear indications of AI's potential for harm. This creation of impairment and disablement by AI is not adequately theorized in disability studies, let alone in the study of AI. Thus, we must urgently challenge the implications of AI tools and consider a disability justice framework for AI. In fact, as disability theorists or scientists working in the field of AI, we have a responsibility to recognize AI as not neutral but perhaps a medium for colonial and imperial violence (Díaz Figueroa et al., 2022). This is to say that AI needs to move away from technical discourse around AI 'bias' as a strictly machine learning anomaly; rather, it needs to be held accountable for what AI has done, continues to do, and may be used for in the future.

In addition to continuing tensions, AI has been used to perpetuate and uphold medical and data colonialism that uses algorithmic bias to perpetuate marginalization and has been implicated in the violence that produces impairment and over-focus on techno-specificities (Madianou, 2019, 2022). In fact, it can be seen to uphold normative conceptualizations of AI that reinforce ableism through the proliferation of science and medicalized conceptualizations of disability and healthcare. Such fields are not immune to the effects of coloniality and modernity but rather rely on them to dismiss diverse orientations to the human body and mind. As such, in this chapter, we trouble the implications of AI as creating conditions that produce disability and disablement despite also being used for the benefit of disabled communities. How do we grapple with such implications? And how do we ensure that AI is being produced, used, and applied responsibly? Most importantly, how do we negotiate this in a manner that is aligned with disability justice? In this chapter, we propose a disability justice framework for AI, to attempt to hold the AI industry and the tools it produces accountable. Particularly, to address tensions of data colonialism and ableism in AI and machine learning, there is a need to move beyond a one-size-fits-all approach in how social policies and care practices are promoted and valorized in the race for effective AI systems. Instead, we argue that nuanced policies governing AI production, use, and consumption need to move away from a cost-benefit analysis. Rather, policies need to account for socio-political and economic realities and implications of AI use beyond dominant technicalities related to efficiency and effectiveness. Unless we deliberately challenge and move beyond such approaches, we can expect to continue to see the operation, normalization, and exaltation of ableist AI systems that systematically erase disabled people and their experiences. As such, a disability justice framework is much needed to address ableism within or through AI. Rather, a disability justice framework requires attention to data injustice, medical colonialism, and the exclusion, violence, and erasure that shape the everyday experience of disabled people.

## Toward a Disability Justice Framework

Responding to individual, rights-based orientations of the disability rights movement in the Global North, disability justice offers a framework to hold AI accountable by moving away from a framework that situates disability as an individual issue, which is met with individualized and limited approaches to care. It emphasizes the interconnectedness and interdependence of socio-political realities by centering on care responses that come from those who are most impacted. In other words, disability justice moves away from state-sponsored solutions to disability care, given the inevitable harm and control it can yield. Instead, a disability justice framework builds on anti-capitalist and anti-colonial politics to advance a framework that questions both the processes and the technologies that enable ableism and its normalization broadly. It facilitates a justice orientation beyond individual, liberal notions of inclusion and accessibility. A justice framework for AI and disability seeks to liberate disability from the socio-political, economic, and environmental remnants of normalcy coloniality. Hence, it emphasizes justice of AI and disability in a way that must yield the liberation of disabled people and ultimately dismantle ableism as it interacts with other systems of oppression governed by capitalist and colonial control by states.

Given the tensions that exist in the prior discussion about the uses and misuses of AI by the state and professionals, we argue that there needs to be a more responsible approach to AI. As such, we put forward a disability justice framework for AI that includes disability justice principles as central and necessary to the utility and implementation of AI models and mechanisms. AI systems function in unidirectional ways that leave out matters of accountability by producing and reproducing predictable, ableist and biased data. A disability justice framework that would better address the predictability and ableist bias involved in AI begins with decentering medical orientations and modalities, as well as moving away from the limited rights-based approaches to disability care. A disability justice framework ultimately centers on the interdependent nature of socio-political and economic relationships that shape social interactions. Given the use of AI for disability care, we argue that this is especially critical for the health, mental health, and disability care contexts. Here, we offer some ways in which disability justice can be mobilized to better hold AI accountable and more responsible for its use, implementation, and consumption. A summary of key principles to be outlined in a disability justice framework for AI include:

1. Centering the social realities of disabled people during the design, development, and updates of AI systems.
2. The focus needs to center on the interconnectedness of social relationships within and between various social systems affecting the everyday experience of disabled individuals and groups.
3. Paying explicit attention to how AI systems have been actively used in wars and armed conflict in ways that inflict colonial violence and contribute to the production of impairment.
4. There is an urgency to move away from focusing on cost-benefits and one-size-fits-all approaches of AI design, development, and updates to center the socio-political and economic implications of AI use beyond the limited technical priorities of efficiency and effectiveness.

## Centering the Social Realities of Disabled People during the Design, Development, and Updates of AI Systems

This principle challenges the focus that AI systems have on technicalities while actively neglecting and marginalizing social realities. In fact, many scholars call out this overreliance and focus. For example, scholars challenge that AI systems focus heavily on technical aspects of algorithms and machine learning and question the blatant neglect of social factors that go beyond considerations of ethics and morality broadly speaking (de Oliveira et al., 2022; Ostherr, 2022; Tilmes, 2022). Although many scholars in the field of AI speak to the ethics of developing and using AI systems, we maintain that the social aspects and implications of using AI continue to have significant impacts on disabled people and communities. A key tension raised here is related to how AI systems rely on the assumption that fosters a universality of knowledge, or a one-size-fits-all approach to disability care, which has been heavily challenged and rejected by many disability justice scholars (Meekosha, 2011; Oliver, 2013). Thus, this principle highlights that social realities are shaped by many nuanced social interactions that have been neglected by AI design systems, their data, and their developers. Instead, we must be willing to center their realities in all aspects and areas of designing, developing, and updating AI systems.

## Centering the Interconnectedness of Social Systems Affecting the Everyday Experience of Disabled People

This principle responds to the lack of protective legislation that exists to protect disabled communities from further state surveillance and control. As we stated earlier in this chapter, AI technologies have been widely used across various disciplines and practice contexts that support disabled people, such as in medical assessment and diagnosis, assistive devices, and communication technologies. However, we have also cautioned alongside many scholars who argue that the benefits that come with AI technological advancements also created significant challenges that need to be mitigated and addressed (Bennett & Keyes, 2019; Land, 2023; Lillywhite & Wolbring, 2020; Marjanovic et al., 2022). Some of these challenges include loss or lack of privacy (Ritter, 2021), concerns over AI use in health diagnosis (Bennett & Keyes, 2019; Whittaker et al., 2019), as well as the overall injustices caused by the over-reliance on AI systems in various disciplines and social interactions (Bennett et al., 2020; Buyl et al., 2022; Lillywhite & Wolbring, 2020; Marjanovic et al., 2022). Particularly, Lillywhite and Wolbring (2020) call out false assumptions that promote "AI for social good" and argue that disabled people are impacted by how these "social goods'' are defined and accessed (typically without any consultation with or consideration for disabled people) or whether "doing good" also helps in preventing "bad" (p. 5). Thus, the focus of many AI-promoting initiatives continues to center on general governance and standardizations while neglecting legislation that protects disabled communities and groups in meaningful and effective ways. Hence, this principle argues that centering the interconnectedness of various social realities does and will affect the everyday experiences of disabled people, thus necessitating the need for their realities to be made central and important.

## Challenging AI'S Complicity in Colonialism and the Production of Impairment

As we have alluded to in this chapter, an alarming issue that has been largely neglected in the development of and by AI systems is the lack of accountability in its use of autonomous weapons and the production of impairment by supporting colonial violence. As such, the lack of social and legal accountability is urgently in need of investigation and research in AI systems. Such lack of accountability and its consequences for disabled people can be seen in the widespread use of AI in military-armed technologies, particularly including automated weapons. Disabled people are subjected to many risks during armed conflicts and operations, and automated weapons further escalate these risks. However, such risks implicate more than disabled people in particular. Rather, these risks are real and detrimental to communities at large, given how armed technologies, automated weapons, and weapons for mass destruction create further impairment. Meekosha (2011) speaks about the colonial dimensions that facilitate the production of impairment and questions the ways in which wars and conflicts have played a major role in supporting violent colonial entities to control resources and materials to serve the interests of the Global North. As AI technologies continue to be adopted and widely relied upon in the Global South, including areas affected by wars, conflicts, and occupations, we argue that a disability justice framework for AI must question how new war technologies neglect taking accountability to and responsibility for those affected by their use. A study by Díaz Figueroa et al. (2022) calls out the use of AI in autonomous weapons and the lack of legislation that controls their accountability and suggests that throughout the international debates and UN discussions on AI and its role in autonomous weapon production and utilization, disabled people were never included. Their rights have been constantly violated by the use of these systems and by the lack of consultation and participation in creating legislation that may prevent further mass disablement. We support Díaz Figueroa et al.'s (2022) assertion that AI systems are not developed in a neutral context and emphasize that they result from the Global North's dominant social and economic priorities that constantly reproduce "disproportionate negative consequences for marginalized groups, and for the global south in general" (p. 286). As such, a disability justice framework for AI must pay explicit attention to the ways in which AI systems are involved in the perpetuation of colonial violence and control in the Global South.

## The Dangers of a One-Size-Fits-all Emphasizing Efficiency and Effectiveness in AI Systems

This chapter has made it explicit that dominant social norms that have normalized experiences of ableism, racism, ageism, and so forth continue to be prevalent in societies. Thus, it is much more important to be cognizant of the ways in which they are being upheld by AI systems and the algorithms that help their decision-making processes. These processes are inherently biased and are shaped by widespread dominant social norms that fail to question systems of oppression and marginalization, such as ableism (Egger, 2021; Lillywhite & Wolbring, 2020; Packin, 2021; Ostherr, 2022; Ritter, 2021; Tilmes, 2022). When ableism is a key feature of dominant social norms, we can expect to see AI continue to evolve in a way that further perpetuates and normalizes ableist assumptions, in turn using that data to teach other AI systems. The key premise of AI systems and their biases is based on their limited algorithmic abilities to connect or account for the complexity and sophistication of social networks that enable people to interact with others and negotiate their everyday social realities. Packin (2021) notes that AI algorithms are mainly built on massive data processing to assess individuals, which fosters wide-scale discrimination in ways that maintain dominant ableist social norms. It becomes clear that "ableism and technology are deeply intertwined in any society" and that privileges are assigned to certain types of bodies depending on two key issues: the kind of technology and how it is used (Packin, 2021, p. 489). As such, decision-making processes that do not question or challenge dominant social norms and what sustains them are inherently problematic. We argue that these decision-making processes directly feed into creating and maintaining oppressive ableist AI systems. It is, therefore, critical to move towards a disability justice framework that would help mitigate some of these inherent flows. The disability justice framework for AI that we propose in this chapter addresses how AI systems can be used to challenge dominant social systems instead of maintaining their existence and facilitating their operation.

## Concluding Remarks

In this chapter, we have put forth a much-needed disability justice framework for AI. While AI continues to evolve and get 'smarter,' it is critical to address the tensions that we have discussed. It is our hope that the reader be reminded of how AI systems and machine learning technology affect marginalized communities such as disabled people and people in the Global South. Thus, a disability justice framework emphasizes the need for more liberatory, ethical, and responsible approaches to the development, implementation, and application of AI. Moving forward, we urge AI developers to include the voices and experiences of disabled people in shaping the future of AI systems and technologies. By doing so, we can imagine a world where disability care is not at risk of state control and surveillance but rather rests in the knowledge that AI can serve as a tool for betterment while also holding itself accountable for the harms it causes.

## References

Bennett, C. L., & Keyes, O. (2019). What is the point of fairness? Disability, AI, and the complexity of justice. *Access: Special Interest Group on Accessible Computing, 125*, 1–5.

Bennett, C. L., Rosner, D. K., & Taylor, A. S. (2020). The care work of access. In *CHI conference on human factors in computing systems*. https://doi.org/10.1145/3313831.3376568

Buyl, M., Cociancig, C., Fattone, C., & Roekens, N. (2022). Tackling algorithmic disability discrimination in hiring process: An ethical and legal technical analysis. In *ACM conference on fairness, accountability and transparency*. https://doi.org/10.1145/3531146.3533169

de Oliveira, L. F., da Silva Gomes, A., Enes, Y., Castelo Branco, T. V., Paiva Pires, R., Bozlon, A., & Demo, G. (2022). Path and future of artificial intelligence in the field of justice: A systematic literature review and a research agenda. *SN Social Science, 2*(180), 1–20.

Díaz Figueroa, M., Henao Orozco, A., Martinez, J., & Munoz Jaime, W. (2022). The risks of autonomous weapons: An analysis centered on the rights of persons with disabilities. *International Review of the Red Cross, 105*(922), 278–305.

Domingo, M. C. (2021). An overview of machine learning and 5G for people with disabilities. *Sensors (Basel), 21*(22), 7572. https://doi.org/10.3390/s21227572

Egger, K. E. (2021). Artificial intelligence in the workplace: Exploring liability under the Americans with disabilities act and regulatory solutions. *Washburn Law Journal, 60*(3), 527–560.

El Morr, C., Kundi, B., Mobeen, F., Taleghani, S., El-Lahib, Y., & Gorman, R. (2024). AI and disability: A systematic scoping review. *Health Informatics Journal, 30*(3), 1–24. https://doi.org/10.1177/14604582241285743

Huq, S. M., Maskeliunas, R., & Damasevicius, R. (2022). Dialogue agents for artificial intelligence-based conversational systems for cognitively disabled: A systematic review. *Disability Rehabilitation: Assistive Technology, 19*(7), 1059–1078. https://doi.org/10.1080/17483107.2022.2146768

Kharbat, F. F., Alshawabkeh, A., & Woolsey, M. L. (2020). Identifying gaps in using artificial intelligence to support students with intellectual disabilities from education and health perspectives. *Aslib Journal of Information Management, 73*(1), 101–128. https://doi.org/10.1108/ajim-02-2020-0054

Land, C. W. (2023). Disability bias and new frontiers in artificial intelligence. *Journal on Technology and Persons with Disabilities, 11*(1), 28–42.

Lawrence, C. D. (2023). *Hidden in white sight: How AI empowers and deepens systemic racism*. CRC Press.

Lillywhite, A., & Wolbring, G. (2020). Coverage of artificial intelligence and machine learning within academic literature, Canadian newspapers and twitter tweets: The case of disabled people. *Societies, 10*(23), 1–27.

Madianou, M. (2019). Technocolonialism: Digital innovation and data practices in the humanitarian response to refugee crises. *Social Media and Society, 5*(3), 1–13. https://doi.org/10.1177/2056305119863146

Madianou, M. (2022). Technological futures as colonial debris: "Tech for good" as technocolonialism. In J. Zylinska & Goldsmith Media (Eds.), *The future of media* (pp. 281–294). Goldsmiths Press.

Marjanovic, O., Cecez-Kecmanovic, D., & Vidgen, R. (2022). Theorising algorithmic justice. *European Journal of Information Systems, 31*(3), 269–287.

Meekosha, H. (2011). Decolonizing disability: Thinking and acting globally. *Disability & Society, 26*(6), 667–682.

Mosleh, M., Dalal, K., Aljeesh, Y., & Svanström, L. (2018). The burden of war-injury in the Palestinian health care sector in Gaza strip. *BMC International Health and Human Rights, 18*, 1–9.

Obermaier, L. (2024). Disabling palestine: The case of Gaza's great march of return. *Race & Class, 65*(3), 27–46.

Oliver, M. (2013). The social model of disability: Thirty years on. *Disability & Society, 28*(7), 1024–1026.

Ostherr, K. (2022). Artificial intelligence and medical humanities. *Journal of Medical Humanities, 43*(2), 211–232.

Packin, N. (2021). Disability discrimination using artificial intelligence systems and social scoring: Can we disable digital bias? *Journal of International and Comparative Law, 8*(2), 487–512.

Panch, T., Mattie, H., & Atun, R. (2019). Artificial intelligence and algorithmic bias: Implications for health systems. *Journal of Global Health, 9*(2), 1–5. https://doi.org/10.7189/jogh.09.020318

Ritter, J. (2021). Digital justice in 2058: Trusting our survival to artificial intelligence, quantum and the rule of law. *Journal of International and Comparative Law, 8*(2), 333–356.

Shew, A. (2022). How to get a story wrong: Technoableism, simulation and cyborg resistance. *Including Disability, 1*(1), 13–36.

Teng, M., & Ren, Y. (2021, December). Application and development prospect of artificial intelligence in the daily life of the elderly and disabled. In *2021 3rd international conference on machine learning, big data and business intelligence (MLBDBI)* (pp. 767–770). IEEE.

Tilmes, N. (2022). Disability, fairness and algorithmic bias in AI recruitment. *Ethics and Information Technology, 24*(21), 1–13.

Whittaker, M., Alper, M., Bennett, C. L., Hendren, S., Kaziunas, L., Mills, M., Ringel Morris, M., Rankin, J., Rogers, E., Salas, M., & West, S. M. (2019). Disability, bias, and AI. *AI Now Institute, 8*, 11.

Zdravkova, K., Krasniqi, V., Dalipi, F., & Ferati, M. (2022). Cutting-edge communication and learning assistive technologies for disabled children: An artificial intelligence perspective. *Frontiers in Artificial Intelligence, 5*, 970430. https://doi.org/10.3389/frai.2022.970430

# Conclusion: Toward Collective Futures of AI and Disability Justice

**Christo El Morr, Yahya El-Lahib, and Rachel da Silveira Gorman**

This volume emerges from the rich, complex, and often contested intersection of artificial intelligence (AI) and disability—a domain with immense potential and significant risks. It is a space shaped by long histories of marginalization, technological innovation, and ongoing struggles for recognition, equity, and justice. Across seventeen chapters, a diverse constellation of scholars, researchers, educators, technologists, artists, and activists confront these issues with critical insight and engaged imagination. Their contributions highlight the urgent need to reframe the AI-disability interconnection, not simply as a technical matter or a site for innovation but as a political, ethical, and profoundly human question. Together, they challenge dominant assumptions about what constitutes intelligence, whose needs are prioritized in design processes, and how value is assigned in our digital futures.

What emerges from this collection is not a single argument or prescriptive roadmap. Instead, it is a **mosaic of perspectives**, each drawing on distinct epistemologies, lived experiences, and disciplinary practices. This plurality is a strength. It resists the simplification that too often accompanies discussions of AI and accessibility, particularly those framed through narrow narratives of "inclusion" or "efficiency." This book invites us instead into a space of critical interrogation—one that probes how AI systems reproduce ableist logics, how they encode histories of racial, colonial, and gendered violence, and how they might be otherwise imagined and deployed in service of justice and liberation.

A consistent thread woven through the chapters is a **rejection of technological determinism**—the idea that AI, by its very nature, leads to social progress or

C. El Morr (✉) · R. da Silveira Gorman
School of Health Policy and Management, York University, Toronto, ON, Canada
e-mail: elmorr@yorku.ca; gorman@yorku.ca

Y. El-Lahib
Faculty of Social Work, University of Calgary, Calgary, AB, Canada
e-mail: yellahib@ucalgary.ca



C. El Morr et al. (eds.), *Beyond Tech Fixes*,
https://doi.org/10.1007/978-3-031-93022-5_18

empowerment. This volume insists that technology is not neutral. AI systems are built within existing social, economic, and political structures, and they reflect the biases, hierarchies, and interests of those who shape them. As such, AI has the capacity not only to replicate but to intensify systemic forms of exclusion. It can reinforce surveillance, restrict access to resources, and devalue ways of knowing and being that do not conform to dominant norms. Whether in education, employment, healthcare, or governance, the deployment of AI can deepen the disability divide—unless it is critically interrogated, reimagined, and grounded in frameworks that prioritize justice.

This volume directly engages with **theoretical models** that push back against reductionist framings of disability. The social model of disability, the disability justice framework, and critical disability studies all provide conceptual tools for challenging the dominant narratives that cast disabled people as passive recipients of technology. Rather than viewing disability as a personal deficiency to be solved by technical intervention, these frameworks position disability as a site of political struggle, creative resistance, and transformative knowledge. The contributions highlight how "crip technoscience," "emancipatory AI pedagogy," and "disability data justice" offer alternative logics of design and use—ones that center interdependence, care, and collective flourishing over individual optimization or productivity.

Importantly, this volume also foregrounds **intersectionality** as a foundational lens. Disability does not exist in isolation from other forms of marginalization. The experiences of disabled people are shaped by race, class, gender identity, sexual orientation, Indigeneity, migration status, language, and geography. The contributors take up this intersectional lens to examine, for example, the compounded barriers faced by forced migrants with disabilities in Germany or the racialized and ableist structures that shape student experiences in Canadian postsecondary institutions. These analyses reject flattening narratives and instead affirm the importance of context, history, and lived experience in understanding how AI systems operate and whom they serve.

Equally striking across the chapters is a commitment to **methodological plurality and innovation**. This book covers a wide range of approaches—from participatory design and co-creation to critical discourse analysis, ethnography, and collective writing. Many of these methods explicitly reject extractive research models and instead prioritize reciprocity, collaboration, and accountability. This commitment is not merely technical; it is ethical and political. It reflects a broader concern with epistemic justice: whose knowledge is recognized, whose experiences are centered, and who has the power to define what counts as valuable insight or legitimate expertise.

As we draw this volume to a close, we do so not with finality but with a call to continued engagement. We resist the impulse to offer neat conclusions or technical fixes. The challenges at the intersection of AI and disability are not problems to be solved through innovation alone. They require structural shifts—in how we design systems, how we understand access, and how we envision the future. We need to move beyond frameworks that seek to "include" disabled people into existing systems and instead work toward transforming those systems altogether. Inclusion without transformation risks reinforcing the very structures that marginalize in the first place.

We offer this book as a contribution to the growing, vital, and urgent conversation about what it means to build AI systems that are not only accessible but also just. We hope it serves as a resource, a provocation, and a site of solidarity for those across disciplines, institutions, and communities committed to reimagining the technological future from the ground up. The work ahead is complex and unfinished—and necessarily collective. It must be guided by those most impacted, informed by critical histories, and rooted in the values of care, equity, and mutual responsibility. In a world increasingly shaped by algorithms, let us ensure that our futures are shaped, too, and hopefully mainly, by justice.

# Glossary

**AAC Augmentative and Alternative Communication** AAC refers to all the methods and means of communication designed to enhance language production including expressive aspects as well as assisting in comprehension.

**Ableism** A system of discrimination and social prejudice against people with disabilities, based on the belief that typical abilities are superior. In the context of AI, ableism manifests through biased data and design processes that exclude or harm disabled people.

**Academic Honesty** Ethical behavior in educational settings, including avoiding plagiarism and cheating.

**Accessibility** The design of products, devices, services, or environments for people with disabilities.

**Achievable Imaginaries** Possible and attainable visions of the future that incorporate the perspectives and needs of marginalized groups, particularly disabled people, in the context of AI and data justice.

**AI Assistive Technologies** AI-powered tools that help individuals with daily tasks and improve their quality of life.

**Algorithmic Bias** Systematic and repeatable errors in an algorithm that create unfair outcomes.

**Algorithmic Governance** The use of algorithmic technologies to make and inform decision-making or off-load governance processes and tasks previously performed by humans in the governance and public sector.

**Algorithmic Humanitarianism** Entails the use of algorithmic and AI-based tools in humanitarian processes, i.e., aid and relief applications, migrant and refugee aid dispersal, and biometric identification interfaces.

**Allocational and Representational Harms** Allocational and representational harms are terms used to describe two significant types of harm caused by biased AI systems. Allocational harms occur when resources or opportunities are unfairly distributed, while representational harms involve reinforcing stereotypes or misrepresenting marginalized groups.


C. El Morr et al. (eds.), *Beyond Tech Fixes*,
https://doi.org/10.1007/978-3-031-93022-5

**Artificial Intelligence (AI) in Accessibility** The application of AI technologies, such as machine learning and reinforcement learning, to improve digital accessibility. Examples include generating alternative text for images, providing real-time captions, and creating adaptive user interfaces.

**Artificial Intelligence (AI)** A branch of computer science that develops systems capable of performing tasks typically requiring human intelligence, such as decision-making and pattern recognition. AI is a site of both potential benefit and harm to disabled communities.

**Assistive Technology** Assistive technology encompasses devices, tools, or systems that support individuals with disabilities in performing tasks or gaining independence. Examples include screen readers for users with visual impairments, AI-driven communication tools for nonverbal individuals, and adaptive mobility aids.

**Autonomous Weapons** Weapon systems that can select and engage targets without human intervention. These technologies are critically examined in the chapter for their role in colonial violence and the production of impairment.

**Bias Mitigation** Techniques used to reduce or eliminate biases in AI systems.

**Bias** A tendency to favor or disfavor certain groups or perspectives. In AI, bias often emerges from training data, developer assumptions, and systemic inequities, impacting disabled people disproportionately.

**Born-Accessible Design** An approach to design that aims to make digital content and technologies accessible to people with disabilities from the outset.

**Capabilities Approach** A framework for evaluating well-being and social justice based on individuals' capabilities to achieve what they value.

**ChatGPT-4** A large language model developed by OpenAI.

**ChatGPT** An AI chatbot developed by OpenAI that can generate human-quality text.

**Co-creation** Collaboration of all stakeholders to identify aspects that are of interest to all parties. In this context, it enables the definition of effective research objectives.

**Co-design** A collaborative design approach that actively involves disabled people and other stakeholders in all stages of the design process to ensure that AI systems are inclusive and meet the needs of diverse users.

**Communication Partner** Someone who interacts with a person with severe motor and communication impairments (SMCIs), often familiar with their nuanced communication methods.

**Community-Based Participatory Research (CBPR)** A research approach that emphasizes the participation and influence of community members in all aspects of the research process, ensuring that research is relevant, respectful, and beneficial to the community.

**Connectionism** One of the models to explain insights into the structure, acquisition, and processing of language in the brain, both typical and disordered.

**Content Creators** Individuals or teams who produce digital content, including documents, websites, and other media.

**Critical AI Literacy** The ability to analyze and evaluate AI technologies, considering their potential benefits and harms, and to engage in informed discussions about their ethical and societal implications.

**Critical Digital Pedagogy** Applies the principles of critical pedagogy to the use of digital technologies in education, examining issues of power, equity, and access.

**Critical Pedagogy** An educational philosophy that encourages students to question and challenge power structures and to become agents of social change.

**D-DCP** Digital disability creation process, a framework for understanding how AI systems can create or exacerbate disability.

**Data Colonialism** The harvesting, storage, and sharing of data along the international axis of ongoing colonial geographic and political hierarchies.

**Data Ethics** The branch of ethics that deals with the collection, use, and sharing of data, particularly concerning privacy, fairness, accountability, and transparency.

**Data Feminism** An approach to data science that seeks to challenge power imbalances and promote social justice by applying feminist principles and methodologies.

**Data Harms** The negative consequences that can arise from the collection, use, and sharing of data, particularly for marginalized groups who may be excluded, misrepresented, or discriminated against.

**Data Justice** A framework that seeks to ensure fairness in the way people are represented and treated as a result of their data, particularly in the context of AI systems.

**Data Sovereignty** The right of individuals or communities to control their data, including its collection, use, and sharing.

**Decolonial Theory** A critical framework which examines and challenges the ongoing colonial relations which shape and inform social, political, and economic spheres and knowledge systems.

**Dementia** An umbrella term for a variety of physical, psychological, and cognitive changes that can impact daily functioning and can have multiple causes.

**Design Justice** A framework that seeks to challenge and redress power imbalances in design processes and outcomes, promoting equitable participation and benefits for marginalized communities.

**Digital Accessibility** The practice of designing and developing online content, tools, and technologies to ensure that they are usable by everyone, including people with disabilities. It focuses on removing barriers so that all individuals can participate equitably in digital environments.

**Digital Divide** The gap between those who have physical access to technology and the skills and resources to make use of it and those who do not.

**Digital Divide** The gap between students who have access to technology and those who do not.

**Digital Economies** Economic systems that are based on the production, distribution, and consumption of digital and data-based goods and services.

**Disability Creation** The process by which AI systems can contribute to disabling situations for people with disabilities.

**Disability Data Justice** A framework that seeks to ensure that data about disabled people is collected, used, and shared in ways that are equitable, inclusive, and respectful of their rights and needs.

**Disability Data** Data that describes the experiences, characteristics, and needs of disabled people, often used to inform the development and evaluation of AI systems.

**Disability Divide** The disability divide refers to the disparity in access, opportunities, and outcomes between individuals with disabilities and those without, often worsened by systemic biases in technology, policy, and society. Bridging this gap requires inclusive practices and innovations focused on equity.

**Disability Evasiveness** The systemic avoidance of recognizing and addressing disability.

**Disability Justice (DJ)** A framework that moves beyond rights-based approaches to disability, emphasizing intersectionality, anti-capitalism, anti-colonialism, and collective liberation. It centers the leadership and knowledge of those most impacted by ableism and other forms of oppression.

**Disability Representation** The way disability is portrayed in media and literature.

**Disability-Led Design** A design approach that prioritizes the perspectives and experiences of disabled people in all stages of the design process, ensuring that AI systems are accessible and inclusive and meet the unique needs of disabled users.

**Disablement** The social, political, and environmental processes that produce disability by failing to accommodate bodily and mental diversity. It differs from impairment, which is the actual condition or difference.

**Disablism** Discrimination or prejudice against people with disabilities.

**Discrimination-Aware AI** Discrimination-aware AI refers to artificial intelligence systems that identify and mitigate systemic biases in datasets, algorithms, or decision-making processes. These systems aim to generate fair and equitable outcomes, especially for marginalized groups impacted by historical inequities.

**Do-It-Yourself Assistive Technologies (DIY-ATs)** DIY-ATs are technologies designed, customized, and/or fabricated by amateur designers and non-engineers to empower users with disabilities.

**Document Accessibility** The practice of making electronic documents accessible to people with disabilities, including those who use assistive technologies.

**Education** The process of acquiring knowledge and skills, often through teaching and learning.

**Emotional Communication** The process of expressing and understanding emotions, particularly challenging for individuals with severe motor and communication impairments (SMCIs).

**Epistemic Violence** Harm caused by the silencing, misrepresentation, or erasure of certain forms of knowledge or ways of knowing, often experienced by marginalized groups.

**Ethical AI** Ethical AI refers to designing and using artificial intelligence systems that prioritize fairness, transparency, accountability, and equity. These systems aim to prevent harm and ensure technology benefits to all users, particularly marginalized communities.

**Eye Gaze Tracking** Technology used to track where a person is looking, used in the study for emotion recognition.

**Featurization** The process of selecting or engineering variables (features) that represent real-life concepts in AI models.

**Fraser's Three-Dimensional Framework** A social justice framework with three dimensions (redistribution, recognition, and representation), encompassing economic, social, and political aspects.

**Generative AI** A type of artificial intelligence that can create new content, such as text, images, or audio.

**Global North/Global South** Geopolitical terms used to distinguish wealthy, industrialized nations (Global North) from poorer, often colonized or formerly colonized countries (Global South). The chapter critiques AI's development and deployment through a Global North-centric lens that harms the Global South.

**HDM-DCP** Human development model and disability creation process, a framework for understanding disability as an interaction between personal and environmental factors.

**Human-Augmenting Technologies** AI-powered tools that enhance or restore human abilities.

**Human-Centered AI** An approach to AI development that prioritizes the needs, experiences, and input of human users, especially marginalized groups like people with disabilities. It emphasizes creating technology that is ethical, inclusive, and responsive to real-world needs.

**Human-Centered Design (HCD)** A design approach that prioritizes the needs and experiences of users throughout the design process, ensuring that products and services are usable, useful, and desirable.

**Identity-First Language (IFL)** A linguistic approach that recognizes disability as a valued and inseparable part of one's identity. It emphasizes disability experiences, cultures, and pride. In contrast to person-first language (e.g., "person with a disability"), one would say "disabled person," "autistic person," or "deaf person."

**Impairment** A physical, mental, or sensory difference in body or function. In the disability justice context, impairment is not inherently negative but is often socially constructed into disability through ableist systems.

**Inclusive Data Collection** Gathering data that includes diverse populations, particularly those with disabilities, to avoid bias and improve AI systems.

**Inclusive Design** The design of products, services, or environments that are usable by people with the widest range of abilities and needs.

**Individual Models of Disability** Models that view disability as a problem within the individual.

**Information Inequities** Disparities in access to and use of, and representation in, information, particularly for marginalized groups, that can perpetuate existing inequalities.

**Inspiration Exploitation** The reduction of disabled people to sources of inspiration or motivation for nondisabled consumers.

**Intelligent Tutoring Systems (ITSs)** A computer program that uses artificial intelligence (AI) to provide personalized instruction and feedback to students. ITSs use AI to track a student's work, adjust feedback, and provide hints. They can also make inferences about a student's strengths and weaknesses and suggest additional work.

**International Affective Picture System (IAPS)** A standardized tool used to elicit emotional responses through images.

**Intersectionality** Intersectionality is an approach to understanding power and identity. Social categories are constructed through situated interactions, as well as norms, laws, and discourses with implications for individuals' identities. People all have multiple social identities, and social inequality is not simply the sum of an individual's categories but rather is created at the intersections of various socially constructed dimensions of power.

**Language Oppression/Language Barriers/Language Discrimination** Situations where individuals or groups are disadvantaged or excluded due to their language use, including limited access to services or opportunities.

**Large Language Models (LLMs)** LLMs are machine learning models that use deep learning to perform natural language processing tasks. LLMs are trained on large amounts of text to learn statistical relationships and respond to user requests with humanlike language. They use neural networks to understand the relationships between words and phrases in a sequence of text.

**Learning Disabilities (LDs)** Also known as specific learning disorders (SLDs), these are neurodevelopmental disorders characterized by a pattern of difficulties associated with the growth and development of the brain, affecting a student's ability to process information. These difficulties can manifest in areas such as reading (dyslexia), writing (dysgraphia), mathematics (dyscalculia), or other cognitive processes like working memory, processing speed, and attention, which are foundational for more advanced academic learning.

**Linguicism** Discrimination based on language use, dialect, or accent.

**Linguistic Hierarchies** The ranking of languages or dialects based on social prestige or perceived value.

**Machine Learning in Accessibility** A branch of AI that uses algorithms to analyze data and make predictions or decisions. In accessibility, machine learning powers tools like text simplification and image recognition for alt text to accommodate user needs.

**Marginalized Communities** Groups that experience systemic disadvantage or exclusion based on factors such as race, gender, sexuality, disability, or socioeconomic status.

**Medical Model of Disability** The medical model of disability defines disability as a health condition or deficit inherent to an individual. Solutions within this framework typically focus on medical treatments or "repairing" the individual rather than tackling external obstacles.

**Models of Disability** Frameworks for understanding and explaining disability.

**Narrative of Overcoming** A narrative that focuses on a disabled person overcoming their disability in order to achieve an acceptable degree of "normal": the discomfort of the audience.

**Nothing About Us Without Us** The principle of "nothing about us without us" in disability advocacy emphasizes that decisions concerning policies, practices, or technologies that affect disabled individuals must actively involve them as co-creators rather than merely as consultants or end users.

**Older Adults Living with Dementia (OALWD)** Older individuals experiencing age-related dementia.

**Operationalization of Disability** How disability is represented and processed in AI data.

**Optimization** The process of improving the performance of AI models.

**Participatory Design** An approach to design that involves end users and other stakeholders in the design process, promoting collaboration and shared ownership.

**Pattern Recognition** A core function of AI systems involving the identification of patterns in data. While useful, this process can reinforce existing social biases if based on flawed or discriminatory datasets.

**PDF/UA (PDF/Universal Accessibility)** An ISO standard for accessible PDF documents.

**Person-First Language (PFL)** A linguistic approach that aims to center the person over their attributes (including disability). For example, instead of saying "disabled person" (an example of identity-first language), one would say "person with a disability." The intent of PFL is to separate the individual from their disability in order to reduce stigma and promote dignity by emphasizing their humanity; however, this approach has faced criticism for further reinscribing beliefs that the presence of disability diminishes one's humanity.

**Physiological Signals** Bodily measurements like heart rate, skin conductance, and pupil dilation, used to infer emotional states.

**Prescriptive AI** AI systems used to support decision-making.

**People with Disabilities (PWDs)** Individuals with physical, sensory, cognitive, or other impairments.

**Racism** Prejudice, discrimination, or antagonism directed against a person or people on the basis of their membership in a particular racial or ethnic group.

**Recruitment** The process of finding and enrolling participants in a research study, particularly challenging for those with severe motor and communication impairments (SMCIs).

**Reinforcement Learning (RL) in Accessibility** A type of AI technique where systems learn through trial and error to optimize actions. In accessibility, RL can be used to create adaptive and personalized interfaces.

**Reinforcement Learning with Human Feedback (RLHF)** A technique used to train AI systems by having humans reward or penalize it for producing certain outputs. The rewards make the system more likely to generate desired content, while the penalties reduce the likelihood of the system producing undesired content.

**Remediation** The process of fixing accessibility issues in existing digital content or technologies.

**Representation Bias** Occurs when a dataset does not adequately reflect the diversity or characteristics of the population it is intended to represent, leading to skewed or unfair outcomes in models or decisions based on that data.

**SARs** Socially assistive robots designed to interact with users and provide companionship and emotional support.

**Section 508 Refresh Act** A proposed bill in the US Congress that would update and strengthen accessibility requirements for federal information and communications technology.

**Self-Advocacy** The ability to articulate one's needs and make informed decisions about one's life.

**Self-Assessment Manikin (SAM)** A visual tool used for self-reporting emotions.

**Sensitivity Heuristic** A rule-based algorithm that helps AI models understand the context.

**Sentiment Analysis** The process of classifying text as being positive, negative, or neutral.

**Severe Motor and Communication Impairments (SMCIs)** Significant difficulties with movement and communication, impacting daily life activities.

**Social Constructionism** A theoretical perspective that emphasizes the social construction of reality.

**Social Determinants of Health** Nonmedical factors that influence health outcomes, such as socioeconomic conditions and access to resources.

**Social Imaginaries** Collective visions of how society could be used to explore alternative social existences and the behaviors and collective notions that underpin them.

**Social Justice** The pursuit of fairness, equity, and inclusion in all aspects of society, particularly for those who experience systemic disadvantage.

**Social Model of Disability** The social model of disability frames disability as stemming from societal barriers, such as inaccessible environments and discriminatory attitudes, rather than personal impairments. This approach focuses on eliminating these systemic challenges to promote inclusivity.

**Social Models of Disability** Models that view disability as a result of social barriers.

**Speech Impairment** A disorder that affects speech sounds, fluency, or voice, making it hard to communicate. Speech impairments can occur at any age with multiple congenital and acquired health conditions such as cerebral palsy, autism, stroke, head trauma, and dementia.

**Structural Ableism** The systemic and institutionalized discrimination against disabled people, often embedded in policies, practices, and cultural norms.

**Surveillance Technology** Tools used to monitor individuals or groups, often disproportionately targeting marginalized populations. AI-driven surveillance is critiqued for enabling state control and exacerbating harm to disabled and racialized communities.

**Sustainability** The ability to maintain a certain level of care or support over the long term.

**Systemic Oppression** The ways in which social structures and institutions perpetuate inequality and disadvantage for certain groups based on factors such as race, gender, sexuality, or disability.

**Technoableism** Technoableism is a belief in the power of technology that sets the elimination of disability as a positive goal and prioritizes fixing disability through technological innovation. It is the intersection of ableism and technological development. It describes how technologies, including AI, reinforce ableist norms by privileging certain types of bodies and minds.

**Technocolonialism** The conception, design, development, and deployment of technological advancements along the axis of colonial relations. This in turn furthers colonial aims and relies on and maintains an imbalance of power and benefits of technological advancement and innovation.

**Token-Level Filtering** A process that filters or modifies specific tokens (chunks of text) in AI-generated content.

**Token** A small chunk of text.

**Tokenism** The practice of including marginalized individuals or groups in a symbolic or superficial way, without genuine commitment to equity or inclusion.

**Transdisciplinarity** A research approach that integrates knowledge and methods from different disciplines and includes nonacademic stakeholders to address complex problems, particularly important in the context of AI and disability.

**Transdisciplinary Approach** A transdisciplinary approach combines insights and expertise from various fields, including ethics, technology, and social sciences, to tackle complex societal challenges. It emphasizes the importance of stakeholder engagement and practical outcomes.

**Universal Design/One-Size-Fits-All Approach** A design strategy that assumes a standardized user, often neglecting the diverse needs of disabled people. The chapter critiques this approach in AI systems that emphasize efficiency over inclusivity.

**Universal Design** A design approach that aims to create products, environments, and systems that are usable by people with the widest range of abilities and needs, without the need for adaptation or specialized design.

**Utopian** Idealistic or visionary, often referring to a perfect society or world.

**Web Content Accessibility Guidelines (WCAG)** A set of international standards for Web accessibility.

# Index




C. El Morr et al. (eds.), *Beyond Tech Fixes*,
https://doi.org/10.1007/978-3-031-93022-5

MIX
Papier aus verantwortungsvollen Quellen
Paper from responsible sources
FSC® C105338

If you have any concerns about our products,
you can contact us on
**ProductSafety@springernature.com**

In case Publisher is established outside the EU,
the EU authorized representative is:
**Springer Nature Customer Service Center GmbH**
**Europaplatz 3, 69115 Heidelberg, Germany**

Printed by Libri Plureos GmbH
in Hamburg, Germany